PRAISE FOR *THE ART OF MONEY*

"Money has always been personal, but the rules of money have changed. Bari Tessler's methodology helps you to do just that—use money as the genesis for self-discovery, self-examination, and self-love."
—**JACQUETTE M. TIMMONS**, *Financial Intimacy*

"Bari Tessler has a gift for helping you dive deeply into your past, current, and future relationship with money in a conscious and compassionate way. This is a must read for creative entrepreneurs and for anyone wanting to truly thrive."
—**JENNIFER LEE**, *The Right-Brain Business Plan* and *Building Your Business the Right-Brain Way*

"I've taught about business and money to thousands of heart-centered and spiritual entrepreneurs, and I'm really struck by the humanness, the practicality, and depth of this book. I know I'm going to be recommending it to our clients and community as a primary resource."
—**MARK SILVER**, MDiv, Founder/CEO of Heart of Business, Inc.

"*The Art of Money* offers a fresh perspective and makes the daunting topic of money approachable and, I dare say, fun!"
—**FARNOOSH TORABI**, *When She Makes More*, Host of "So Money" podcast

"Dive into these pages if you are ready to be free of your fear and resistance to all things money. Follow the injunctions and you will feel more clarity, direct connection, and overall coherence as the artist of your money world."
—**KATIE TEAGUE**, documentary filmmaker, "Money & Life"

"Bari Tessler's approach to getting mindful about money is full of compassion and love. She shines a gentle light in all the places we don't want to look, and from there, change is possible."
—**ANDREA SCHER**, Founder of SuperHeroLife

"I feel so much joy holding this book! It's packed with time-tested wisdom, mature strength, and loving support. *The Art of Money* process is built on decades of refinement and a deep, heartfelt mission to improve lives. If you want to improve your relationship with money (and life and love and legacy), this book will help and you will thrive." .
—**CHRISTOPHER PECK**, *The Resilient Investor*

"*The Art of Money* offers a sacred and essential bridge between money pain and shame and our deepest dreams for financial well being. Bari Tessler has the rare gift of holding space for healing AND inspiring action. If you desire a new relationship with money—an empowering one, worthy of your highest self—this is the perfect place to start."
—**WOKIE NWABUEZE**, Executive Coach and Speaker

"Bari strikes a potent balance between vulnerable stories, brass tacks practices, and an overarching spiritual framework. At long last, we have a compassionate guide to help us feel at home in one of the most taboo (and troubling!) areas of our lives—money."
—**SARA AVANT STOVER**, *The Way of the Happy Woman* and *The Book of SHE*

"This book is a rare gem filled with honesty, integrity and real solutions for anyone who wants to deeply explore their relationship with money. A true pioneer in the financial therapy field, *The Art of Money* should be required reading for everyone, but especially for financial service professionals and therapists."
—**DEBORAH PRICE**, *Money Magic* and *The Heart of Money*, Founder/ CEO of The Money Coaching Institute

"Wise, warm, and eloquently written, *The Art of Money* is for everyone who desires more clarity and confidence in their money relationship. In her seasoned style, Bari helps your head and your heart journey together toward more peace and prosperity."
—**LISA GRACE BYRNE**, Founder of WellGrounded Institute and author of *Replenish*

"Bari Tessler has found a masterful way of mixing her money methodology with the encouragement we can all appreciate when we face our money fears. *The Art of Money* could be your rite of passage to a fulfilling life and the bank account balance to fulfill on it. You'll feel the revolution from the first page until the last."
—**GLORIA & RICARDO MCRAE**, Co-Founders of Wedge15.com

"*The Art of Money* is a deep salve for one of our most hidden wounds. Bari Tessler's storytelling, grounded practices, and sage wisdom have offered me hope and new way, which I'd never considered before, and would have never found without it."
—**RANDI BUCKLEY,** Coach and Founder of Healthy Boundaries for Kind People

"Bari Tessler says that deep money work isn't magic. But I found, by taking her astute, delicate and wise lead, and following her program diligently, my relationship with money transformed magically. Bari's wisdom will help you welcome money back into your life consciously, with great care and grace. "
—**MARTHA J. HARTNEY**, Attorney

"In *The Art of Money*, Bari Tessler gracefully unfolds an elegant and gentle pathway from the provocative point of looking money in the eye to deeply honoring its teachings and allowing ourselves to heal in its presence. This spiritual and practical map is a beautiful read inviting us to pay attention and soulfully shift our relationship to our resources."
—**NANCY LEVIN**, *Worthy: Boost Your Self-Worth to Grow Your Net Worth*

"How often in your life has money, the elephant in the room, eluded your grasp? Gently nurturing, wise, and always compassionate, Bari is our mahout, as we ride atop that magnificent animal, guiding us with every step, making sure our journey with money is safe, fulfilling, and effective and offers new and expanded vistas along the way."
—**APRIL BENSON**, *To Buy Or Not To Buy*

the art *of* money

A LIFE-CHANGING GUIDE TO FINANCIAL HAPPINESS

Bari Tessler

PARALLAX
PRESS

Berkeley, California

Parallax Press
P.O. Box 7355
Berkeley, California 94707
parallax.org

Parallax Press is the publishing division of
Unified Buddhist Church, Inc.
Copyright © 2016 by Bari Tessler
All rights reserved
Printed in Canada

Edited by Rachel Neumann
Cover and text design by Debbie Berne
Cover photograph © Danielle Cohen

Printed on 100% post-consumer waste
recycled paper

Library of Congress Cataloging-in-
Publication Data is available upon request.

ISBN: 978-1-941529-20-1

1 2 3 4 5 / 20 19 18 17 16

contents

an elephant worth friending

YOU BELIEVE A good life is a conscious one. You reflect deeply, question the status quo, and infuse your decisions with good intentions. You might not have it all figured out, but you're pretty sure the meaning of life has something to do with being as loving, compassionate, and mindful as possible, in big choices and teensy ways, every day: from smiling at passersby to being a conscious parent to finding a way to make a big, positive impact on the world with your one beautiful life.

Normally, you'll look the toughest taboo in the eye. (Heck: you'll pour it a glass of wine and share a few laughs.) From body image to spirituality, diet to a meaningful career, you've gotten brave, gotten honest, and worked to create healthier, more intimate and mindful relationships with yourself, with others, and with the different aspects of your life.

But there's one nagging exception. An area of your life that you'd rather not think about, let alone talk about. One last taboo that can still turn your palms sweaty and give you that icky, pit-in-the-stomach feeling. It's the elephant in the room.

MONEY.

Money was the elephant in the room during that family dinner when you announced your new career—and watched your parents panic. Money was the elephant sitting between you and your sweetie that weekend you gave each other the cold shoulder after fighting about whether to take a vacation this year. Money was the elephant in the room when you berated yourself after splurging on those boots you weren't sure you could afford.

Probably, money has been the elephant in the room your whole life. Because here's the truth: no one has taught you how to *really* deal with him.

You've tried following mainstream "money guru" frameworks and creating super-strict budgets to whip the elephant into submission. But you inevitably fall off the wagon and feel like a failure.

You've toyed with more spiritual ideas of "money as energy" and tried to cultivate a mindset of abundance. But without grounded practices and financial know-how, this quickly devolved into mere wishful thinking.

You've tried turning your back on the elephant, sticking your head in the sand, and tossing bank statements, unread, straight into the trash. But the elephant is still there . . . and ignoring him is getting awkward.

You're not alone. When I introduce myself as a "financial therapist," someone who helps people with their relationship to money, I invariably get the response, "Oooooh, I need that!" Since teaching my first financial workshop in a cozy living room over fifteen years ago, I have been fascinated to learn that absolutely everyone, regardless of age, race, gender, economic background, or musical taste, has shame and stuck places around money. Yet we also all have our strengths, dreams, and gifts in the financial realm.

Money isn't just about the numbers: it's also about our relationship with *ourselves*. In order to shift our relationship with money, then, we must untangle old patterns and challenge our assumptions about ourselves. This is tender work, and I have learned that a nurturing, gentle, and radically un-shaming approach is the *only* way. The compassionate path is far, far more effective in creating sustainable transformation than the self-critical one. Yes, it's challenging! Yet when we embark on this journey, we can also cultivate greater awareness, peace, and joy than we ever thought possible.

Along my journey with money, both as a financial therapist and in my personal life, I have reexamined the toxic and unhelpful idea that money isn't "spiritual" or compatible with a creative life. I have learned, instead, that building a healthy relationship with money helps ground *all* aspects of life. If you already have a mindfulness practice, expanding it to include how you handle money will strengthen it by leaps and bounds, and if you don't have a mindfulness practice, money is, perhaps surprisingly, a beautiful place to start.

. . . . .

While nothing is taboo in my approach to money (and *all* of you is welcome here), there are certain aspects of money that you won't find thoroughly examined in this book, simply because they're not my specialty. One of these is the "macro" side of money: the long lens and big picture view of global economics, historical trends, systems, social activism, and cultural structures. This "macro" side of money is real, worthwhile, and important stuff, and I love learning more about it from my favorite economists (see the Resources section for some suggested reading). Yet the methodology outlined in this book focuses first and foremost *inside* rather than *outside,* on what I call the "micro" side of money: our individual, internal relationship with money. I've chosen this approach because it makes the most sense to me—yet also because I've seen, over and over again, just how powerful it is. Like a pebble falling into a still pond, the benefits of personal money work ripple out into our close relationships, larger communities, and beyond. You heal an old money wound deep inside . . . then find a little more patience for your sweetie during *his* money freakout . . . then he makes a brave financial choice at work . . . and the ripples continue onward and outward. From this deeply intimate starting point, then, we can create a global conscious money movement. Goodness knows, we could use one.

I emphasize these deep places within our money relationship, rich with personal meaning, because in my experience, unless we first turn *within* and heal our emotional relationship with money, no external changes (no matter how savvy) will stick.

However, I also love teaching the practical, external side of money, and have learned how empowering and important this is. Put nuts on bolts, tighten them down, and get things done. In this book, then, you will find many of the money practices and tools I've found indispensable—yet I will always invite you to make these practices your *own*, and to define financial maturity, success, and ease for yourself. You might end up learning how to "spend less and save more" in this book, but it won't be in the way you think . . . and it certainly won't be the main thing you learn. Together, we will approach money in ways that nourish your body, mind, and spirit as much as your bank account.

· · · · ·

In that first money workshop I taught many years ago, one woman joked nervously, "It's easier to talk about my sex life than my credit score!" While I passionately advocate for more openness and honesty about money, I also realize how difficult this can be. That's why, from the start, I've taught about money through sharing my own money challenges, riddles, and triumphs. This book is full of these stories, as well as the stories of some of the many different kinds of people I've encountered in this work, from young to old, broke to flush, urban mid-career professionals to rural farmers. My hope is that these stories will inspire you to shine compassionate light on your own Money Story. Because when we speak the truth about money, deep healing happens. Taboos are broken, veils lift, and radiance breaks forth.

I believe our money work is never done, but rather evolves, right along with us, from cradle to grave—and I am no exception to this rule. That's why, in this book, I share so openly about my challenges and lessons learned about money, both past and present.

That said, I have moved mountains within my relationship to money. I have deepened my understanding of value, worth, and right livelihood, and applied these concepts to my own life in profound and practical ways. I have broken through one "money ceiling" after the next, growing a business that is both financially sustainable and creatively fulfilling, providing for my family and serving my community. I have reexamined old money wounds from my upbringing and deepened my compassion for my parents (and *their* relationships with money). I have strengthened my marriage and parenting through open, intimate conversations about money. I have made my money practices my own by infusing them with body-based mindfulness, playfulness, and dark chocolate. Through all of this, I have become a seasoned guide through the emotional, practical, and psycho-spiritual facets of this thing we call money. I have looked this elephant in the eye . . . and now show others how they, too, can sit down with him, pour a cuppa, and make friends.

Throughout this book, you will be invited to look deeply within yourself. You will create beautiful, meaningful practices and rituals around money. You will draw upon what matters most to you for guidance. You will cultivate your value, challenge your perfectionism, celebrate each tiny victory, and apply mega-doses of self-love, forgiveness, and un-shaming.

Deep money work isn't magic. It's conscious transformation: tiny step after tiny step, day by day, breath by breath.

If you are nervous, terrified, or skeptical—it's OK.

If you are excited and hopeful—it's OK.

If you are overwhelmed, numb, impatient, irritated, lonely, or grieving—it's OK.

Engaging with money this way is a rare, fulfilling, and challenging journey. Yes, there may be rough spots. The road may twist; we might traverse a foggy patch when we can't see the way ahead. But we will also laugh and rest and take dark chocolate breaks along the way.

Deep breath. Take my hand. Here we go . . . .

why are you *really* here?

The Eight Money Areas

Many of us grow up learning that, when it comes to money, thou shalt keep thy head firmly in the sand. See no money. Hear no money. Speak no money.

Then, for many of us, there comes a moment. A wake-up call. The realization that we must come to terms with this *thing* called money.

Sometimes, this call is unmistakable and deafening: a bankruptcy, an inheritance, a career change, or having a child. Yet many people hear smaller whispers, for years: quiet, subtle invitations, drawing their attention ever closer to this crucial, sorely neglected area of life.

One of my mini wake-up calls came the fateful day when my first student loan bill arrived. I stared at the minimum monthly payment in horror: *How do people DO this?* I thought. After briefly considering skipping the country, it hit me: I couldn't ignore the elephant in the room a day longer. It was time for me to finally look money in the eye and figure out how to make friends.

As I started the emotional and practical work of healing my relationship with money, I quickly realized: that student loan bill was the tip of a massive iceberg, and that monthly "payment due" amount was far more than a number. I was coming face-to-face with my struggle to value myself and the education I had just poured years into, my doubts that I was smart enough to learn the language of money, and all the despair and resistance I had around concepts like success, maturity, and ease. As I looked beneath the surface of my financial reality, I began to encounter the *real* longings and quandaries that had brought me to this "money stuff": quintessential things like value, hope, and peace. *These* were the real reasons I was drawn to this "money stuff." These were the qualities I felt missing from my life, but that I sensed I could access and cultivate, if I kept finding the courage to continue my money journey.

I'm not alone. Over the years, everyone who's walked through my door looking for money guidance has been chasing their own longings, just as aching and urgent as mine were. Often, they only knew the surface reasons that brought them to money work: that career change or ongoing fight with their sweetheart. But almost always, they could recognize those deeper, more emotional issues they were seeking to find solutions to through their money work, once I named them. "Yes! Clarity and ease!" they'd exclaim, with a sigh of relief. Once they articulated these deeper desires, the steps ahead of them along their money journey came into focus.

Over time, I noticed trends in these longings, and eventually identified eight key areas that bring most people to this deep money work. These eight areas incorporate what many people are truly longing for in their money relationship—and beyond. They are the facets within our money relationship, skills in which we may either excel or feel our lack of education. As we heal our relationship with money, we cultivate these eight areas, turning them into reliable and joyful companions that may serve us in every aspect of our lives. These are the gems waiting for us at the bottom of the iceberg, making the entire journey oh-so-worthwhile. While they show up a little differently for us all, it's important to begin tracking these deeper currents, right from the start of this journey.

I've listed these eight areas in no particular order, as this journey is not linear. As you read them, you may notice a rush of pride with one area or a pang of longing with another. For now, please just notice and welcome these feelings. All of your experience—and all of you—is welcome here.

1. CLARITY

About half the people I've worked with have sheepishly admitted to me at some point that they have *no idea* how much money they're earning, spending, and saving each month (let alone the total amounts of their assets and debts). A protective fog of ignorance obscures their view of their financial situation, and they're desperately ready to slice through it—yet also terrified by what they may see.

Clarity might already be a natural financial strength for you, but for most people, looking squarely at their numbers is a Big Scary Deal. Clarity asks that we take a deep breath, extend a firm handshake, and say, "Hello! Nice to meet you, money!"—perhaps for the very first time. This is Square One in creating an honest, engaged partnership with money. If you're longing for this kind of clarity, but even reading this paragraph sends shivers up your spine, don't fret: we will move forward slowly, gently, and with compassion for ourselves.

2. INTIMACY

You know yourself pretty well. Perhaps you take your morning coffee black. You love ketchup but hate tomatoes. You forgive almost anything except an insult to your friends. In many areas of life, you are the expert on yourself: your strengths, your challenges, and all of your idiosyncratic patterns. Yet, for most people, this intimacy stops short at money's door. You may not know how you behave with money, what your spending patterns are, or how you really feel about earning. You may not know what your strengths, challenges, and quirks are around money. As with most things in life, when we don't know what's motivating our behavior—or perhaps even *what* our behavior is—there's very little chance of it changing.

Intimacy with ourselves around money entails bringing a curious, compassionate mind to our behaviors and what's motivating them. It means paying gentle attention to what we do and don't do with our money, to how we talk about it, to our thoughts and the whole range of emotions around it, from subtle to overwhelming. This self-awareness opens the door to choice, transformation, healthy control, and an expansion of joy.

3. KNOWLEDGE

The language of money can feel like some sort of jabberwocky, concocted by a malicious madman determined to make things as hard and confusing (not to mention boring) as possible. Many people feel financially illiterate, and are understandably intimidated by this area of life—especially because most of us never received a real financial education, in incremental steps, from childhood on up.

Here's the great news: the language of money actually isn't that difficult. If you're motivated to learn, and (this is the key) practice patience and self-compassion as you climb that learning curve, you really can do it. You *can* learn how to use and enjoy a tracking system (even if you're "bad at math"). You can learn what all of those different financial professionals do, and begin making long-term plans around money. You can make the whole experience pleasurable and rewarding, rather than another miserable to-do. Let me tell you: learning the language of money is crazy-empowering.

4. EASE AND PEACE OF MIND

As I have learned in my role as a financial therapist, many people experience significant stress and anxiety about money, regardless of how much (or how little) they have. A 2015 study by the American Psychological Association found that almost three-quarters of people surveyed experience financial stress, and a recent survey by SunTrust Bank revealed money as the leading cause of stress in relationships.[1] Couples fight dirty about money, even when they're conscious, skillful communicators in every other area of their relationships. Money evokes a constant stream of worry for most entrepreneurs I know. But, I promise: it's oh-so-possible for your financial anxiety and stress to drop way, way down.

If you're seeking more ease around money, it's helpful to identify the true source of your financial stress. You might be surprised. An overwhelming number of my community members have found that simply getting clear on their numbers is a huge relief: their stress stemmed not from a lack of money but from a lack of money *clarity*. You might access greater ease once you're consistently engaging with

---

1 Kelley Holland, "Fighting with Your Spouse? It's Probably About This," CNBC, last modified February 4, 2015, http://www.cnbc.com/2015/02/04/money-is-the-leading-cause-of-stress-in-relationships.html.

your money in a regular, ongoing, and conscious fashion. Or, you may achieve more peace of mind when you learn to flex that savings muscle, get some professional support with your taxes, or learn to greenlight all of your big emotions around money instead of stuffing them down. On a deeper track, many people enjoy a soul-level peace around money as they learn to trust the natural ebbs and flows of their financial lives.

5. SUCCESS

There's a reason I didn't call this book "a guide to financial success." For many people, "success" conjures images of external achievement: climbing the corporate ladder or a flush retirement fund. So many of us want to feel successful, yet have never taken the time to ask ourselves what success actually means for us.

Success is incredibly subjective, so I encourage you to discover (or create) your own definition of it. Success for you may mean earning twenty-five percent more income this year—or it could mean gifting more to charity or feeling more calm and confident around tax time. An entrepreneur might feel financially successful when she's able to charge the rates she *really* wants, and state this amount clearly and easefully to potential clients. Success might mean having safe, supportive, fun conversations with your honey about money. Not only is your definition of "success" your very own, it is also fluid and dynamic, often changing over time alongside your shifting life circumstances, goals, and values.

6. VALUE

Have you noticed that some of these areas have you jumping up and down, saying, "Yes! That's me! I need *that*," while others don't hold nearly as much charge for you? In my own life, *value* was the big, big nut to crack, when it came to money. For most people, value is intimately intertwined with money, and many of our struggles with money are, at heart, part of a quest to find, feel, and claim our own self-worth.

If some of your patterns or discomfort around money stem from self-worth and self-esteem issues, please be extra gentle and patient with yourself. Value is woven from deep, essential stuff: connecting with our unique gifts, finding meaningful work in the world, shifting our relationship with power, releasing anger and self-judgment, and on and on. This is tender work that takes time. Please know that as you move courageously and compassionately forward with your money work, you are already taking steps to value yourself, your time, your energy, and everything that truly matters to you.

7. HOPE

Some people arrive at this money work in near or complete despair. They feel trapped under a mountain of debt or think they'll never find that career that actually feels good *and* pays well. Others have all but given up hope that they'll ever be able to talk to their partner about money without fighting or shutting down. Some are convinced they simply "aren't good at money," and never will be. Many of us have "despair triggers": we feel hopeless when our account dips below a certain number, when tax season rolls around, or when that one uncle asks about our job.

Hope is the gift of believing that things can be different. Hope whispers encouragement in our ear: "It can get better. It will. You can do this." Hope is practical, too: it motivates us to tackle daunting tasks, keeps us showing up to those bookkeeping dates and tough money conversations, and fuels our growth in the rest of these eight money areas. Hope cracks open a sun-drenched window in what looked like a brick wall. If you're here, you have some hope. Each step you take forward in your money journey, no matter how tiny, will grow and deepen your hope.

8. SUPPORT

"Pull yourself up by your bootstraps. Take responsibility. Be self-reliant. Just do it!" Many of us grow up hearing messages like this and repeat them to ourselves for many painful years to come. One place where our culture's love affair with this harsh version of individual responsibility runs most rampant is within our relationship to money. So many of us harbor the belief that we need to do this "money stuff" all alone. "If I don't know how to reconcile a checkbook, there's something wrong with me. If I can't stick to a budget, I just need to grow up, already."

We haven't been taught to ask for support within our money relationship. Many people don't realize this kind of support even exists—or, if they do, they don't allow themselves to receive it. We simply were not taught how to relate to money (let alone acknowledge our emotions around it) from grade school on up. Receiving some form of support is essential for so many of us: talking through our emotional reactions to our debt with a therapist or friend, plotting out a monthly spending plan or discussing debt repayment options with a financial coach, or even getting an accountability buddy to meet for monthly tea and money dates. Creating a financial support team isn't a shameful act that means you're weak, dumb, or lazy. Getting help is one of the smartest, most pro-active and empowering things you can do.

the three phases of
deep money work

ON A SUNNY August afternoon in 2001, I found myself stuck in an apple orchard outside of Sebastopol, California, running late to my first-ever meeting as a freelance bookkeeper. I had almost arrived at my new client's house when I encountered a gleaming white pickup truck blocking my path, parked cattywampus across the backwoods gravel road.

This is the last thing I need today, I thought as I sat fuming in my beat-up old Subaru. I stepped out of my car, smoothing my maroon velvet skirt with sweaty palms, and cleared my throat to have words with Mr. White Truck. The man who emerged from behind the truck had a full silver mustache, a halo of grey hair, and, as he saw me, a huge smile.

"*Bari?* What are you doing out in California?"

Mr. White Truck turned out to be Warren, an old friend and acupuncturist I'd known years before, when I lived in Colorado. That day in Sebastopol, he would change my work-life journey forever.

When I told Warren that I was on my way to my first client meeting as a freelance bookkeeper, he laughed, thinking I was joking. I was used to that reaction. Most of my friends, family, and community thought I was taking a seriously bizarre detour into all of this bookkeeping and "money stuff." I had just earned my graduate degree in somatic psychology, spent all my free time dancing, and considered myself too creative to talk to friends or family about money. It wasn't that I had a *bad* relationship with money, back then. I had *no* relationship with it. I pooh-poohed the whole "money thing" as far too boring. Bank statements would arrive in the mail . . . and I'd toss them directly into the trash. If I thought about them at all, it would be to wonder, *What do people DO with these?* before closing the trash lid.

For most of my life, I harbored the belief that, since I wasn't good at math, I couldn't possibly be smart about money. Like so many people, I was never taught how to manage money, let alone my emotions around it. Though my family rarely talked about money, it loomed like an otherworldly elephant in the room during most fights, sticky conversations, and big decisions. No wonder, as an adult, I didn't want to think about it, much less talk about it.

My path to becoming a bookkeeper was a bit peculiar. I was working long hours and frequent overnight shifts in the mental health and hospice fields when the mental health clinic I worked at asked if I would like to spend five hours a week taking care of their bookkeeping. I leapt at the opportunity, thinking it might provide a little respite from the graveyard hours and emotionally challenging work I had been doing.

A dear friend taught me Quicken and QuickBooks (the gold standard for accounting software), and, to my shock and delight, I understood it. It was as if the clouds parted, the angels sang hallelujah, and I realized that the half of my brain associated with math and money and other strange, esoteric arts actually worked! Not only that, *I loved it.*

Soon, I took on a second job as a bookkeeper at a local bakery. I began tracking and reconciling my own personal expenses for the first time in my life. I devoured every financial and accounting book I could get my hands on, wondering: *Who am I turning into?* By the time I moved out to California, I was hanging dinky blue flyers at local yoga studios and grocery stores, promoting myself as a bookkeeper for healers and other artsy folk.

When I shared what I was up to with Warren, he insisted I meet his friend Tamara Slayton, who lived close by. Tamara had spent most of her life teaching women's work and rites of passage, but had recently become fascinated with money. "She sees money as something that goes way deeper than numbers and cents," he told me. "I think you two would have a lot to talk about."

Hearing Tamara's name was the second serendipitous twist that day. Six years earlier, a thesis advisor had given me one of Tamara's newsletters, a gorgeous and artistic pamphlet called *Cycles*. It had such a profound effect on me that I'd kept it all those years and even brought it with me on my big move from Colorado to California. Clearly, that truck was in my path for a reason: Tamara was about to become my first money mentor.

A few days later, Tamara and I finally met. She was a fiery redhead, artist, teacher, philosopher, and mama of five. I told her about my longing to merge healing, creative bodywork with my new fascination with money—including all of the external tools and practices of bookkeeping.

She *got* it.

Over the next two years, Tamara and I worked closely together. We visioned. We philosophized about money and life and wisdom. We went on walks through apple orchards. We talked about economics, rites of passage, and money *as* a rite of passage. We talked about bookkeeping and numbers, creativity and purpose, financial institutions and right livelihood.

Gradually, over those two years, Tamara helped me bridge my two worlds. She urged me to integrate my bookkeeping work with my deep healing work, years before the term "financial therapy" broke into the mainstream. That day I encountered Warren on that gravel road, he literally stopped me in my tracks. Bookkeeping and all this "money stuff," I soon learned, weren't a temporary detour from my therapeutic career; my life's work would be integrating these two worlds, helping people create mindfulness, joy, and peace *through* their money relationship. Tamara's vision sparked my initiation into my money work: within my *own* relationship with money and, simultaneously, as a mentor for others through theirs.

I applied the same subjective rigor to my money work as I had in my psychotherapy training before: I knew that I would need to become my own, vulnerable-as-heck case study, and shine lights into the deepest, darkest crevices of my relationship with money if I wanted to guide others through their own tender places healing journeys. So I began applying all of the body-based mindfulness and therapeutic practices I'd learned in my psychotherapy training to my Money Story.

I examined my early money memories, my relationship with my parents, grandparents, and money, and how I had hooked money to power and safety. I recalled the shame I felt when I couldn't afford to bring anything to a friend's potluck, the abject terror I felt when my first student loan bill arrived, and how painful it was to have no idea how I could create a comfortable, sustainable living *and* do deeply meaningful and creative work. I taught myself all those things we really should be taught about money from grade school on up. I learned the language of money. I educated myself about bookkeeping and accounting, tracking systems and budgeting. I zoomed out to the grandest possible view of money and life: how money can either make us miserable or help support the realization of our deepest dreams.

I named my business "Conscious Bookkeeping" and began teaching six-week classes to small groups. I assembled a team of financial coaches and bookkeeping trainers under the Conscious Bookkeeping umbrella, and referred clients to outside accountants and financial planners.

Since those early days, I've transformed my business model a number of times. I expanded into a whole team of bookkeeping trainers and financial coaches. I pared down to a one-woman-show when I had my son in 2008. I moved my business online and slowly grew into a passion-driven team leading an international conscious money movement, with over four hundred participants per year from more than twenty countries around the globe. Over the years, I have honed and refined my methodology—but it wasn't clear to me from the start.

Over fifteen years ago, when Tamara Slayton first announced to me that it was time for me to teach about money, I was terrified. How on earth could I articulate and structure the insights I was just beginning to understand, myself? I felt it deep in my bones, though: this was the work I was here to do. With my first workshop looming, I took my questions into the woods behind my home, determined to return with answers.

I walked. I prayed. I implored the trees and the sky for answers. "Everyone in my life is in so much pain around money—how can I help them? What am I supposed to bring back to them? Please give me a framework, some concepts, *something* to ease their suffering." I walked and breathed and listened some more.

After many hours I returned to our ridiculously tiny cottage with . . . something. With the help of my then-boyfriend (now husband), Forest, I mapped everything out. Flip chart paper everywhere. Colored markers. Four hundred square feet of wild excitement. Somehow, an elegant solution appeared seemingly out of nowhere. I believe there was an audible *zap.* We had mapped out a three-phase methodology:

Phase One: Money Healing
Phase Two: Money Practices
Phase Three: Money Maps

Since that day in the Sebastopol woods, these three phases have deepened, changed names, and evolved—but the core of what they represent has remained the backbone of my methodology, from that day forward. Including all three phases in deep money work is crucial, because I've seen time and time again how painfully ineffectual any fractured approach to money is.

Example One. You sit yourself down to "do money stuff"—whether it's paying bills, balancing your checkbook, figuring out if you have enough money to take that vacation—yet become so emotionally triggered/overwhelmed/depressed/numb/ashamed/scared that you give up (or find it *really* hard to continue).

This is what happens when we focus on the external practices in our financial life and neglect the inner, emotional work. This is why Phase One, Money Healing, is so important.

Example Two. In a flash of insight, you realize something about your emotional relationship with money that should change *everything*. Perhaps this flash comes as you debate asking for a raise, and realize you've undervalued your work (and maybe even yourself) for a long time—something you learned from one of your parents. You *know* you'll never be the same, after this revelation, and vow to never forget it. Yet within a few weeks, you've fallen right back into old habits. You had no framework, systems, or rubber-meeting-the-road practices to translate this insight into a daily reality.

This is what happens when we only do the introspective, inner work around money and neglect the ongoing, nitty-gritty, practical component of our money life. This is why Phase Two, Money Practices, is so important.

Example Three. Just when you think you've got your "money stuff" handled, a big life transition sweeps through—a career change, a divorce, the birth of a baby, or a health crisis—and you're back to Square One. Budgets fly out the window, old ways of earning, spending, and saving become obsolete, and you have to find utterly new footing in your relationship to money.

Money isn't something you figure out, once and for all, and then comfortably coast through for the rest of your life: it evolves, deepens, and changes over time, right along with you and your shifting life. This is why Phase Three, Money Maps, is so important.

These are the three different kinds of work we must engage with to create healthy, sustainable changes in our money relationships. Because most other approaches to money only incorporate one (or *maybe* two) of these phases, it's no wonder the insights and practices they recommend don't stick.

Money reflects and affects *every* area of our lives. That's why we need a truly integrated framework if we want to examine, honor, and mature our relationship with it. Here are the phases in more detail.

PHASE ONE.
MONEY HEALING

This is the emotional work of creating an honest, mature relationship with money. Here, we dissolve shame. We get clear on the "Money Story" we've accumulated over the course of a lifetime (and all the patterns we've inherited from our family of origin, lineage, and culture). We identify and unwind patterns that no longer serve us. We claim our value. We learn emotional and body-based practices to support our journey, and ensure we are working with self-care, acceptance, and love along the way.

PHASE TWO.
MONEY PRACTICES

This is the practical, nuts 'n' bolts, number crunching, systems and habits of an ongoing and clear-eyed relationship with money. Here, we gather data. We learn the language of money. We set up daily/weekly/monthly/annual practices to engage with our numbers. We strive to do all of this in ways that are personally meaningful, aligned with our deepest values, and feel creative, playful, and life-affirming. (Bye bye, dry, dusty budgeting. Hello, values-based bookkeeping!)

PHASE THREE.
MONEY MAPS

This is the big picture of your goals, dreams, and plans, how they're unfolding, and how money can fuel them. Here, we learn to make great money decisions, based not only on the numbers but also on your values, phase of life, and more. We look at where you've been in your life, what's on the horizon, and how this moment fits into the grand scheme of your money relationship—and your precious human journey.

The Money Healing phase gives us the emotional support and foundational tools to dissolve the resistance, shame, or other emotional patterns we all have around money. The Money Practices phase translates these deep insights into real-world actions, breathing them to life.

Finally, the big picture visioning of the Money Maps phase situates all of this within the unfolding narrative of our unique lives—and infuses it with personal meaning.

Ultimately, the Three Phases aren't a linear, step-by-step program. They are fluid and organic. Interwoven. Each phase is always happening, and each one affects the other. Once you have learned about them, I hope you will learn to use them in any order, according to what you need, moment-to-moment. You may uncover an old pattern around money from your childhood (Money Healing), then realize you want a better way to track your spending, so you stay mindful of this pattern (Money Practices), then go back to some deep journaling around your resistance to structures and authority (more Money Healing) before zooming out to the bigger picture and your numbers for the entire year and seeing how they meshed with your dreams, values, and goals (Money Maps).

This kind of spontaneous engagement with all three phases can happen once you've delved deeply into each one. But, I recommend practicing them first in order. Master the structure first, then get creative, then return to the structure, as needed. Along the way, take special care to honor your own enthusiasm *and* your stuck places. Linger in a phase, if you like. Or return to it, again and again. Remember: this journey is yours to enjoy. It isn't a sprint, and the finish-line isn't as important as experience. Make the whole process as luxuriously slow or lighthearted as you like.

money healing

· · · · ·

Welcome to the first phase of our journey together.

Here, we explore the vast terrain of our hearts.

We trace the intimate details of our past.

We practice loving awareness.

We dissolve shame.

We unwind old patterns that no longer serve us.

We claim our value.

We forgive.

And we celebrate.

My, oh my, do we celebrate.

This deeply personal, inner work is our foundation.

It is gentle and deep, universal and uniquely yours.

Deep breath. Let the healing begin.

healing money shame

NOAH THREW HIMSELF in the middle of our bed the moment he got home from school. His blue eyes rimmed with red and his bottom lip trembling, he transformed my bed into a tangle of feather pillows and hot tears. I stroked his hair and invited him, as gently as I could, to tell us what was wrong. His soft, warbling voice finally broke through the lump in his throat, and he recounted the affronts of the day:

"I can't read as well as this other girl—and I'm in first grade, but she's only in kindergarten. I'm just not good at *anything*!"

I gently reminded Noah of all the other things he's good at, and that he was learning to read at his own pace. But try as I could to soothe him, he was forehead-deep in swirling shame and sorrow and could not come up for air.

This is shame, pure and raw, and in this case unrelated to money. It is a universal human experience, able to cut us all to the quick, whether we're six or ninety-six. Though its sources shift over the course of our lives, it never loses its potency. When it comes to money, shame is present somewhere in us all, whether it's right at the surface or swept under the rug, prompting big changes or holding us back from even starting our money healing journey.

Learning to recognize, understand, and transform money shame is a cornerstone of Money Healing.

We all carry money shame. Women, men, black, brown, white, young, old, short, tall, gay, straight, billionaires and paupers, spreadsheet enthusiasts and number-phobes, self-made entrepreneurs, welfare recipients, and trustfunders. Money shame is an equal opportunity affliction, and it does not discriminate based on who you are, where you're from, how much money you earn, what percentage you save, whether you pay your taxes on time, or what your credit score is.

I have worked with people earning under $20,000 a year and people earning several million a year. Everyone, every single one, has had some sort of money shame. So, above all, do not shame yourself for having money shame! Second, know that there *is* a way out. But first: let's un-sweep money shame from under the rug and get to know it. After all, it's an illuminating, opportunity-filled, and misunderstood little beast.

What *Is* Money Shame?

Money shame might be a universal human experience, but each of us carries our own types and flavors of it, which are as unique as our fingerprints. Your money shame might be tied to a specific experience in your life, your upbringing in general, or none of the above. Here are some variants I've heard:

"I'm just not good with money. I can't be trusted with it."

"I earn plenty, but I still seem to spend too much—how do I have this much debt?"

"I'm too right-brained, creative, and bad at math to be good with money."

"If I make a lot of money, I'm betraying my working-class roots."

"I should be further along with my savings/earnings/debt payoff/ investment."

"People who have money are bad."

"I'm so flaky around money. Why can't I get it together?"

"I can't believe how bad I screwed everything up. I'll never be able to fix this."

"I used to be so good with money—what happened?"

"Why can't I earn more/save more/spend less/pay my bills on time?"

"I should have more money by now—the fact that I don't means something's wrong with me."

"I'm too reliant upon my parents/husband/daughter for money. Why can't I be more financially independent?"

"People like me shouldn't make money; it's dirty and unethical."

"I only deserve money if I work really, really hard for it. Lazy people (like me) don't deserve money."

"Wanting more than 'just enough' money is selfish."

Here are some of the ways money shame can show up:

- That queasy pit in your stomach as you approach the check-out line, wondering if your card will be declined (or if you're simply buying more than you "should")
- Pangs of guilt when you decide how much to charge for your new product or service (if you're an entrepreneur)
- Feeling hot, sweaty, and anxious when the topic of money comes up in your extended family
- Feeling sleepy, bored, "checked-out," or out of your body a little when you pay bills

- Guilt, frustration, and disempowerment in your personal and business life
- Procrastination, "freezing," or denial around paying your taxes, setting up an estate, or some other money-related item on your To Do list
- Anxiety around talking about money
- Fear or guilt that you don't have way more saved for your future
- Rabid self-criticism
- A leaden cloak of grief that's always with you
- Rage toward the world, your family, your boss, etc., that you even have to *deal* with this part of life
- Longing for someone to swoop in and save you from your money struggles or issues
- Utter hopelessness and despair that you'll ever figure it all out

. . . . .

If you recognized yourself in any of the above, or in all of it, you're in the very best company. In fact, I've never met a person who *didn't* carry at least some money shame, at some point in their lives—even people who call themselves "money experts."

Back in my social worker days, one of the heaviest pieces of money shame I carried was the belief that I shouldn't try (or even *want*) to earn a comfortable income: that would be too materialistic, shallow, and un-spiritual. Instead, I told myself I should just do good work in the world and be happy with that. Unfortunately, this shameful money belief only fed another: I was supposed to earn more money and "be a grown-up" about it. Satisfying both of these demands wasn't just difficult, it was utterly impossible. Indeed, when we look directly at money shame, we can start to recognize all of those sneaky contradictions and impossible double-binds it puts us in. It took me years of reflection, forgiveness, and practice to let go of these beliefs about money, and throughout this book I'll share many of the insights and tools that helped me. But the first and foundational step in healing money shame is acknowledging, as gently as possible, that it exists.

A SPECTRUM OF INTENSITY

Suzie was convinced she'd never be able to show her face in public, again. The beautiful house she had bought the previous year (her first house ever and a huge source of pride) was falling apart around her. The foundation was cracked, and years of rain damage had begun separating the entire front wall of the house from the rest of the structure. The repairs would cost more than the value of the house itself and were far beyond her means. She had sunk her entire life savings and a generous loan from her mother into the down payment. She spent months fine-tooth-combing every contract, inspection, and document she had signed, looking for some way to keep her home. She talked to a dozen lawyers, contractors, and government officials; she researched short sales, foreclosures, and government assistance.

As for many people, there was no legal recourse for Suzie; the only option she had was foreclosure and bankruptcy. Crushed and ashamed, she moved into a modest apartment a few blocks away. For the next several years, she couldn't drive by the house without falling into despair. She cried at work, at home, and in public. She even began avoiding her favorite people and places for fear she'd burst into tears. She berated herself for creating this mess: obviously, she told herself, it was all her fault, because she was bad with money and didn't deserve such a nice house. Suzie talked about her money shame with a therapist, who helped her see she hadn't done anything wrong, and this situation happens to many people. Berating herself for not being savvier about money was an old, ingrained pattern that *felt* helpful but actually kept her stuck. It took Suzie several years and a lot of work, but she eventually cultivated more compassion for herself and everyone involved with the house. Eventually, she was able to hold her head high, delighted to know that she truly could live through anything life threw at her—even this, her idea of a worst-case scenario. Yet for a long time before this point, her money shame felt like a full-time job.

Some money shame feels acute and all consuming, like Suzie's. Yet there are also more subtle forms of money shame, and some of us only experience fleeting pangs of it here and there, when a memory surfaces or a late fee arrives, for example. Kate, a dear colleague of mine, drew a blank when I asked about her money shame. "For me, 'shame' refers to something so intense, I can't even talk about it without fighting back tears," she explained. Yet, sure enough, within a few moments, she shared recent stories of when she'd felt embarrassed, inadequate, or immature around money. Despite a huge leap in her earnings over the previous few years, Kate hadn't saved more than a couple hundred dollars: as soon as money came in, like the tide, it went right back out. Kate was usually able to witness this aspect of her financial life with lightness and compassion, but when she talked about money with others in her field, considered buying a home, or projected long-term, her jaw tightened, her gut sank, and she wondered when she would ever "grow up" and learn how to save.

Money shame can feel like anything from a tightened jaw to a queasy stomach to sleepiness, anxiety, or grief. While it's often tempting to stuff down the unpleasant feeling of money shame, it is far more helpful to recognize it when it arises, and call it by its name—no matter how huge or small it feels. By noticing, naming, and honoring even this challenging emotion, we crack a doorway into other, gentler, more reassuring states of mind.

If we took all of these various flavors of money shame, put them in a pot, and simmered them down to their fundamental quintessence, it would be something like: "Something's wrong with me. I'm not OK. I'm bad, deficient, not good enough. I'm doing something wrong in this area of life." For the vast majority of people, this essential core of money shame brings along its buddy, *comparison*. Like money shame, comparison can take many forms: "If only I'd grown up in a different family, I would've learned about this money stuff . . . If my parents had been richer, I wouldn't struggle with money so much . . . If my parents hadn't been so wealthy, I wouldn't struggle so much . . . If I were a different type of person . . . If only . . . If only . . ." Comparison boils down to: "Other people have this figured out, so why don't I?"

Many of my clients not only compare themselves to other people, they compare themselves to an idealized version of themselves: the version of the self who was born into a wealthy family, who instinctively knows how to budget, or who fights gracefully for that pay raise. Then, they torment themselves for not living up to this imaginary standard.

This cycle of self-abuse only perpetuates shame. Real, sustainable transformation never occurs in this way.

Where Does Money Shame Come from?

I've asked thousands of people: "Were you given a financial education, on an emotional, practical, or spiritual level?" The crazy-ubiquitous answer: "Nope."

Most of us were simply not taught about money: how to manage it, how to talk about it, and least of all how to navigate our feelings about it. In an ideal world, we would learn money skills and tools for understanding it and practices for relating to it and how to talk about it, all in incremental, age-appropriate ways, from grade school on up.

In the absence of this much-needed education, we project like crazy onto money: we conflate it with our identity, our sense of worth, our definitions of success and maturity, beliefs inherited from our community, lineage, culture, spiritual aspirations, and on and on.

Given that most of us simply were not taught how to make sense of money in any conscious way, is it any wonder, then, that we flounder and fall in this money territory?

As shame and vulnerability researcher Brené Brown explains, "Shame needs three things to grow exponentially in our lives: secrecy, silence, and judgement."[2] We've already seen these three ingredients in action: most of us keep our money shame to ourselves, never (or rarely) speak it aloud, and berate ourselves for even having it. As we'll explore in more detail later—and as I hope you're already beginning to *feel*—simply naming and speaking money shame aloud is an important step in healing it. As Brown continues, "Shame cannot survive being spoken. It cannot survive empathy."

Gentleness: The Only Way Out of Money Shame

One of the trickiest things about money shame might be its ability to shapeshift. I've seen money shame masquerade as many, many different

2 Brené Brown, quoted in "Brené Brown on Shame: 'It Cannot Survive Empathy,'" HuffingtonPost.com. Last modified August 27, 2013. http://www.huffingtonpost.com/2013/08/26/brene-brown-shame_n_3807115.html.

things. For example, cynical judgments that wealthy people are spoiled and heartless might hide a deep shame of being raised by a poor single mother. The belief that a welfare recipient is lazy may stem from a guilty unease around the privileges you've been handed. Perhaps the most ubiquitous mask money shame wears is that of the helpful self-disciplinarian: *"I have to keep beating up on myself about this money stuff so that I toe the line!"* Please do not be misled by such rhetoric. As helpful and mature as this "tough love" approach might sound to you, this is often unhealed money shame, yet again, keeping you under its thumb.

Shaming ourselves is an old, unconscious pattern. Telling ourselves, again and again, that we are not doing it right, that we're not good enough, or that we're unforgivable is self-directed violence. It's unhelpful and flat-out inaccurate.

The path out of money shame is *not* getting smarter or working harder or restricting your spending more harshly. You hold the shaming whip in your own hands and it won't stop hurting if you lash yourself harder or in a new spot. When Noah cried about not being able to read as well as he wanted to, I didn't tell him everything will be OK once he can read. I reminded him that I love him right now, right here, just how he is—and that I know he will learn to read at his own pace, on his own timeline. Likewise, "tough-love" approaches to money, while they might work on a practical level for a time, never create sustainable, positive healing. Saying you'll heal your money shame by getting your act together with budgeting is simply madness. The path out of money shame isn't shaming yourself harder; it's finally putting down that lash, releasing those unrealistic standards, and cultivating every last drop of forgiveness, self-love, and compassion you can muster. Tough love is simply not an effective way to heal emotional wounds.

Two Stories of Letting Go of Shame

I settled into the plush, overstuffed couch, taking in the beautifully appointed space around me. I was in the San Francisco home of a dear friend, colleague, and client, Rebecca. That day, on that beautiful couch, we would record an interview about a rarely spoken sort of money shame: shame of wealth.

It was money shame itself that first prodded Rebecca to address her relationship with money. Like many people, Rebecca didn't hear one single, big "wake-up call" about her money shame, but rather experienced it on a subtler level for many uncomfortable years before reaching out for support. "I carried this secret shame: I didn't have a clue about money! But I thought I was the only one who had an issue with it, because I saw friends or family who seemingly 'had it together.' I finally got brave and said, 'I'm tired of feeling this way, being this way, spending this way.'"

Rebecca's "secret shame" about not knowing how to manage her money might surprise people who were raised in middle-class or working-class families. In the small groups I've taught for many years, as soon as someone raised their hand and mentioned growing up in a wealthy family, it was as if all the oxygen was sucked out of the room, and I could practically hear all of those icy judgments: "Well, I'd sure love to have *that* problem! If only *I'd* been born into a wealthy family, all of my money issues would disappear." But as I've learned—and as Rebecca so bravely shared—there are challenges and strengths from every type of financial background.

Rebecca continued, "Because I came from a wealthy family, I felt like I shouldn't have *any* issues, in any area of life. I'd been given so much, so who was I to complain? Who am I to say that I'm struggling, or have had pain, here? It took me a long time to validate that pain for myself."

Rebecca listed several "flavors" of money shame common to people who'd grown up in wealthy families:

Alienation. Others assume I've had everything handed to me on a silver platter, and throw epic judgments and projections my way.

Entanglement. Family money often arrives with strings attached, complicating the already challenging process of getting to know yourself and becoming your own person.

Guilt. Who am I to have these resources, when others in the world are struggling, even starving?

Fear. I've been given so much, but do I deserve it? Am I worthy? Will I ever be able to accomplish enough, share enough, or make a big enough difference in the world with this money?

Self-doubt. Could I have made it on my own? Could I ever truly be self-reliant and earn without help, just from my gifts, sweat, and brilliance?

Hearing Rebecca talk, I could see the shame lift. Her face brightened and she spoke with more confidence. Shame thrives in the dark, silent lands of taboo, so bringing the light of consciousness and courageous truth-telling can dissolve even the deepest, oldest shards of money shame. There is such healing in speaking the truth about money. *Especially* when it comes to releasing old patterns of shame and blame.

Another striking story of releasing money shame comes from a colleague of mine, Fabeku. At the tender age of eighteen, Fabeku suffered the unexpected loss of his father, who died from cancer. In the thick of this grief, Fabeku received a sizable inheritance: $60,000. (Which, as he put it, felt like $40 million at that age.) While he invested some of the money in computer equipment for his graphic design career, he spent the rest on frivolities and luxuries, including treating his three best friends to an extravagant trip to the West Coast. Within nine months, he had spent the entire $60,000, and within a couple years, he was literally homeless, living out of his car. "I remember the shame," he shared. "A few years ago, I had $60K! Now, I'm sleeping in my car. How does *that* happen? I had a ton of guilt around that, for years."

It took Fabeku years and a lot of inner work, but he eventually healed his money shame around this episode of his life. In fact, he even drew a cache of wisdom from it. Fabeku's process included accepting on a deeper level just how young he had been when his father died, and forgiving himself for doing the absolute best he could with a large sum of money and extremely limited know-how. When we spoke, he could still recall the weird mix of horror and relief he felt as he watched his bank account dwindle. It took Fabeku years to understand that one reason he had spent that money so rapidly was how grief-stricken and ambivalent he felt about its origin: the loss of his beloved father. Eventually, Fabeku came to cherish this experience with money shame as a crash course in what he refers to as his "superpower": *freedom*. "Having this pile of cash felt like instant freedom: I could buy whatever I wanted. But later, looking back, I realized: there's unrestrained freedom, and there's *balanced* freedom." As it turned out, a little structure and balance were necessary to sustaining the feeling of freedom over a period of time—and while there might have been easier ways to learn this lesson, going from wealthy to homeless made the lesson stick for Fabeku at a very young age.

After he recounted this story and the hard-won insights he had gleaned from it, Fabeku admitted that he'd never shared it publicly before our conversation. Money shame keeps us tight-lipped, even with those closest to us. As Fabeku quipped, "People talk about [money] like it's this dirty little secret. We can't talk about it or, the flipside, we can only talk about the good stuff. So you feel like the one jerk who's had a hard time. On one level, it's silly. But on another level, it's crazy harmful."

My own money shame stayed pretty hidden until that fateful day I received my student loan bill. I knew I had to find some way to sort through and heal the flood of money shame I was suddenly faced with. So I turned to my training in somatic psychology and created what I call the Body Check-In: the simplest and most fundamental practice I teach and one of the best ways I know to begin healing money shame.

the body check-in

AS I WATCHED my son Noah whirl and splash at the water's edge, I dug my toes deeper into the warm sand. I pushed my sunglasses onto the crown of my head so I could see more clearly. My husband sat beside me, holding my hand lightly. I turned to watch the sun and shadows dance across his closed eyelids, and I could almost see the grey fog of stress and exhaustion roll off of him, into the healing sand and ocean air.

Santa Cruz was, mercifully, our final destination along one of the wildest, most beautiful, and most challenging adventures our little entrepreneurial family had ever undertaken. For the past seventeen days, my son, husband, mother-in-law, and I had traveled down the West Coast of the United States, filming a mini travel-and-money documentary. We had sat with, broken bread with, and filmed video interviews with a number of colleagues and members of my year-long program, getting intimate and real about their personal journeys with money. While all the conversations, hugs, and enthusiastic feedback on the web episodes were nourishing, the trip had also been far more challenging than expected.

Just imagine: three adults and a six-year-old, in a small RV. Eight towns in seventeen days. Stiff beds, leaking toilets, carsickness, a young child *literally* bouncing off the walls. Pre-camera primping in campground bathrooms, next-to-no exercise, and all of it at a breakneck pace so we could film our interviews, edit them, publish them on our website from the RV, and immediately hit the road for our next town. It was a beautiful adventure, and I adored meeting so many people face-to-face (a rarity in my online teaching model) and sharing their stories through film. But those weeks of fast work and hard travel took a toll on us all. By the time we reached the finish line—that gorgeous Santa Cruz beach—we were discombobulated burnt toast: beyond done.

But there, on the sands of Santa Cruz, I watched my little family come back to life. The sun, ocean, and beachy breeze all worked their healing magic on us. We perked up, woke up, and let loose. *Ahhhhh.* But a haze of anxiety haunted the afternoon sunshine. We were scheduled to fly home to Boulder the very next morning, and my nervous system was still haywire from our epic work-travel journey. I was dreading the return to normal life, work, and rush—and craved just a few more hours of healing downtime.

Suddenly, an idea struck me like a genius thunderbolt: we should stay in Santa Cruz for a few more days before heading home. This had a certain kind of logic: we'd just lived through one of the toughest work-and-travel periods we'd ever experienced and, once we got home, we would dive right into the busiest time of the year for our business. But it wasn't just the logic that made this idea most compelling to me. It was how it *felt.* I have learned to listen to and honor my body's signals, and in that moment, everything in me was telling me to stay. I knew that we desperately needed a few days of beach, rest, fun, and chill-time. Whatever it took, I needed to make this happen.

But quickly, the not-so-fun reality of this plan sank in. This was a money decision. A big one. We would need to change our flights and pay for three extra nights at the hotel, in addition to incidental and recreational expenses. I made a mental estimate, and felt an icy wave of fear rush through me: this was going to be expensive. Plus, we were in the middle of the registration period for our year-long program (which earned the lion's share of our income for the whole year), so I couldn't know exactly how financially risky this was. Within me, hope battled fear, soul-knowing duked it out with heady skepticism, and deep long-ing fought financial logistics. Adding another layer of complexity to this mix, this wasn't my decision, alone: Forest and I would need to come to an agreement about it, and I wasn't sure if he would be on board with my little California dream.

This was a complex money decision. But, thanks to the technique you'll learn in this chapter, I was able to get extremely clear about what I wanted, quickly. Of course, I felt fear and stress and doubt arise. But using the Body Check-In, I was able to move through these challenging reactions without being paralyzed by indecision or anxiety.

The Body Check-In is my absolute favorite tool for conscious money work. It has been the cornerstone of my approach since the very first group I taught, over a decade ago, and I return to it again and again because of its simplicity, elegance, and profound power to support us through challenging emotions and stressful situations. It helps us remain present, empowered, and conscious when things get tough (*or* when things are so fabulous, you can't believe it). It supports us along steep learning curves and through deep, inner exploration (two things money work demands of us frequently, and often simultaneously). I recommend it to both the newest and the most veteran money adventurers. It's the perfect foundational tool to empower you right now, along the first leg of your money journey. While it only takes a moment to learn, don't let its simplicity fool you: when practiced regularly, it is massively supportive and utterly life-changing. Pinky swear.

....

HOW TO DO A BODY CHECK-IN

It all starts with a pause. Stop whatever you're doing. Take a moment for yourself. Gather up all of your attention and turn your gaze within yourself.

Take a few deep, slow breaths. Close your eyes, if this feels good and helpful to you.

Adopt an attitude of openness and curiosity. Without judgment or any attempt to change anything, simply notice. Start with your physical sensations: become aware of how your body feels on your chair or how your feet rest on the earth. Notice sensations of movement and stillness: the breeze across your skin or the quiet stability of your pelvis. Notice how your breath feels, moving in and out: is it deep, shallow, cool, tight?

Next, gently observe the emotions moving through you. Do you feel angry, anxious, annoyed, or awestruck? How do these feelings *feel*, in your body? Is your jaw set in hot determination, or do you feel a flutter of excitement in your belly? Allow yourself to simply be aware of these emotions and how they feel in your body.

Also notice any thoughts, images, memories, or self-talk. Like clouds floating through the sky of your mind, simply notice them. No need to cling to them *or* push them away—simply acknowledge them. Are self-criticism, judgment, or other challenging sensations arising? Notice. Are elation, excitement, or other expansive sensations arising? Notice these, too.

As you scan your body, emotions, and mind, you may like to ask yourself if there's anything you'd like to remove from or add to your situation. If you notice your jaw is tight, perhaps you'd like to wag it loose. If you notice your breath is shallow and quick, you might gently lengthen and deepen it. Come home to your body, here. Follow your breath. This isn't about perfecting or even changing anything—it is simply about being *aware*.

....

That's it! You just did your first Body Check-In. You might spend a relaxing ten minutes doing this, or twenty seconds might do the trick. Think of it as a compassionate treasure hunt: you may find clues, patterns, or insights about whatever you're feeling. If writing these down in a journal feels good to you, then make that part of the process, too.

Once you've done your first Body Check-In: repeat, repeat, repeat. I recommend this practice before, during, and after every money decision or any of the money interactions you face throughout your day, from teensy to monumental. When you're in the checkout line at the grocery store, or the parking lot at the mall. Before you go online to look at your balances and pay bills. After that stressful conversation with your credit card company. Smack dab in the middle of a money conversation with your sweetheart, your parents, or your business partner.

Especially in tough times, when you're feeling triggered, stressed, or simply "off." Certainly as you delve into the deep and often turbulent waters of Money Healing, as you encounter pieces of money shame, work through your Money Story, or take yourself on a Money Date (a practice we'll explore in Phase Two of this book).

This practice is simple—yet utterly profound. The Body Check-In can become your reliable companion on this whole money journey. It will bring you back home to yourself. It will unravel levels and layers. It will soothe frayed nerves and dissolve mental fog. It certainly did all of this for my family and me, as we faced that tricky financial decision on the beautiful Santa Cruz beach.

· · · · ·

I gathered my beach bag and headed back to our hotel room, determined and excited to share my brilliant idea to stay in Santa Cruz with my husband. Forest had already gone inside, and I found him sprawled on the bed, in a sea of laptops, recording equipment, techie doodads and gizmos. He was back in work mode, intently focused on editing our latest video interview so we could share it in our online newsletter. I could feel the buzz of work overtaking the healing calm of the beach, inside my husband, inside the room, inside myself. I sat next to him, slid off his headphones, and announced—as gently as I could—my idea to stay in Santa Cruz for another three days.

"No way, Bari," he scoffed immediately. He proceeded to list all the reasons we couldn't stay. "We have no idea how this registration period will go, and I can't make a decision like this without seeing the numbers. So—no. We are absolutely not staying here and spending a bunch more money for a few more days on the beach."

Forest put his headphones back on: he was back in his work-cave. I sighed. On the one hand, he was totally right: the cost for three more days in California would be terribly steep, and we truly did not have a clear picture of our finances. Yet, even if the numbers weren't totally clear, my heart was. I knew we *did* have the immediate cash flow to make it happen (without racking up credit card debt). I knew that if we *didn't* stay, the cost to our emotional and physical well-being would far outweigh the hotel and flights. Every cell in my body was telling me to make this work, no matter the price. I motioned for Forest to take his headphones off again.

As we talked through this money decision, my passion crashed like a storm front into Forest's fear and doubt. The harder I said "yes," the harder he said "no." My "yes" got bigger, stronger, faster and Forest retracted farther and farther into his "no."

I knew this wasn't just about the numbers. I could see the fear and stress on my husband's face. "I see what's happening with you," I reassured him. "I see you shutting down. I want us to stay connected through this."

Forest begrudgingly agreed it was worthwhile to just *see* what the actual cost might be. So I took the phone out onto the hotel balcony and drank in the view of the ocean. As I negotiated prices with airlines and travel agencies, my body began swaying. This flowing movement was my doorway into embodied mindfulness—functioning much like a Body Check-In—back to this space where I feel rooted and light, centered and present.

I first developed this habit of moving my body when I was stressed back in my angsty teenage years. Back then, my emotions often felt so huge and overwhelming, I had a hard time even articulating them, let alone working through them. Instead of ignoring my feelings, though, I would lock myself in my bedroom, blast Madonna and The Cure, and dance, not only to the music, but as a way to express my huge emotions. I discovered that if I relaxed and allowed my body to express these emotions in an unfiltered, raw way, I could understand them (and myself) better. I always emerged from my bedroom with greater presence, clarity, and self-trust. It became second nature to move my body and "lean into" challenging emotions instead of fleeing from them. Eventually, I would follow my fascination with this body-based practice to a wonderful graduate program in somatic psychology, where I studied mindfulness, body-based wisdom, and emotions to their fullest extent.

Over the years, regular practice of mindful movement and the Body Check-In has supported me through a wide range of my life's ups and downs. Whenever I was stressed or overwhelmed with emotion, I knew it was time to get back into my body. The Body Check-In helped me through a period of immense grief, when I lost one of my dearest friends. It helped me dissolve an old, addictive pattern of overeating by showing me what hunger and fullness *really* felt like (something I had been disconnected from all the way into my mid-twenties). To this day, I still rely on Body Check-Ins to help me make most decisions, big and small: from where to go on date night to what sort of program to create next in my business to what publisher to choose for this book. Whenever I get stressed or overwhelmed with emotion, I know it's time to get back into my body.

The Body Check-In is so versatile and effective because, in many ways, we are a mystery to ourselves. Countless times a day, in countless ways, we "check out" of our bodies. We keep shoveling ice cream in our mouths when we're full; we snap at our beloved partner or child; we hide under the covers when our excitement about a new project reaches a critical mass. The Body Check-In brings us reliably, gently, and compassionately back to the present moment, and back home to ourselves. It is only *here* and only *now* that we can meet ourselves, understand ourselves, and transform ourselves. Here, in this embodied mindfulness, we can experience and work with our "money stuff." From this open, curious, and fully present place, we may choose a new pathway out of old patterns. Using the Body Check-In within our money relationship brings us to transformation's Square One: awareness.

Awareness → Understanding → Transformation.
In your money life . . . and beyond.

Many of us have mindfulness practices in other areas of life—on the yoga mat, in conversation with our sweetie, or while eating—yet neglect to bring this same awareness to money. When confronted with an overdue tax bill, even the most mindful among us tend to get scattered, overwhelmed, or numb. That's why one of the first things we become aware of when we start practicing the Body Check-In is just how *unaware* we typically are.

After a few months of regular Body Check-Ins during her shopping trips, Shelby, a mother of two teenagers, noticed an odd pattern: as soon as she pulled out her credit card at the cosmetics counter at the mall or surfed over to an online shopping site late at night, a woozy, dreamy feeling would wash over her. The more present and aware the Body Check-In made her, the more she noticed just how unconscious she habitually became at the moment of a transaction. This is one reason the "just do it" approaches to money management often fail: how can you possibly stick to a budget or limit your credit card spending when you "check out" at the checkout counter? Awareness comes first, then understanding; and finally, transformation.

Tuning into the content of your inner experience is a way of honoring it and yourself. This pause is, in fact, a radical act of self-love. It sends the message that you matter, and what's arising inside you deserves attention. This compassionate and attentive self-care is particularly important when we encounter vulnerable facets of ourselves (like money shame). Regularly practiced, it builds our confidence that we can take good care of ourselves, which makes us feel safe to continue learning, growing, and moving forward, even when the territory is as unknown and anxiety-producing as deep money work. The Body Check-In also primes us for new experiences by cutting through distraction and overwhelm, which slam the brakes on our ability to metabolize new information.

After a financially contentious meeting with her landlord, Aurora, a middle-aged office manager, took herself around the corner to the park, a safe space to practice the Body Check-In. At first, she noticed anxiety. But as she followed the sensations arising in her body, she noticed shame . . . and then grief. Memories of trauma bubbled up, as well as the challenge of redefining her financial identity and breaking out of a scarcity mentality. Finally, glints of hope broke through all of this darkness; Aurora felt her own vulnerability, and reminded herself that what was most called-for, and *within her control*, was kindness and gentleness. She called up her best friend for a little cheering on, treated herself as kindly as she could, and honored those shimmering glimpses of hope. While it often feels centering and calming, the Body

Check-In never glosses over the complexity of our emotions, but often reveals new depths—both positive *and* challenging.

Grace, a young graphic designer, shared the mini-triumph of doing a Body Check-In while in line at the grocery store. While this had historically been a stressful, frightening spot for her as she worried whether she had enough money to feed herself, on the day in question, she approached the conveyer belt confidently and happily. She had just received a large paycheck from a new client who had signed up for a six-month retainer project, and Grace had fully mapped out her expenses for the month. For one of the first times in her adult life, she felt well paid, knew she wouldn't go hungry, and could buy her groceries with confidence. It occurred to her to practice the Body Check-In, so she could truly *feel* the *good* feelings she was experiencing: safety, "enoughness," clarity, and groundedness with money. She exuberantly shared how memorable and profound the experience of *truly* allowing herself to feel the good things was. Indeed, it can often be just as challenging to fully feel our positive, expansive emotions as it is to deal with our stress and fear. As you make progress in your own money journey, the Body Check-In will reveal your evolution to you—and may even feel like its own reward.

Many people are scared to fully go into their feelings with a Body Check-In. They have the fear that if they fully open to a feeling, it will swallow them whole. For the most part, this fear is unfounded. In the same way that dancing to Madonna in my teens helped me deal with the turbulence I was going through then, allowing ourselves to fully feel our emotions actually helps them move through us, often surprisingly quickly, leaving us more informed and whole than before.

Move at your own pace through Body Check-Ins, as slowly and gently as you like. Give yourself permission to dip your toes into a feeling, see how you respond, and then wade in deeper only if it feels right. If you feel particularly overwhelmed or raw, invite your favorite furry friend into the process, or take your emotions to a park, creek, or garden. Nature, animals, friends, candles, and chocolate (especially chocolate) can all provide invaluable support when emotions get hairy.

A word of caution: if you encounter some particularly overwhelming emotions, old wounds, or trauma, please do not deny yourself the support you need and deserve. Reach out and get help: from a professional therapist, a help line, a friend, whoever is available to you. You do not need to go through this alone.

· · · · ·

In the Santa Cruz hotel room, after almost two hours on the phone with various airlines, travel agencies, and the hotel itself, I felt like I'd found the answer. I rushed inside from the balcony with good news to share with my worried husband. While I was dancing, I had successfully negotiated a fabulous deal for us to stay in Santa Cruz. It would still cost us a significant amount of money, but it was less than half what the airlines had originally quoted us to cancel and rebook our flights. Plus, the hotel was allowing us to stay in our beautiful ocean-view room (which they'd originally told us was booked). With a travel agent still on the line, I explained the good news and asked my husband if he could find a "yes," so we could stay by the beach, rest, and heal for another few days.

A dark shadow crossed Forest's face, and for a few long moments, he was silent. He later described what he experienced in that hotel room as a very young, frightened, preverbal place within him. Silent and dark. It was his core money issue, wrapped in shame and anxiety, and very close to a fear of dying. Not only were we debating a large expense, and not only were we in the dark about how much money we would have access to, but he needed to make a decision within a matter of minutes, while the travel agent was still on the phone.

Despite all of this stress, within a few moments on that gadget-strewn bed, Forest was able to sort through his powerful emotions and say, "I'm scared. I can't see clearly into our financial future. I barely have words right now . . . but let's do it." He had practiced his own version of the Body Check-In to help him through these challenging emotions. He was able to stay connected to himself and to me, and come out the other side with a clear money decision.

Later, he explained,

When I first started working on my "money stuff," I thought that once we made enough money, my core money issues would just go away. I'd never have to feel this fear, this dark feeling, again. That's what I hoped, at least. Once we earned significantly more money, sure enough, a couple years went by without those dark feelings coming up. But I always had the nagging suspicion that the issue was still there, in the background, waiting for the right combination of triggers to arise. On that day in Santa Cruz, I learned: Oh . . . yep! There's that same money issue. Right there. It was just waiting for the right conditions to rear its head.

Here's what I've learned from working with this core issue over the years: deep money issues aren't about the numbers. If you make more money, they don't go away. Making more money won't heal them—*awareness does.* The marker of growth isn't necessarily that your issues disappear. It's that you're able to move through them when they arise, and you can prevent your core money issues from making major money decisions *for* you.

Feel your feet on the floor, feel the grief in your belly, lower your shoulders, let it roll through you. First comes *awareness* of what's happening—however challenging or stressful it may be. Then comes *understanding* of what's happening—beliefs, habits, ingrained patterns shine forth, illuminated. Finally, a doorway opens, and hope beckons with a golden finger: *conscious transformation* is possible, here. You *can* choose a healthier pattern. You can un-shame yourself. With practice, you can move through all of this faster and faster, more and more easily.

We can't expect to exterminate our reactions or emotions around money. But we can tone down the emotions and soften the triggers. We can catch our reactions, honor them, work with them, be loving and gentle with them, learn from them, and be more fully present. In this way, your relationship with money will deepen and evolve. In the case of our Santa Cruz decision, there was so much beauty on the other side of this stressful decision. A few weeks later, Forest shared:

> Every moment of those four days in Santa Cruz felt
> heightened, like a hyper-real dream: with every breath of that
> warm California air, every whoosh of the waves—I was very
> aware that I wouldn't have experienced any of it if I hadn't
> hopped on Bari's vision-train, worked through my money
> issues, and stayed. I'm so grateful that Bari had the clarity to
> see what we all needed. I'm so grateful that I didn't let my old
> money patterns make my decisions for me. I recognized the
> pattern, was patient with it, stayed in connection with Bari,
> and made a new decision. It was wonderful. Those four days in
> Santa Cruz are turning out to be a highlight of our year so far,
> and I have a feeling they will remain that way in my memory.

This is another of the many benefits of regularly practicing the Body Check-In: not only do stressful emotions become easier to manage, joyful emotions become more vivid.

Of course, your emotions around money won't simply disappear, and your personal "Money Story" will stay with you (unfolding and evolving) throughout your life. But by practicing the Body Check-In, you can bring more and more love and awareness, honesty and compassion, smarts and empowerment to your relationship with money. You can move through your emotions *more quickly*, with less self-shaming and more self-love. When life gets tough, it's tempting to escape our experience by checking out of our bodies. But trust me: the answers are never out there. The way out ... is in. With a little practice, Body Check-Ins can become second nature and emotional honesty your preferred M.O. You can show up with more patience and power, every single day.

The next time you pay a bill or bump into an old belief about money, pause and check in with your body. You may find this practice particularly useful as you read the next chapter, where we'll begin exploring the oldest roots of your money relationship: your personal Money Story.

your money story

I SLAMMED THE screen door behind me and stomped down the sidewalk toward the car, kicking every rogue rock in my path. I was sixteen and wanted to make sure *everyone* within ear- or eye-shot knew my displeasure. *Especially* my father. He was cool and comfy inside the air-conditioned house, while I, halfway to the car, was already sweating in Chicago's summer mugginess.

That day, my father had instructed me—insisted, despite my protestations—that I find a part-time summer job. In fact, he decided that I should apply for at least a half-dozen jobs that weekend, reporting back to him at regular intervals to share my progress. I was aflame with adolescent angst. I hated the push and rush of it all. Most of all, I hated feeling controlled—especially by my father.

The memory of this angst-ridden summer day came flooding back to me a few years ago, smack-dab in the middle of a live-streamed interview. An online learning company had invited me to host an interview series with my dream-team lineup of financial colleagues, visionaries, movers and shakers. One of my most-anticipated interviews was with Barbara Stanny, a pioneer in the field of women and money and a delightfully tough cookie. Partway through our interview, she turned the tables and asked *me* a terribly vulnerable question: "Close your eyes . . . what is your earliest memory of money?"

I like to think of myself as a gracious interviewer, game for spontaneous experiments and experiential surprises. So I did my best to report honestly and fully the earliest memory that I could find. The memory of job-hunting on that hot summer day came to my mind and refused to leave. While it might not have been my *earliest* money memory, it was a defining moment in my money relationship. In fact, it cut deep enough that I couldn't keep my voice from shaking as I shared it with Barbara—along with a virtual audience of thousands! This little memory unleashed a torrent of emotions, beliefs, and associations within me. It perfectly illustrated the point Barbara was trying to make: something *happens* in our earliest encounters with money that shapes us for the rest of our lives.

Barbara isn't the only money coach who guides people through this sort of visualization, but she has one of the best explanations of *why* it's so powerful. As she explains, when we access our earliest memory of money, freeze-frame it, and really examine it, we will inevitably find that, there and then, in that moment, we made a *decision* about money. *Money is dirty. Money equals power. Money is for those other people, not me. Money equals survival. Money equals happiness.* This decision, however irrational and unconscious it may be, drives and shapes our money relationship for the rest of our lives. Sometimes, it will serve us; at other times it will shackle us. It will show up loudly, in big money decisions, and sneakily, in seemingly insignificant ways (that might add up to big, life-long patterns). As conscious adults, when we shine the light of awareness upon this seminal memory, re-experience, understand, and lovingly witness it, we empower ourselves with choice. We can liberate the gifts locked within that memory and cut loose any tethers that had bound us to it, against our will.

After I shared that early, job-hunting money memory with Barbara (and the live, worldwide audience), Barbara kept me on the hot seat for a few more minutes. She asked me to slow that memory down—way, way down—and to feel into what decisions, judgments, and associations I had made about money, back on that summer day. I took another deep breath. In a flash, I saw it: all of the challenges and gifts of my financial upbringing—the paradoxes of middle-class life—were crystallized and preserved within this one, tender memory.

I remembered the car I drove to those job interviews: my father's dream car, a black Mustang that we kids got to drive. That Mustang symbolized the upside of my financial upbringing: my parents were generous, my siblings and I always had enough, and there were, undeniably, nice things in my life. Yet that memory also contained the darker side of my relationship with money: I was *scared* to apply for those jobs—and rather than teach me how to pick the right one, give me advice on how to give a good interview, or offer any support for my extreme anxiety, my father ordered me to simply do it. That day, my father taught me without words to *be tough, push through, emotions be damned, go make something happen, and earn money.* That summer afternoon contained all the tangled emotional conflicts I would associate with money for years to come: nice things *and* emotional disconnection; generosity *and* abandonment; fear, anger, and domination.

Of course, my father was doing his best to teach me something that had been invaluable in his own life: the ability to *be tough.* This was part of his own money lineage: his parents had instilled this hard-knuckled drive in him, and it had served him well growing up and in the rough and tumble world of Chicago real estate. But as he tried to pass this tough-as-nails attitude and work ethic along to me, I railed against it. I decided that day that I would never, ever rely on a man for money; I would honor my intuition; and I would never sacrifice my heart's calling for any old job, but would insist on a career that set my heart aflame. I had no idea how I would pull all of this off but I was determined, all the same.

None of these decisions were fully conscious that muggy afternoon. But they would operate beneath the surface of my mind, informing my relationship with money and work, for the rest of my life. In my twenties, unbeknownst to me, these beliefs influenced crucial steps along my career path. In my thirties, they fueled my hesitation to get married until I had done a metric ton of inner work and found a man I could feel was my equal partner. In my forties, these early money decisions compelled me to embrace a nontraditional, creative, and values-based approach to entrepreneurship. In countless ways, I have adhered to, rebelled against, and struggled to integrate the money decisions I made that day.

Barbara Stanny's own earliest memory about money affected her just as deeply as mine affected me, though in very different ways. In Barbara's earliest money memory, she was three years old, perched atop a miniature step stool, brushing her teeth before bed. Suddenly, a question popped into her mind, and she turned to her mother to ask, "Mama, how much allowance do *you* get?" Her mother remained silent but gave Barbara a withering stare. In that moment, Barbara got the message (and made the decision): *one does not talk about money.* Years later, as she navigated extremely difficult financial circumstances, she kept silent about them. Even in her sessions with a therapist, where she could talk openly about everything else, she couldn't bring herself to talk about money. This early memory, then, set Barbara on a path of neglecting money for many years—and ultimately paying a steep price for it.

This sort of money neglect is incredibly common—yet it's never too late to turn it around. I often refer to money as one of life's "gardens," one of those important aspects of our life we need to consciously cultivate. Like spirituality, sexuality, or food, these gardens are there whether we're aware of them or not. Without loving attention, they can wither or become overgrown with weeds; with too much watering and pruning, they may become soggy or fragile. It is up to each of us, at every phase of life, to discern the just-right amount of attention and care our money "life garden" needs. These earliest money memories are much like the first seeds planted in these gardens, eventually growing into the central, imposing fixtures of our financial lives. They are the focal points, the towering oaks, around which whole ecosystems grow, even though we often remain unaware of their existence.

As conscious adults, when we bring these early money memories into focus, we can choose how to care for them: we can prune them back or even encourage them to stretch their limbs along a beautiful new trellis. We can pull the dead limbs off of that old sycamore, plant daffodils around its base, and even adorn it with a hummingbird feeder, a tree house, or twinkling lights. With compassion and awareness, we can nurture our Money Garden, making it beautiful and bright.

Thankfully, these initial seeds in our Money Garden (our earliest money memories) aren't always painful; sometimes, they reveal long-hidden financial strengths. When Amy, an emergency room nurse, went digging for her own earliest money memory, she recalled herself at eight years old, holding a small, treasure-filled blue box. She flipped the secret switch to unlock it and pulled out a carefully folded stack of cash: many months' worth of allowance, birthday money, and earnings from shoveling snow from neighbors' driveways. Next, in a thrilling power reversal, her mother poked her head into the doorway and asked if she could borrow a little money. Like most Saturday mornings, Amy's mother had just spent several hours at the dining room table, surrounded by a stressful explosion of bills and paperwork. As Amy counted out the cash to lend, her mother exclaimed, "Gosh, you're so good with money! How'd you save all this?" Amy beamed, feeling awfully proud and grown-up to be able to help her mother with money. Yet she also felt a twinge of warning in her mother's praise: *Just wait till you're a grown-up—money won't be so easy then,* she imagined her mother saying. In that moment, Amy decided two things: first, "being good with money" meant having a lot saved; and second, once you're an adult and have responsibilities, money is impossibly hard, and you'll never have enough. As she gently examined this early money memory, Amy discovered just what a Catch-22 it presented to her adult self. How could she be good at money if being an adult meant she would never have any? By unpacking the conflicting messages in this early memory, Amy was able to forgive herself for the debt and financial gaffes she'd made in her early twenties, while also dusting off one of her long-forgotten strengths with money: her ability to save it.

Meet Your Money Story

As pivotal as these initial money memories can be, there's much, much more to your relationship with money. Whether or not you could afford college, for example, and if you did go, whether or not you had to work when you were there, may be a big part of your story. You may have relied on a partner for part of your twenties, lost your financial footing due to a layoff, or received a big inheritance. You may have been financially self-reliant from the age of sixteen on up, or your money relationship may always have been intertwined with your family. Perhaps you turned your financial relationship around dramatically when you started your own business—or maybe you took a risk in the stock market and lost your life savings.

This panoramic view of your past and present relationship with money is what I call your Money Story. Your Money Story is the entirety of your relationship with money, from the tiny details to the major events. It's as unique as your fingerprint and includes the whole shebang: the historical facts of your financial life; inherited patterns from your family of origin, lineage, and culture; how you take on or rebel against them and integrate your own beliefs and behaviors around money; and all the sensations and emotions that get stirred up in this terrain.

When I introduce people to the concept of a Money Story, I tell them to start by looking at their current relationship to money—*then* go back to the past. I learned this the hard way. Years ago, in my work with small groups and individuals, I instructed them to begin their Money Story work in the past: with their childhood, family of origin, and ancestry. Inevitably, my gentle instructions were met with looks of raw terror and overwhelm. This approach went too deep, too fast. That's why I now suggest you begin exploration of your Money Story in the present moment. First, center yourself with a Body Check-In. Then, look at your current relationship to money: how you feel about earning, spending, saving, and so on. Once you feel current and aware, you can begin the next phase of the journey, into the past. You can gently explore memories and lovingly turn over rocks. Clear the cobwebs and shine lights. Perhaps you can push even further into the past, examining what messages you've received about money from your religion, ancestral lineage, or culture.

Once you've assessed your current relationship with money and your past history with it, you can make the crucial leap of connecting the dots between the two, noticing if you're echoing spending patterns your mother taught you, or rebelling against your grandparents' strict beliefs about savings by splurging any chance you get.

When we can clearly see the past *and* its influence on our present relationship with money, a whole new world of choice opens up for us. Perhaps you realize that the inheritance you received from your grandfather was created in ways you consider unethical—knowing this, you can choose how to be a conscious steward of that wealth. Maybe your parents lost all of their money in a stock market crash, which instilled a deep distrust in you from an early age. Becoming *aware* of this inherited belief and *understanding* where it comes from and how it affects you sets the stage for liberated *transformation*: you can choose a new path for yourself and your future. Perhaps your immigrant parents each worked three jobs, teaching you that your worth equals how hard you work; becoming *aware* of this belief may free you to enjoy a deeper sense of your own value, just for being who you are, even if you only work one job and never miss your annual vacation.

If I have learned anything in my years as a financial therapist, it's that we have the power to rewrite our Money Stories. We can sift through our histories and distinguish the facts from our subjective experience, interpretation, and the meaning we've made of them. Through awareness, understanding, and un-shaming, we can heal our Money Stories, reframe old beliefs, shift patterns, and create utterly new, delightfully meaningful beliefs and practices around money.

Money Memoirs

A few years ago, I invited thirty-three colleagues, friends, and community members to get brave and share their Money Stories on my blog. I didn't just include "money experts"; I talked to mamas, papas, young people and old people, white-, blue-, and no-collar professionals, artists, unconventional entrepreneurs, healers, waitresses, and musicians. Every single person I interviewed had stories to tell, shame to unravel, insights to liberate, and strengths to celebrate. For some, the stories flowed with ease and readiness; for others, it was hard to access early memories or speak the truth about money.

A successful business consultant recalled her father's instruction about money: "Money is like the dirt on your hands—brush it off before it clings to you." This ambivalence about money suffused her early interactions with it, until she decided to make it reflect her own commitment to generosity. Another woman admitted that she had spent years pushing money away because of how her family seemed to "worship money over love."

A wildly talented artist and successful entrepreneur shared the tension, frustration, and scarcity that surrounded money during her childhood. She also identified the brilliant gem at the heart of this scarcity: she developed a gift for budgeting and saving that served her well into adulthood.

An author and entrepreneur recalled her childhood with a father who dealt with all things financial and a mother who pursued her passions without any pressure to monetize them. The money message Tara internalized was, "girls do what they love; men take care of money." It took years for her to break out of "little girl mode" with money, and bring all of her smarts and passion into her financial management.

Beliefs like these spring from fleeting moments at the dinner table or half-heard phone conversations from the other room. They accumulate over generations, from our family of origin back through our cultural heritage and seemingly into the very strands of our DNA. They overpower us during a crisis and topple when challenged by a truer truth. In many ways, our personal, unconscious definitions of money come to define us. That's why bringing awareness to them is so doggone important.

· · · · ·

I maneuvered the black Mustang into a strip mall with a gym, an ice cream parlor, and several restaurants. My father's assignment for me that day was to apply for a minimum of six jobs, and then report back. In one afternoon, I filled out application after application, wrangling those awkward clipboards and practicing my most mature, self-assured smile (while underneath, I was anxious and angry). I applied at the health club, the miniature golf course, and eventually at the little ice cream parlor in the strip mall, where I would soon don a hideous green apron and work my first job.

I hated almost all of that crummy ice cream parlor job. I loved the part about eating all the ice cream I wanted. (Double dark chocolate fudge daily!) I loved depositing a paycheck every two weeks; earning money felt wonderful. But I despised the work itself. It felt arbitrary and dull, and it offended my adolescent idealism.

The resentment I felt toward my father for making me get this first job has since softened into appreciation and understanding. Now, as a mid-forties entrepreneur and mother, I can look back at that summer job and recognize what my father was trying to accomplish. A self-made middle-class entrepreneur, my father prized hard work, responsibility, and self-reliance. Thanks to his hard work, we always had enough money to cover our needs and most of our wants. While I am incredibly grateful for the abundance of my upbringing, our moderate wealth carried with it its own challenges, too. I saw my father work long, stressful hours to provide for us; there was often a lot of tension around money—and yet, we weren't supposed to talk about it. While I had friends who were much wealthier and much poorer than us, for me money was simply always there. I think my father recognized how this level of comfort might lead to a dangerous complacency. His insistence that I get a job that summer was his way of teaching me a work ethic and the value of paying my own way.

The last thing that freckled fifteen-year-old in her ice cream parlor apron thought she'd become was an entrepreneur, especially one focused on money. From an early age, I noticed how many people respected my father as a successful, aggressive businessman. But I also learned to associate "business" with stress, frustration, and lawsuits. I knew I benefitted from his hard-earned wealth, but I also hated the ugly underbelly of business, at least how I judged my father's version of it. Even my friends' focus on career and money bored me; many of my neighborhood friends jumped right from college to very profitable careers, and everyone seemed to put "high earning potential" toward the top of their personal life goals (and the list of qualities they wanted in a potential spouse). This career-centric lifestyle felt stifling to me, especially because I was a little slower to find my true passion and career.

My personal progression from unconscious enmeshment with my family's money beliefs, into rebellious rejection, and finally into integrated synthesis is common. I've seen it play out, to some degree, with many of my financial therapy clients. Our relationship with money goes through a maturation process, very much like that of a child. All of us grow, evolve, and unfold our relationship with money, and while every person's journey is unique, there are common themes and stages that many of us go through.

How "Grown-Up" Are You, with Money?

Over the years, hundreds of people have admitted to me that when it comes to money, they still feel like children. When a financial stress arises, their wits and emotional sophistication fly out the window, and they instantly feel like an infant, a toddler, or an adolescent. They might throw an inner tantrum (like a two-year-old), crumple into a preverbal haze of fear and confusion, or even explode into a rebellious, "I hate the world!" teenager.

Such childlike reactions around money are hardly surprising. Many of us truly *are* like children when it comes to money, simply because we have not worked with it consciously or enough to mature our relationship with it yet. One of my favorite stories of this kind of childlike money behavior happened (perhaps not surprisingly) in the Apple Store. My client, Rachel, a biochemical engineer expecting her first child, walked into the gleaming computer store a little shaky, but armed with a plan. Her laptop had been stolen out of her car, so she was already shaming herself for being so careless—but her plan was to stay grounded and make the best decision she could about buying her new laptop. Before heading in, she had done some research and mentally earmarked the medium-level model as best fitting her needs and budget.

But all that reason and "maturity" flew out the window when she stepped into the shiny, happy retail wonderland. The salesperson asked her the same questions Rachel had asked herself: what features did her old laptop have, what would she be using it for, etc. As she chatted with the salesperson, Rachel could feel her teenage self emerging, growing in desire. She was tantalized by all the gleaming things around her: the top-of-the-line screen, the additional RAM, and all the fancy bells and whistles she didn't need, but that would be oh-so-nice. Didn't she deserve it? And couldn't-she-just afford it? And how often do you buy a laptop, anyway? By the time Rachel regained her composure, her "adolescent self" had justified and rationalized and convinced her to buy a significantly more expensive computer, one that was really more than she needed or could afford.

Rachel paused. She took a few deep breaths. She realized this was an opportunity to make a clear, empowered money decision. She needed a little more time to center herself and get clear, so she excused herself and walked out of the store, a brave act in itself. Rachel took herself for a walk around the block, practicing her Body Check-In as she moved. She followed her breath and gave herself full permission to feel her feelings. Her "teenager self" was clamoring for attention, so Rachel took another breath and decided to listen. "Hello, you," she cooed. "Tell me what's going on."

For a few minutes, Rachel simply listened to this inner adolescent voice. She listened to her raw desire and sharp rationalizations. She didn't cave in to her or shut her down, she merely listened, with openness, compassion, and curiosity. "My teenage self is extremely rebellious. If she doesn't feel listened to, she mows me over in no time. I've had to learn to be really loving, gentle, and strategic with her, to give her room to have her say, and validate her."

After about twenty minutes, Rachel felt ready to return to the store. Having honored her adolescent desires, she felt less overpowered by them, and ended up buying the medium-level computer she had originally planned on purchasing. "It was such a small thing, but it was a huge triumph for me. Not just because I didn't spend that extra money, but because I actually got into relationship with this adolescent part of myself around money."

So many of us are afraid to slow down and listen to these younger parts of ourselves. We might already judge ourselves for not being more of a grown-up around money, and we're afraid that, if we listen to that rebellious teenager or anxious toddler, they will take us over. Yet it is only when we take the time to truly honor and get to know these younger parts of ourselves that we can create a relationship with them, become whole, and move forward into clear-headed maturity.

Ripping out the early pages of our Money Story doesn't help anyone. It's by rereading these old stories, unraveling these ancient patterns, and honoring these young voices within us that we can integrate them and eventually write a few new chapters.

· · · · ·

When we stagnate in a young or immature phase with money, it sometimes takes a dramatic act or crisis to spark change. George, a theater set designer in his early thirties, reached out to me from a thick haze of guilt and overwhelm. Back in his adolescence, his parents, both scientists, had strongly disapproved of his choice to go to college for theater. In the years since, his theater career had started blossoming, but his relationship with money remained stagnant.

George, like so many people, had shut down and tried to run away from his money problems. Like many of us, he had never been taught how to file his taxes, track his spending, or review his money patterns. Yet (also like many of us), he thought he somehow *should* already know how to do all of these things, and shamed himself into a complete shutdown around money. For over five years, George didn't file his taxes, and ignored notice after notice from the IRS. Finally, he woke up to find the IRS had filed a lien on him, laying claim to his house, car, and other personal property.

George couldn't ignore his finances any longer. Yet instead of berating himself for not being more "together" with money (thus triggering more avoidance, less action, and even more childishness), George chose a new path. He began practicing the Body Check-In regularly, allowing himself to acknowledge his emotions—even the challenging ones. Once he *felt* his feelings, he could notice his self-sabotaging patterns and break free from them. He stopped shutting down and started getting support. He hired an accounting firm to file his taxes.

George's financial transformation wasn't all-sunshine-and-roses, though. He began tracking his spending, only to become overwhelmed by the software program he'd chosen. As with any education, George took leaps forward, fell down, and picked himself back up again. He woke up to find himself "like a child" with money, and though he desperately wanted to "grow up" around it, he accepted the time and energy this would take, and began looking forward to each new chapter in his Money Story, even the turbulent teenage years.

You can choose to update your financial identity anytime you like. I developed a strong appreciation for this truth when I spoke again with Fabeku Fatunmise, the colleague whose inheritance story I shared with you in Chapter 1.

As a successful entrepreneur, Fabeku experienced some rapid income growth. One day, as he reviewed his income for the past quarter, his jaw dropped: his mind was utterly blown. He realized the Fabeku looking at those numbers was the *old* Fabeku, a previous version of himself, who wasn't yet used to earning much money, and had no clue how to manage it. It was time to update his financial identity, plug into who he was, right then, and go from there. Fabeku began updating his financial identity, asking himself on a regular, almost daily basis: "Who am I now? What's my current identity, with money? How does this person earn, manage, save, and spend?" He quickly found that he needed both inner and outer updating to keep up with his evolving relationship to money. Within himself, he felt more strongly rooted in valuing himself, more mature and free, and he needed to let that sink in and shift some old beliefs. On a practical level, his increased earning meant he needed to hire a new accountant better versed in his new income bracket.

Your financial identity is fluid and subjective.
Update it anytime you like.

. . . . .

I don't remember how much money I made at that Chicago ice cream parlor the summer I was sixteen, but I do remember that I loved earning it. More accurately: I loved *spending* it. I wanted things and, when I wanted them, I *reallyreallyreally* wanted them. I'll never forget the pair of purple Gloria Vanderbilt corduroys that I needed desperately or that aqua-blue blouse I ordered from the Esprit catalogue.

The moment I tore off my chocolate-splattered apron and tore into my very first paycheck, my financial identity shifted. Suddenly, I had more control, more power, and more freedom. I didn't have to borrow money from my little brother to buy that candy and I didn't have to coo nicely to my mother to get me those clothes. I had started the long journey of financially individuating from my parents and *that* felt wonderful.

Individuation is a huge theme in deep money work. Whether we're familiar with our inherited Money Stories or not, many of us go through periods of breaking free from our parents' ways of doing things. While sometimes it feels wonderful and liberating to individuate, the process can also be painful.

Layla, a stay-at-home mother in her forties, received a shock a few weeks before Christmas. She had ordered a huge quantity of toys for her children online, and while they arrived safely, they were stolen right off of her porch. The toy company and delivery service refused to replace or refund them, and she knew her children would be crushed. Layla reached out to her community for help and created an online fundraising campaign to replace the toys. She felt proud of her resourcefulness and thought it was a great step forward to receive support from others in this way. Yet her little bubble of pride popped the moment she shared her idea with her mother, who was horrified. Layla's mother was raised with very little money, and developed strong, strict beliefs about self-reliance and image. She was disgusted that Layla had asked for help in this way, and didn't hesitate in telling her so. At first, Layla was deeply hurt. Then, as she reviewed her own Money Story, Layla recognized that, though she was well into her forties and had a family of her own, she had gotten lost in her *mother's* Money Story. It was difficult and sobering, but from that point onward, Layla stopped chasing her mother's approval around her money decisions and started making her own judgments.

. . . . .

As we trace our Money Stories, most of us bump into this universal truth about money: we have all received certain advantages and disadvantages. We were *all* born into a lot in life. At a certain point, many of us enter the sticky, sometimes tender territory of comparing our Money Stories with others. Our hearts break when we see our parents working long hours into their seventies, just to make ends meet, while others live in opulent mansions. Or we feel guilty for our own abundance when others have so little.

Some of these disparities stem from systemic injustices and ingrained, inherited hardships on a grand scale. This points to that "macro" view of money, which, while certainly important to educate ourselves about, isn't my personal focus (see the Resources section for more reading on this subject). For some people, this sense of injustice becomes part of their calling in life, so they spearhead economic equality or do social justice work—and this is beautiful and necessary. Yet even more often, I have found that the question of "fairness" around money emerges from young, hurt places deep within ourselves. When we feel anger, grief, or anxiety as we compare ourselves to others, it is often a warning bell that we have gotten stuck focusing on our disadvantages rather than our gifts. Every lot in life affords its own set of challenges and gifts, and it's never all good or all bad. Each of us has a different path to walk and each of us has the ability, to different extents, to influence where that path leads us. It is up to each one of us to do something with what we've been given. Something better. Stronger. Different. Beautiful.

. . . . .

As a mother, I have the great privilege—and responsibility—of watching my son's Money Story being written. My husband and I try to bring as much awareness as we can to the elements of our own Money Stories that we're handing down to our son, so we don't unconsciously pass along unhealed wounds or unforgiven chapters. *Have I let go of that resentment, yet? Do I need to update my thinking on this thing?* I want to carry forward positive elements of my upbringing—the value of work, for example—while releasing other, less helpful pieces. The goal here, I remind myself compassionately, cannot be perfection: as much as I strive for mindfulness and loving awareness, we all pass along some unconscious beliefs and patterns to our children. Yet my husband and I are doing the very best we can to offer our son as much education about money as we possibly can, knowing he will formulate his own experiences and personality, gifts and challenges—in short, his own Money Story—as he grows.

Whether you're a parent or not, this process of sifting through your Money Story and releasing pieces that no longer serve you is important, challenging, and beautiful. We cannot truly heal a wound without forgiveness. Writing new chapters in our Money Story usually involves completing old ones, which means seeing them, learning from them, and letting them go. There is beauty in this release. With a little guidance, we can honor old parts of our Money Story, and gather their wisdom, while gently, cleanly cutting our ties with them.

....

MONEY STORY VISUALIZATION

Create a safe, sacred space for this exploration. You may want
to light a candle, say a prayer, or pour yourself a cup of tea. Take
your time. Move gently. Insert Body Check-Ins before, during,
and after. If you find yourself rushing, slow down. You may want
to answer all of these questions at once, or you might insert a
few moments or even days between each section. Explore with
compassion and curiosity. Let this be an act of mindfulness and
self-love.

1. DESCRIBE YOUR CURRENT RELATIONSHIP WITH MONEY

It's always best to begin in the present moment. Spend a few
moments thinking or writing about your current relationship with
money. How do you feel about earning, spending, saving, giving,
borrowing, loaning, and receiving money? What feelings or memories do these activities stir within you? Slow down. Do you notice
any beliefs, patterns, or conditions attached to these areas?

2. VISUALIZE YOUR MONEY PAST

Get centered in your body and take a few deep breaths. From this
grounded, mature place, let your mind travel back into your childhood memories. Look around, see your home and its surroundings. What did you learn about money, here? What beliefs did you
receive? What decisions did you make? Do you recall others who
had more or less money than you? What did you feel about that?

Now, think about your family. What was your mother's role,
in terms of family finances? What messages did she give you
about money, verbally and through her unspoken behavior and
emotions? In what ways have you echoed her role or rebelled
against it? Ask these same questions about your father, your
grandparents, your siblings, and anyone else significant to you in
your childhood.

continued

Did you receive messages about money from your religion, culture, or lineage? What were they?

Trace the ups and downs of your life in relation to money. Did you experience any big financial successes or hardships? How have they affected you, your life, and how you relate to money?

3. CONNECT THE DOTS BETWEEN PAST AND PRESENT

How are you keeping the past alive in your relationship with money? Considering everything you were taught (and not taught) about money, how are you living out old or inherited beliefs, patterns, and stories? Have you repeated the past, rebelled against it, or struck out on your own?

How is your past Money Story affecting your relationships with your parents, siblings, friends, boss, clients, or larger community? How does it show up in your self-talk, in your behaviors, and in your thoughts about the future?

4. GIVE YOURSELF A HUG

Congratulations! Even if you answered just a few of these questions, you deserve a huge pat on the back. However you might be feeling at this point—energized, angry, grieving, or overwhelmed—please know this: you are brave, you are awesome, and you are making great progress in your Money Initiation. Please take time for self-care and integration after this significant exploration. Dance, draw, paint, sleep, hike, play with the dog—do whatever you love to do, to honor your courage and let these insights seep in.

CHAPTER 4

forgiveness, completions, and letting go

THE VERY FIRST money workshop I led began with ten men and women gathered in a circle in a cushion-strewn living room. These brave money adventurers swore they wanted to create new, healthier, and happier relationships with money. But despite their hope and determination, something held each one of them back. It was as if heavy chains were keeping them anchored to painful elements in their money stories: outdated money beliefs, shameful secrets, unresolved relationship dynamics, and even to practical To Do's they hadn't checked off their lists. As genuinely as they desired their bright new futures, they simply could not move forward until we paused, looked into their past, and addressed what was tying them to it.

Some of these first clients already knew what was holding them back from the moment they signed up for my money workshop:

"I haven't paid my taxes in three years, and the shame is killing me."

"My inheritance caused a family rift, and I can't see my brother without fighting about money."

Other issues were more subtle and didn't fully surface until we'd done some digging into their past:

"That time I stole money from my Mom's purse when I was seven still haunts me."

"I can't believe I signed that pre-nuptial contract without reading it. Wow, I sure didn't know how to value myself back then—and I'm paying for it!"

Sheepishly, one by one, people admitted their money secrets and stuck places. They usually thought they were the only one with a Big Dark Secret or unfinished business around money, and they inevitably sighed with relief when they found out we *all* have our "money stuff" from the past that needs to be completed, released, forgiven, and grieved.

As you dredge up your Money Story, you will likely encounter pieces that you are ready to release, loose ends you're ready to tie off, and old money beliefs you've reexamined. Sometimes, resolving these old chapters of your Money Story is simple: mail that tax return, set up a payment plan with the collection agency, or have that chat with your brother about the money he owes you. Often, though, the work of releasing, forgiving, and letting go is a little harder, more subtle, and more internal. Here, we don't just need action: we need deep money healing before we can move forward and write that new, more hopeful chapter in our Money Story.

This is the tender realm of forgiveness. Here, we come full circle back to money shame . . . and release it. Gently, baby step by baby step, with as much mindfulness and courage as we can muster, we transform our shame. We grieve, forgive, complete, and let go.

No act of forgiveness is too small if it liberates energy for you.

The Levels of Letting Go

As with most everything in our money relationship, there are levels to completing lingering bits of your Money Story.

Practical: Hire an accountant, get yourself organized on TurboTax, clear the clutter from your desk, organize your files, pay off that credit card, collect money someone else owes you, set up a manageable payment plan with the IRS, make an appointment with a consumer debt advocate, coach, or other financial professional who can offer you support.

Emotional: Speak your truth to someone (in reality or through a letter you never send), release old emotions, stories, and dynamics that no longer serve you (but keep knocking on your door), let go of some adolescent rebelliousness, honor your need for support through this healing journey by working with a financial therapist.

Mental: Sift through your beliefs about money and consciously affirm or reject each one.

Spiritual: Voice anything unspoken (especially grievances) in your relationship with whatever your conception is of something greater than yourself (even if you don't have such a concept at all). We all define this spiritual level of money in our own way, but for me, it's about working with deeper levels of trust, thriving, and tithing, and shedding negative, stuck energy within myself regarding money.

As you complete various bits of your Money Story, you may find that tying off one loose thread reveals a dozen more issues. You might think a completion is merely practical, then uncover emotional, mental, and/or spiritual components within it, ready to be released. Everything is normal. All of you is welcome.

The Gifts of Forgiveness

"Practicing forgiveness means letting go of self-righteous anger, blame, and resentment. That's hard. The combination of self-righteous anger, blame, and resentment is one of my favorites. Umm. Umm. Umm. Drink it up! Unfortunately, I think it's toxic and eats you alive from the inside. It might go down like a milkshake, but it burns up your insides like battery acid." —Brené Brown[3]

---

3 Brené Brown, "Imperfect Parenting—Forgiveness," *BreneBrown.com*, last modified August 28, 2008. http://brenebrown.com/2008/08/28/2008828imperfect-parenting-forgiveness-html/.

....

BABY STEP: COMPLETIONS

Find a quiet, comforting time and place, free from distraction and disturbance. Surround yourself with things that comfort and reassure you. Do a Body Check-In and anything else that helps you relax and connect with yourself.

When you're ready, ask yourself: What would I like to complete in my money relationship? What am I ready to let go of, release, or say goodbye to?

Take it slow and gentle. Remember, you don't need to recall everything on your first try—you can come back to this at any time. If it helps, consider each of the four realms: physical, emotional, mental, and spiritual. You may find it helpful to consider any secrets you keep about your past, as these are often wrapped around incompletes.

Then, if you're ready, brainstorm. For each one, what are possible action steps to complete, let go, or forgive?

....

There are always two sides to forgiveness: the letting go and the moving forward. Looking back to the past and stepping forward. Releasing and creating anew. It seems paradoxical, but when we look back at our pain from the past, honor it, and release it, we can also move forward in new, more liberated ways. We let go of old beliefs about money and choose what new beliefs we want to bring forward with us, into the future.

Forgiveness is tough work. It is a *journey*. But the rewards are *huge*. I'm not just talking about being able to mail that letter or file that tax return. I'm talking about liberating your energy reserves and vastly expanding compassion for yourself and others. The stories below illustrate some of the gifts that await you on the other side of forgiveness.

THE GIFT OF PEACE

"Forgiveness is not always easy. At times, it feels more painful than the wound we suffered, to forgive the one that inflicted it. And yet, there is no peace without forgiveness." —*Marianne Williamson*

When we cannot (or will not) forgive, we are, effectively, haunted by our past. We may harbor unprocessed sadness, rage, fear, insecurity, or a host of other emotions, beliefs, and dynamics. Common indicators of hauntings include: sweaty palms when you sit down to pay your bills, your eyes glazing over when you pull out your debit card at the market, or the lump in your throat when a new client asks about your rates.

As I learned when I did grief and hospice bereavement work, we can't simply snip those chains tethering us to our past. Try as we might, even if we really, really want to, grief simply doesn't work that way. It is an active process, and you can no more resolve old money stories by turning your back on them than you can forgive a friend by pushing him or her out of your awareness.

Instead, we must bring our old money patterns, hurts, and unfinished business into loving awareness. Only then can we loosen their hold on our hearts. I often refer to Clarissa Pinkola Estés's beautiful writings on grief and *descansos* during this part of money work. *Descansos*, she tells us, are crosses on the roadside (common in the American Southwest and Mediterranean countries) that mark a death. They are often inscribed with a name and adorned with flowers, and indicate that someone's life journey ended there. Yet Estés wisely invites us to broaden our use of *descansos*, to mark all of the

> ... roads not taken, paths that were cut off, ambushes, betrayals, and death. . . . They must be remembered, but they must be forgotten, at the same time ... the aspects of yourself that were on their way to somewhere, but never arrived. . . . *Descansos*

marks the death sites, the dark times, but they are also love notes to your suffering. They are transformative. There's a lot to be said for pinning things to the earth so they don't follow us around. There is a lot to be said for laying them to rest.[4]

I believe we all experience varying levels of hurt, loss, and trauma, from large to subtle—and thinking in terms of *descansos* can be incredibly healing for our Money Story. We need to grieve the career that ended, mark the end of a marriage (and the financial partnership and dreams that died along with it), honor the moment we turned down that high-paying job, lay to rest the shame of a bankruptcy or loss of a house. Peace comes when we find ways to honor these parts of ourselves, these dreams that didn't come to fruition, these metaphorical deaths (both large and small). Peace comes when we write love notes to them, adorn their graves with flowers . . . and let them go. Then, we can move forward, lighter, freer, and at peace.

THE GIFT OF COURAGE + PERSONAL POWER

"The weak can never forgive. Forgiveness is the attribute of the strong." —*Mahatma Gandhi*

Gayle and Mike, a happily married couple in their fifties, had lived in their beautiful California home for nine years before everything changed. After trying to refinance their home and fighting their mortgage company for some time, they finally accepted that they needed to complete a short sale on their home. (A short sale happens when there are debts and/or liens on a property that the owner cannot afford to repay; the sale of the property will fall short of the debt balance, but the property is sold with all proceeds going to the lenders, who agree to accept less than the total amount owed.)

Losing a home is one of the biggest financial traumas that can befall a person. Gayle and Mike needed to say goodbye to the home in which

---

4 Clarissa Pinkola Estés, *Women Who Run with the Wolves* (New York: Ballantine Books, 1996), 396-397.

they had lived, loved, and raised their son for nearly a decade. Yet, in doing so, they were able to find something on the other side of this loss.

Gayle and Mike wanted to mark the closing of this chapter of their lives as mindfully as possible, so they spent the last few months in their home in a grieving process. They said goodbye to the rose bushes and prolific vegetable garden out back. They said goodbye to their neighbors. They created a photo album of cherished memories in their home. They grieved the possessions they needed to let go of as they moved into a smaller space and questioned their beliefs about how much stuff and square footage they truly needed for a good life. They even grieved their idea of the American Dream, and what it meant to them to be "middle class."

Now, three years after losing their house, Gayle and Mike have emerged stronger than they had ever expected. They have settled into a new home and Gayle is working on a blog and book to share their story with others facing similar challenges. While they still miss things about their house from time to time, they have found that sharing openly about the experience with friends, family, and others has eased moments of sadness and even helped them become more courageous.

"This was a difficult decision as well as being quite stressful at times, yet it has also turned out to be an empowering, hope-filled process for our family. In the end it's been a great opportunity to explore what constitutes a meaningful life. Facing a big money challenge head-on and with an open heart can increase one's courage in so many areas of life," Gayle shares.

Not every completion is as huge and traumatic as Gayle and Mike's. Yet whatever their size, we can bring loving awareness and conscious forgiveness to the endings and transitions in our financial life. We can walk away with a bit more resilience, having learned just how strong we truly are.

THE GIFT OF APPRECIATION + PRESENCE

"The present moment is filled with joy and happiness. If you are attentive, you will see it." —*Thich Nhat Hanh*[5]

Geneen Roth is a teacher, author, and pioneer in the eating, body image, and spirituality movement. She also wrote a book on money, *Lost and Found*, about her experience losing most of her life's savings to Bernie Madoff's fraudulent investment scheme.

When I interviewed her about the experience, Geneen shared with me that, when she got the call that her family's thirty years' worth of savings was swindled and gone forever, she cycled through a painful rainbow of emotions, including shock, terror, denial, self-blame, and more shock. Once she could reach out from her fog, she called her trusted friends, each of whom reassured her that "nothing of any true value has been lost." At the time, Geneen bristled at what she saw as their optimistic mumbo jumbo.

As time passed, though, Geneen recognized the wisdom in this positive spin. She could still breathe. She still had her husband and dear friends. She began leaning into her decades of meditation practice. Every time her mind wandered into shame, terror, or blame, she brought herself back to the present moment: her easy breath, her warm teacup, the blue sky outside her kitchen window. Slowly, it became easier for her to focus on the good in her life, the "enoughness." She still had a roof over her head; there was food in the pantry. As long as she didn't stray from the present moment, there actually did not seem to be any problem.

Geneen insists that, within one week of that terrible phone call, she found herself very happy, and changed forever. Not only did she tap into resilience she did not know she had, she also realized that she could always be happy and have enough, as long as she was truly present and grateful. As she shared with me in an interview,

---

5 Thich Nhat Hanh, *Peace is Every Step: The Path of Mindfulness in Everyday Life* (New York: Bantam Books, 1991), 17.

"Enough" isn't out there; it's a relationship to what you already have. Unless you work on that first (or simultaneously with how you're making money), you will never feel like you have enough, and you will always feel poor. It's possible to feel fat when you're thin, and to feel poor when you're rich. The thing that changes is your relationship with "enough."

Geneen certainly went through stages of grief about her lost money. She had to let go of those many thousands of dollars because they simply weren't coming back. She had to let go of her rage and betrayal because they would have poisoned her. She also had to let go of blaming herself for falling for the scheme—because there was nothing that blame could accomplish. As she laid all of these things down to rest, she was able to recognize just how bountiful the present moment truly was.

THE GIFT OF COMPASSION

When Chris, an executive and personal coach in her sixties, sat down to explore her Money Story, she was nervous. She knew there were a lot of things in her financially challenging childhood that still haunted her. She lit a candle, put on her favorite soothing music, and did a Body Check-In. Then, she traced her Money Story from childhood on up, cataloguing the important money messages and events she had inherited and experienced throughout her life. (You can find the questions she used at the end of Chapter 3.) Chris returned her mind to her breath every few moments to help her work through the big emotions and old memories that surfaced. One of the most powerful stories that bubbled up to the surface had occurred in a hotel room when she was just a toddler.

In her childhood, Chris's family lived, as she described it, in "abject poverty." For several months, they all lived in one old, dilapidated motel room. One night, after finally receiving a little money, Chris's mother stepped out of their hotel room to get food and medicine for Chris's sister, who was ill. Unfortunately, Chris's mother locked herself out of the hotel room, and panicked as she heard the young children crying inside. After a few terror-filled moments (on both sides of the door), Chris's young mother broke the window to crawl back in.

As Chris recalled this intense episode, she not only identified with her own role in the scene, but, for the first time, with her mother's perspective, as well. Waves of grief and fear coursed through her as she imagined how her mother felt that night: young, impoverished, and terrified for her children. Any judgments about her parents' financial savvy or commitment to her well-being evaporated as she felt the love her mother surely felt for her and her sister washing through her own body.

Inspired by the beauty and intensity of this reframing of an old memory, Chris went on to catalogue some of the "limiting beliefs" about money that she had accrued during the rest of her childhood that were still active within her as an adult, including:

> It's not OK to ask for what I want.
> I should over-give and take care of others before my own needs.
> Men are responsible for providing for women and children.
> People who save money are stingy and greedy.
> I should spend money as fast as it comes in.
> I'm not good with money.
> I should not have more, or nicer, things than others.

Simply naming these old beliefs shifted Chris's understanding of her Money Story and even her financial identity. She experienced a newfound appreciation for her father and how much he had worked and sacrificed to raise her family out of poverty. She walked away from the exercise filled with deep compassion for both of her parents.

It's so common to hold on to resentment toward our parents for how we were raised, including the money beliefs they instilled in us, from a young age. When we can muster the courage to recognize that, no matter how harmful someone's actions may have been toward us, they were being driven by their own habits and Money Stories, we can experience true healing compassion.

One of the most important people to forgive is yourself. We have all made mistakes in life—yet I truly believe that we all do the best we can, with the knowledge and resources we have. If you are harboring resentment and judgments toward yourself for money mistakes in your past, grieve those choices, recognize that you did the best you could, and let go of that self-blame so you can move forward.

THE GIFT OF WHOLENESS

> "I call all of my power back to me now. I am whole and complete."
> —*Danielle LaPorte*

Once you are able to identify some of your old wounds and begin forgiving those who inflicted them, you may recover parts of yourself that went into hiding long ago. You might rediscover that little boy you used to be—the one who played with Legos and dreamt of being an architect, but was told "you have to follow the money, not your dreams, to be successful," and for years couldn't pass by a construction site without getting angry. You might revive that little girl within you who loves collecting and sorting things, from stamps to seashells to money—but was chastised and told, "holding onto things makes you stingy, greedy, and bad."

Forgiveness actually calls these parts of ourselves home from exile, so we become whole again. One of my favorite stories of this was told to me by Kate, a life coach in her mid-thirties.

Ten-year-old Kate could not escape the summer heat. There was a drought in Missouri that year, and her family's home didn't have air-conditioning. Their utilities got shut off due to nonpayment, and to make matters even worse, they suffered an outbreak of fleas thanks to a houseguest's cat. Both of Kate's parents had big debts, divorces, and the steady stream of financial emergencies that arise when you don't have much money. One day, Kate's father took her to the grocery store, and announced that he had $20 to feed their entire family for the next two weeks. They turned this difficulty into a game: what could they buy that would stretch the farthest? Kate suggested pancake mix: it was cheap, filling, and you only needed to add water. For two weeks, they lived on pancakes: breakfast, lunch, and dinner. After that, it wasn't until she went to graduate school that Kate could stomach pancakes again.

As she reached her early thirties, Kate became more and more aware of how many money habits and beliefs she had carried with her from her childhood. Even though she had begun earning a very comfortable living as an online entrepreneur, she never saved money. Once her basic needs were met, she spent every last penny on "fun stuff": an amazing dinner with friends, a cute pair of shoes, a weekend getaway to wine country. At first, Kate shamed herself for her "reckless" spending: *Why can't I get it together and save, like an adult?* Finally, she connected the dots between her current splurging and her childhood: ten-year-old Kate was still alive inside thirty-four-year-old Kate, and this little girl carried the money belief that no matter how good things seem, all the money could be gone in a flash, so you'd better spend it, now, on a guaranteed good time.

As Kate tried to release some of her self-criticism around her spending, she entered a dialogue with her younger self. *Hey, you and I? We're collaborating now. I'm an adult, and I've got your back. Please trust me, OK?* By inviting that tender, scrappy little girl into the conversation, adult Kate paid her the highest honor. Paradoxically, the more Kate's younger self within felt cherished and listened to, the less she felt the need to overpower Kate's spending.

After this experience, adult Kate got to consciously choose when to indulge. Sometimes she chose to take a spontaneous vacation, or "throw money at a problem" instead of working herself to the bone to create a DIY solution. Other times, she held back her spending and instead invested in a retirement fund—to her surprise, investing money in her future became its own sort of "party time" fun.

Five Myths About Forgiveness (And What to Do Instead)

We often harbor misguided ideas about what forgiveness is that hold us back from practicing it.

Myth #1.
Forgiveness means condoning, letting someone off the hook, or excusing them from any wrongdoing.

"You stole my money, but that's OK. I forgive you."

Reality: True forgiveness is more about letting yourself off the hook than the other person. Chronic anger, resentment, and blame are not free. They cost us energy. And energy that's bound up in the past is energy that's not available to us in the present. Forgiveness, therefore, is primarily about self-care: cutting the ties to the past in order to more fluidly move forward with conscious, intentional use of our energy. You can absolutely forgive someone (including yourself) without condoning their behavior.

Myth #2.
Forgiveness means whitewashing the impact of someone's actions.

"You raised me to believe girls can't be good with money, but I guess that didn't really mess me up that much, so I forgive you."

Reality: Acknowledging the harm done is often an important first step toward forgiveness. But we can also find compassion (for others and ourselves) by acknowledging that we all have our own Money Stories. Each time someone hurt you around money, their behavior came out of their own deep patterning, unconsciousness, and pain. Recognizing the poignancy of our shared, flawed human condition can help us forgive *and* stay in connection (if we so choose). This compassion (or at least neutrality) can dissolve blame.

Myth #3.
Forgiveness is unnecessary, as grievances will fade away on their own, over time.

"I hate that my sister screwed me out of my inheritance. But I'm not going to think about it. I'm sure I'll get over it, someday."

Reality: Sometimes, pain softens on its own, but it can also crawl underground and fester, stinking up a whole relationship. Time alone does not wash away strong anger; anger is potent energy that stays lodged in our body-mind system until it is transformed or released. Suppressed anger curtails freedom and creativity. Often, it leads us to compulsively manage our lives to avoid contacting this internal material. When we inevitably bump into it, we get "triggered" and lash out, reactively. You may be well aware of people you haven't forgiven, or you might have long-standing grievances that have burrowed underground. In that case, you may need to re-acknowledge some pain first, fanning the flames of old anger a bit, before working with forgiveness. Keep in mind: most of us have a longer list of grievances toward *ourselves* than anyone else.

Myth #4.
Forgiveness is an all-or-nothing proposition: flip the switch and all is forgiven.

> *"It's been ten years, and I still can't forgive myself for defaulting on that loan. I guess I never will."*

Reality: There are stages and phases and levels of forgiveness and letting go, and most people move through them gradually, over time. As Clarissa Pinkola Estés reassures us, 'Forgiveness has many layers, many seasons . . . the important part of forgiveness is to begin and to continue. The finishing of it all is a life work."[6]

Myth #5.
There is one way to forgive, and we should all do it the same way.

> *"My mother forgives so easily! There must be something wrong with me for still being upset about that bankruptcy."*

Reality: We all forgive in our own way, in our own time. Some personality types are more "hard-wired" to cling to resentment, while others

---

6 Clarissa Pinkola Estés, *Women Who Run with the Wolves* (New York: Ballantine Books, 1996), 400.

may be champion repressors who only appear to forgive. You may find it helpful to explore a personality typing system like the Enneagram (my personal favorite—see the Resources section) to become acquainted with your own patterns, gifts, and challenges around forgiveness.

. . . . .

Forgiveness is the inner work of letting go and moving on. Without this inner work, resistance often wins out, and we don't have a real hope of acting on the practical, nitty-gritty To Do list in our financial life. Imagine yourself procrastinating to set up that meeting with your lawyer to discuss your inheritance from your father. The "tough love," just-get-it-done-already approach to money would see this as a purely practical problem: just schedule the meeting and be done with it, already! But you and I both know: that's *never* the full story. Perhaps you feel conflicted about how your father earned that money and need to process your grief and ambivalence about him and his business practices before you'll be able to receive that money. This kind of resistance invites us into the tender realm of forgiveness, grieving, and letting go. Have compassion for your past decisions and behaviors. After all: what's the point in trying to update your financial life if you feel aggressive and critical toward yourself the whole time?

Letting go is an ongoing process. You might uncover a large portion of your old money beliefs in one fell swoop, but chances are, you will continue to encounter memories and beliefs in your money relationship that you wish to release, over time. The more practiced you become with completions and forgiveness, the more quickly and easily you may find yourself letting go of new slights and beliefs in the moment. Instead of beating up on yourself for paying that bill late (and incurring a stiff late fee), you may choose to release your shame and blame within a few moments, and make that phone call to see if you can get the fee waived. If you discover that outpatient surgery you scheduled was far more expensive than planned, you can take a deep breath, remind yourself that you are learning to advocate for yourself in this confusing insurance-and-medical-stuff realm, and find out if you can reschedule the procedure someplace more affordable. And when you discover you've been paying for that gym membership all these months (when you *thought* you had cancelled it), instead of beating up on yourself for the money you've lost, you can choose to pause, celebrate that you've noticed it today, and make that phone call to plug that "money leak."

These small acts of forgiveness and letting go can make all the difference in your money healing journey. But, as we'll see in the next chapter, you can bring even more beauty, sacredness, and meaning to this experience.

CHAPTER 5

money healing rituals

"Life is a ritual of love
Life is a ritual of union, and
Life is a dance of the divine"
—*Vishwas Chavan*[?]

FORGIVENESS, GRIEF, AND letting go are ongoing practices that affect us all in personal ways and on many different levels. If you find yourself face-to-face with a particularly large, deep, or old part of your Money Story that you're ready to release, and you like the idea of infusing your forgiveness with some extra beauty, meaning, and sacredness, you might want to create your own Money Healing Ritual.

What Is Ritual, and What's It Got to Do with Money Healing?

If the word "ritual" makes you a little anxious, allow me to dispel a few common misconceptions. First, ritual does not have to come from (or connect you to) any religion, magic, or traditional spiritual practice. Certainly, many rituals are associated with particular lineages, cultures, and traditions. Perhaps you have some from your own or your parents' beliefs, which you cherish and that connect you to those who have come before. Traditional rituals, because they have been passed down for so many generations and in different places around the world, can be incredibly powerful. More than anything else, though, I adore creating

---

7 Vishwas Chavan, *SoulBliss: A Poetic Tale of Love* (Maharashtra, India: CreatiVentures, 2013).

my own, *personal* rituals. When we relate to ritual as a creative process, born directly from our own beliefs, aesthetics, and deep desires, it can become even more powerful. These personal rituals may draw upon elements from traditional sources, if that feels good to you and (respectfully, of course), may weave traditional elements with utterly new and personal ones. Or they may emerge directly from your own heart.

Secondly, rituals do not need to be elaborate, long-winded, or even public. Even the simplest daily tasks can become deeply meaningful and transformative when infused with mindfulness and intention. Sipping your morning coffee with the newspaper might be a ritual, so is pausing for a moment of gratitude at the start of your meal. I practice a personal mini-ritual before every interview: I spritz my favorite essential oils, light candles, and take a few deep breaths through my heart. Mini-rituals like these can ground us in the present moment, recall our deepest intentions, and open a space for our highest calling to live through us.

Finally, rituals do not have to be somber and serious. They can be celebratory, spontaneous, and lighthearted, like a wedding or a birthday party. Rituals can be fastidiously planned, one-time-only, ongoing, utterly minimalistic, richly sensual, reverent, irreverent, solitary, communal, daytime, nighttime, woodsy, indoor, silent, musical, traditional, and unique.

As you explore your personal Money Story and begin consciously crafting your relationship to money, ritual is one way to help you take the insights and desires that bubble up and integrate them into your life. Through ritual, we give embodied form to our deepest intentions, speak aloud what matters most to us, and surrender into the felt experience of our deepest selves. Ritual aligns our inner and outer worlds and affirms our commitment to transformation and healing. It pulls our intentions into the material world, and infuses everyday reality with sacred awareness.

There are several different types of rituals you may want to create to support your own journey with money.

THE TYPES OF MONEY HEALING RITUALS

RELEASING, FORGIVING, LETTING GO

Cut the chains to old money patterns, beliefs, or identities that no longer serve you.

Examples: Release your belief that money is "bad" or there will never be enough of it. Forgive your parents for the unhealthy money patterns they bestowed on you—or for not giving you sufficient money lessons. Let go of the identity that you "just aren't good with money." Forgive yourself for your financial "mistakes."

MARKING A TRANSITION

Cross a threshold into a new identity, chapter, or relationship with money.

Examples: Shift into married life, with all of its implications for financial merging. Switch from paying rent to owning a house. Take a leap from a corporate job into creative entrepreneurship.

CELEBRATING

Too often, we jump from one accomplishment to climbing that next mountain, without taking a breath. We need to take the time to celebrate our successes, so we can integrate them and appreciate the goodness in our lives. Celebrations get us re-inspired and propel us forward.

Examples: Pay off that credit card, loan, or mortgage. Begin a new money practice. Raise your rates to better reflect your value.

BLESSING

Send something out into the world with loving intentions.

Examples: Bless that big check you send to the IRS, that it may help those in need. Forgive a debt owed to you, and send the note with a prayer of blessing. Finish your manuscript and pray that it find its way to everyone whose life may be helped by it—and that it support you, too, along the way.

You can perform a ritual before, during, or after these transitions—even years after a transition, if you didn't fully integrate, honor, and acknowledge something at the time.

Ritual is one way to *love* yourself into transformation, rather than shaming or yelling yourself into change. One of my favorite examples of a personal Money Healing ritual comes from a dear master ritualist friend of mine named Julie.

When I first asked Julie if I could interview her, she was excited—but realized how much she needed to do her *own* Money Healing Ritual first, before sharing her teachings on the topic with my community. Julie had been working through my methodology for some time, and had become increasingly aware of her money shame. It came up every so often, sometimes quietly and sometimes more dramatically. As ripe and ready as Julie was to step into a new money relationship, her money shame was keeping her tethered to old, unhealthy dynamics. Julie knew that she couldn't simply *think* her way out of these old, shame-filled patterns around money. She needed a ritual to support her transition. Pivotal transitions and thresholds like these are often the perfect moment for rituals. In ritual, we declare our readiness for change. We honor and release our past, consciously affirm our choice, and step toward our future with clear intentions.

To begin dreaming up her personal Money Healing Ritual, Julie started with the Money Story Visualization (see the end of Chapter 3). Safe and cozy in a quiet space, Julie traced her history with money, from childhood on up, listing out the beliefs and big events in her Money Story. Soon, a theme emerged: memory after memory surfaced of her receiving money, always with a distinct posture: hand held out, head hunched in shame.

The emotional weight of this posture was palpable, and showed up again and again as Julie retraced her Money Story. Yet she soon realized she wasn't the one who'd created it. Julie recalled being a child in the mid 1960s and seeing this same posture (and attitude) in her mother, a divorced woman struggling to make ends meet. From time to time, Julie's mother accepted financial support from family members. Each time, she hung her head in defeat. Without speaking a word, Julie's mother had passed on this belief: *"Money is a struggle, and you will need handouts to survive, and you will feel shame when you receive them."* At least, that's how Julie interpreted her mother's stance.

Julie knew that unhooking money from shame would be the first half of her Money Healing Ritual. Yet she didn't quite know, yet, what new attitude or posture she wanted to step into. Sometimes, we can't quite envision the new relationship we want with money: we only know what we're done with. That's fine. If you haven't found your "yes," yet, start with your "no."

Once Julie was clear about her "no" (that posture of shame-filled receiving), she simply sat with it for a few moments, relaxing into a space of "not-knowing," wondering what sort of new money relationship she truly desired for herself. Before long, a new posture popped into her awareness: tall, head held high, feet firmly on the ground, connected to both the stability of the earth and the light of the sky, heart open. Julie recognized this image and the feelings it represented as what she calls "the natural posture of the nobility of the soul." *This* was how she wanted to relate to money, from now on.

This is the striking paradox of letting go: when we release our old, stagnant beliefs about money, we have room in our hearts to create new, happier, healthier beliefs of our own choosing. As Julie so elegantly put it, "The more we're willing to remove the veils, the more radiant we become."

As Julie probed deeper, she realized her money pattern was far older than her, or even her mother. In her mind's eye, she caught glimpses of her grandmother and great-grandmother embodying the same story. This money shame was interwoven throughout her entire matrilineal heritage. This raised an important question: How can we release those old, painful money beliefs when they're associated with people, memories, or even places within ourselves that we truly love?

Many of us deeply cherish elements of our family and our heritage. Yet, at the same time, our family and ancestors are often the sources of much of our negative, limiting money beliefs. Shelby, a middle school teacher in her fifties, shared with me her memories of a series of personal rituals she performed years ago in an attempt to heal deep past trauma. She burned every photo of herself she could find, and gave away even her most treasured mementos. "I was so desperate to move forward that I literally torched my past," she recalled. Years later, she deeply regretted the loss of her photos and mementos: these fiery rituals, intended to heal her, became a new sort of trauma, keeping her stuck in a ghostly grief cycle, unable to fully let go of her past. When she felt the desire for a Money Healing ritual stirring again, years later, she was understandably anxious.

Stories like Shelby's reinforce my conviction that we must honor our past even as we release it—especially in ritual. We can let go of our past, and even ritually burn or bury it, yet we must also appreciate it for getting us to the present moment, where we are strong enough to move beyond it.

For Julie, this paradox inspired her to "invite" her entire matrilineage to her personal Money Healing Ritual. Even as she bid farewell to the unhealthy money dynamic she had received from them, she appreciated and loved them for giving her life and courageously facing their life's challenges.

Ritual as a Creative Process

Personalized Money Healing Rituals connect us ever more deeply to ourselves. There is something powerful about crafting a ritual of your very own and lovingly attending to each detail, so everything reflects what matters most, to you: from that hawk's feather on your altar to the photo of your grandfather to the fragrance of your favorite incense. Your personal Money Healing Ritual should support you, encourage you, clarify you, and connect you to what matters most to you.

In this way, personal Money Healing Rituals help us cultivate and access the deeper mysteries of our lives, our selves, and even what is greater than us. Each of us needs to go inside and access the voices, movement, wisdom, and languages that will guide us as we create our own healing.

. . . . .

Julie performed her ritual in a place that felt sacred to her: a grove of eucalyptus trees near her home. She meditated quietly for a few moments, with all of her curiosity and shame and hope, to truly "arrive" in that place, in that moment. Suddenly, her quiet reverie was interrupted: a man had entered the grove, walking a golden retriever, and was singing—joyfully, at the top of his lungs—"House at Pooh Corner" by Kenny Loggins:

I've wandered much further today than I should
And I can't seem to find my way back to the wood
So help me if you can
I've got to get back to the house at Pooh Corner by one . . .
Back to the days of Christopher Robin and Pooh.[8]

Julie laughed out loud and cried with happiness and relief: she had adored Christopher Robin and Pooh since she was a girl, and in this synchronistic flash, that stranger with the melodic voice embodied for Julie what she wanted to connect to money: a joy, innocence, and childlike playfulness—the girl she was *before* she took on all of this shame and worry. The form of her ritual now complete and clear to her, she looked at the blue sky, connected to the earth beneath her feet, laughed a bit more, and began walking, following the gently curving lines of eucalyptus trunks, embedded in the ground as a serpent line.

As she walked, she focused on that old posture of Money Shame: hand held out, head hanging down; and she simply let it go. She walked and released, walked and released. Scraps of memories and shards of trauma surfaced in her awareness, and she let them fall from her, piece by piece.

Julie tapped into that younger, more joyful and innocent girl within her, who had been there long before she took on this money shame. Adult Julie felt love and compassion for this part of herself flood her awareness—she didn't want to leave her behind! So she invited her

8 Kenny Loggins, "House at Pooh Corner," Nitty Gritty Dirt Band, *Uncle Charlie and His Dog Teddy*, Liberty, 1971.

child-self to "drop the veil" and release whatever weighed her down, keeping her from being her fullest, most radiant self. Much to Julie's delight, she felt a gentle shift within. This loving part of herself *already* embodied precisely the kind of relationship with money Julie so hoped to cultivate! Julie envisioned herself walking hand-in-hand with this younger part of herself as she continued down the eucalyptus grove.

As Julie reached the bottom of the grove, she found herself naturally holding that new posture she had envisioned for her money relationship: head held high, feet connected to the stable earth, heart brimming with light. Her walk complete, she concluded her ritual with a few moments of gratitude: she thanked her ancestors for being with her; she thanked the earth and birds and eucalyptus trees; she thanked that dear, young part of herself; and she thanked her adult self for making time for this sacred, loving Money Healing Ritual.

As Julie's story illustrates, a personal Money Healing ritual need not be elaborate, complex, or lengthy to be deeply transformative. When we slow down and trust the body's wisdom, it will reveal to us what we most need. While everyone's ritual will be different, there are several elements I've found that support any type of ritual—all of which Julie incorporated into her lovely walk through the eucalyptus grove.

Seven Elements of a Personal Money Healing Ritual

1. SELECT AND INSTRUCT YOUR WITNESSES.

Your ritual may be a solo journey, or you may have one or more trusted witnesses present (even a whole community). If you choose to include others, tell them clearly what you want from them: silence, words of encouragement, a celebratory mood, or somber reverence. Articulate what's true for you before you begin, because your clarity will help your witnesses be more fully present.

2. HAVE A CLEARLY DEFINED BEGINNING, MIDDLE, AND END.

You could begin by lighting a candle, ringing a bell, or bowing to bring focus to the present moment. You may choose to read a piece of sacred literature or poetry, or call in your ancestors or spirit guides, or bow to the four directions. After the middle—the main process—your ending could be as simple as blowing out the candle, bowing out, or chiming the bell again, or you may decide to hold a celebratory feast.

3. HONOR THE OLD AND CALL IN THE NEW.

As eager as you may be to move forward and invite new things into your money relationship, it always helps to smooth and integrate the passage by giving loving attention to what you're letting go of, and honoring the gifts it has brought to your life. Only after you name and honor what you're releasing should you call in the new.

4. RELY ON METAPHOR.

Ritual is a creative, embodied bridge between your inner intentions and outer expression. Do your best to match your desires to acts that embody them. Fire is a common metaphor for completions, but you might prefer to bury something in the ground or release something to the wind. You could step over a line in the ground to symbolize a transition, plant seeds to symbolize a new chapter in your life, or soak in a bubble bath to emerge cleansed. You may incorporate your body through dance, or include objects, photos, or meaningful mementos. Use your imagination to identify ways you might represent your inner experience (and the shift you want) in physical form.

5. PAY ATTENTION TO THE SPACE.

What do *you* need to make your surroundings feel sacred and beautiful? If you hold the ritual in your home, you may choose to tidy up or rearrange things, first—or you may clear stagnant energy by burning sage or ringing bells. I am a fan of simplicity and love bringing in flowers, a few meaningful objects, lighting candles and nibbling a bit of exquisite dark chocolate. Perhaps your ritual includes an altar of sacred objects and artwork. If you prefer a public space for your ritual, perhaps you'll want to bring water and blankets to feel comfortable, or select a time when it's less crowded.

6. BE AS PRESENT AS POSSIBLE.

Ritual loves mindfulness. Focus your attention and bring your whole self to the moment. You may choose to meditate for a few moments or do a Body Check-In before you begin your ritual. And remember, you can be reverent and light-hearted at the same time!

7. HONOR YOUR TIMING AND RESISTANCE.

Only you can know when it's right for you to do a personal Money Healing ritual. Do Body Check-Ins, journal, speak to someone you trust. And when you feel sparks of curiosity, follow them and see where they lead. Take the pressure off and take one step at a time.

· · · · ·

So . . . what does "success" look like, with a ritual? This will be different for everyone—it is up to you to decide. For Julie, her Money Healing Ritual sparked more joy, ease, and spaciousness around money in the days and weeks that followed. She felt less heavy and shameful about it—even on tax day. She didn't eradicate *all* shame or difficult emotions about money, but she was more conscious of her feelings, and able to bring more loving awareness to herself, even in her challenging moments.

Money Healing isn't an all-or-nothing proposition. It is a journey of baby step after baby step. Allow yourself to embrace the incremental changes, and experiment with personalized rituals to support any step along the way. Each new sliver of hope is beautiful. Every step closer to yourself is worth celebrating. All of this is welcome and essential to your relationship with money, which, as we'll see in the next chapter, is never *just* about the money.

it's never just about the money

WHEN FOREST AND I first moved in together, finances were tight. We were living in a tiny cottage in the redwood forest of Sebastopol, California, and, combined, we made enough money to cover our rent and basic necessities, but not much more. But we both valued locally grown, organic food enough that we agreed to prioritize this expense over anything else (like attending concerts or dining out). Once a week, we made our pilgrimage to the co-op and pricey health foods market in town.

I'll never forget how reverently we carried those precious paper bags back to the car each week. I'll also never forget the look on Forest's face as, every week, he sat in the car for a long moment, staring at the astronomical receipt and spiraling into a dark, terrible place. Sometimes, as he cycled between terror and numbness, I could reach him and pull him back to the present moment with me. Other times, it seemed he was spinning in his own private black hole, with no hope for escape.

While those grocery trips were certainly a financial stretch for us, they never put us at the edge of eviction: we could afford our organic produce by living extremely frugally in other areas of our life. Something deeper was going on here. Forest's weekly freakouts in the store parking lot were directly connected to old childhood trauma and his inability to feel safe in his financial world, in his body, and in life at large. Sitting beside him, I felt heartbroken and helpless. Since then, I have learned not only how to support others through situations like this, but also just how common such feelings of un-safety are around money, even for people who have all their basic needs met.

Money is directly tied to our most primal survival needs: food in our bellies and roofs over our heads. This is why money can be such a vulnerable part of life, and why financial stress can even trigger feelings of *physical* peril. But safety is only one of the deeper issues we may discover when we scratch the surface of our "money stuff." Our money relationship brings us into direct contact with a whole range of deep, complex themes, including:

Our relationship to pleasure, abundance, and thriving

How we access feelings of "enoughness" and safety

Our capacity to feel worthy and valuable

Our self-confidence, self-reliance, and resilience

Our ability to get vulnerable and ask for help

These themes are roiling just below the surface of our interactions with money, though many people go their whole lives without recognizing the deeper issues fueling their money challenges. This is why a simple late fee can send us spiraling into catastrophic shame, or why that spat with our honey about the vacation budget can make us feel so powerless or rageful. This is also why money issues can feel like emotional quicksand—a "simple" evening of paying bills may trigger a confusing cascade of self-doubt, shame, and memories of old trauma. It's about the money, but it's never *just* about the money.

We all have our own constellations of challenges, patterns, and essential inquiries associated with money—and, like peeling back the layers of an onion, new and deeper issues reveal themselves the longer we work with our money relationship. Money always mirrors our inner world: the unresolved issues, suppressed gifts, and growing edges. So when we get brave and bring love and mindfulness to our money relationship, it can become a sacred training ground where we unravel old knots, practice new skills, and learn to tango with these tender, essential elements of life. This rich work is what continually fascinates and excites me about money work. It is utterly life-changing.

Over the years, I have seen themes emerge for people in their money work, again and again. Five of the most common are: Safety, Enoughness, Responsibility, Value, and Power. You may identify closely with one, two, or three of these issues—and you will find practices here to support their unfolding. But even simply acknowledging some of these deeper currents in your money relationship can help you relax into the healing process—as long as you keep bringing gentle, loving awareness to whatever you find within yourself.

Safety

During those lean years Forest and I spent in Sebastopol (with those weekly grocery store freakouts), I learned just how frightening it is to earn barely enough money to cover basic expenses. That's why it's so important to me to empower people with the emotional and practical tools they need to afford the basics and beyond, achieving a comfortable or even ultimate lifestyle level (which, as we'll see in Phase Three, looks different to everyone). But the truth is, even the most "secure" job could be downsized, the most luxurious homes can be swept away by natural disasters, and a health crisis could wipe out your retirement fund. These external trappings of *security*, while important, are different than the deep, inner sense of *safety* that can help you weather even the toughest financial storm. And if safety is one of the underlying emotional issues you'd like to address in your money relationship, more money in the bank rarely does the trick.

Imagine you're reviewing your financial numbers and discover that you might not have enough money to make ends meet this month. Maybe you had some unexpected vet bills or a new client you were counting on backed out at the last minute. As soon as you see the cold, hard numbers, you start to panic: your nervous system shifts into a fight-flight-freeze fear response, hijacking your rational mind and wreaking havoc on your heart. Now, imagine you could interrupt this pattern and shift from posttraumatic stress to (as one of my clients put it) "post-traumatic growth." As you're about to see, this truly is possible, and there are a number of practices to help you feel safety on a deeper, nonmonetary level. But all of them require, first and foremost, that we be as gentle and patient with ourselves as possible when we feel triggered, unsafe, or anxious.

One of the first ways I was able to cultivate more safety within my money relationship was by tracking my income and expenses. Even though I wasn't making much money at the time (and you might assume seeing that would cause anxiety), getting clarity about exactly how much money I *did* have helped me feel clear-eyed, calm, and grounded. Even though my spending choices were limited by my low income, knowing exactly what my reality was saved my imagination from making up scary stories, and I could feel good and safe about the choices I made.

However, some people need to do the exact opposite in order to feel more safety in their money relationship. Adam, a bartender in his twenties, had a habit of compulsively checking his bank balances (or counting his stash of cash)—sometimes a dozen times a day. Tracking his numbers was an *expression* of his anxiety, not a cure for it. For him to relax and feel more safe, he actually needed to spend *less* time checking his balance. I suggested he cut back to once a day, at first, and eventually once a week. Adam practiced going for a walk in nature or simply sitting still and noticing his breath—inhale, exhale—during those ten-minute bouts he used to spend worrying. Accessing and growing your own inner safety, then, is a task unique to you. Always check in with yourself and see what ingredients *you* need to feel more safety in your money relationship.

Here's the truth: we all go through different phases and cycles in life. Ups and downs. Abundance and scarcity. But we can learn to cultivate a deep inner sense of safety that helps us feel calm and secure, no matter what's happening around us. This inner safety soothes the impact of challenging times, makes good times more enjoyable, and opens up our ability to imagine new, creative solutions.

My favorite approach to cultivating safety is somatic or body-based. These practices are often deceptively simple, but incredibly powerful ways to help us self-regulate, self-soothe, and find safety within ourselves, no matter what.

Four Somatic Practices for Cultivating Safety

While our minds might race, our bodies are always in the present moment. Tuning into the body, then, helps us feel more physical *and* emotional stability and balance. In this way, we can get calm and present, experiencing the full spectrum of our emotions without getting overwhelmed or numb.

The somatic term for this feeling-safe-in-your-body-no-matter-what's-happening is "self-regulation." The following four somatic practices draw from Peter Levine's work on Somatic Experiencing® and are designed to help you cultivate this self-regulation. You might think of them as an expanded version of the Body Check-In (see Chapter 2) and practice one the next time you want to feel more deep, inner safety.

1. SLOWING DOWN

Our minds move at a much faster pace than our bodies. The first step to getting more "into" your body, then, and into that inner, embodied safety, is to slow down. Relax into the slower pace of your body. Feel the rhythms of your in-breath and out-breath.

To try this, give yourself thirty seconds to simply stop, close your eyes, and focus on your breath. Inhale and exhale slowly and regularly. You might count your breaths or even repeat a phrase to yourself (or mantra) like "slow and sweet . . . slow and sweet," or a favorite from Zen teacher Thich Nhat Hanh, "Breathing in, I calm my body. Breathing out, I smile. Dwelling in the present moment, I know this is a wonderful moment."[9] After a few moments, open your eyes—but remember to retain this slower, gentler pace as you return to your tasks. If you're paying bills online, type a little more slowly and take mindful pauses between tasks, even for just a moment. In this way, your money practices can start to become a refuge of relaxation and safety.

2. GROUNDING

We're so used to working hard and effort-ing. From a very young age, many of us are taught to feel responsible for carrying our own weight,

---

9 Thich Nhat Hanh, *Being Peace* (Berkeley, California: Parallax Press, 1987), 15.

both physical and metaphorical. Yet the earth is always there, supporting us. It can be an exquisite relief to relax, let go, and consciously
experience just how supported and safe we truly are.

There are many ways to ground. If you're sitting, you might feel
your bottom and back on the chair, and simply notice how your weight
is fully supported. If you're standing, you could pour your awareness
into your feet, and feel them held by the floor or ground. You may
even want to practice grounding while you move, being mindful of how
gravity settles and stabilizes you as you walk, hike, or bike.

3. RESOURCING

If you find yourself feeling unsafe, you can gently shift your awareness
to sensations, images, or even objects that nurture and support you, and
draw ease and safety from them.

Start with a Body Check-In: slow down and scan your body,
noticing any places where you feel good or even neutral. Then, pour
your awareness into that good (or neutral) place for a few moments—
whether it's your big toe or the back of your neck, or even a particularly
fond memory, like the feeling of your grandmother brushing your hair.
Simply allow yourself to "live" there for a few moments, enjoying the
sensation.

Another way to resource is by focusing on the Earth or natural
elements. You might go for a walk around the block, noticing the trees.
You could pet a furry friend, sniff a favorite essential oil, or even keep a
small stone in your bag, and take it out whenever you pay bills or need
to make a money decision. Whenever you draw on soothing feelings,
memories, images, or objects, creating an environment that helps you
feel settled and safe, you are resourcing. Any time you feel unsettled or
unsafe, you can draw strength and safety from your inner and external
world. Anytime.

4. TITRATION

Most people think of money work as a laundry list of To Dos: deal
with that tax situation, find an accountant, have that hard talk with
a business or personal partner, and on and on. That list can get very

overwhelming very fast, no matter how much enthusiasm and momentum we start with, especially because each item on our list usually involves several smaller actions. I've seen too many people burn out, get overwhelmed, and disengage from money work when they try to do too much, too fast.

Titration is the antidote to overwhelm. It's the practice of giving yourself the time you need to integrate each tiny step before moving on to the next. For example, if you are learning a bookkeeping system (which involves countless small steps), you might start with one (like downloading the system), and stop here, breathe, check in with yourself, and allow any feelings of danger or fear to dissipate before moving on to the next step. Once you're ready, tackle the next step (perhaps it's spending five minutes learning how the system works) and then again, pause, integrate, breathe, and even celebrate this baby step. Any time you start feeling overwhelmed, you can give yourself a moment to settle and feel safe. In this way, you can push your edges gently, while honoring your limits.

. . . . .

Enoughness

I stared wistfully at the long, lush display of chocolate bars. Dark, extra dark, milk; fair trade and organic; pure chocolate, popping with raspberries, swirled with sea salt, spiced with chili flakes. It was a gorgeous clear day in Boulder, and I was making a quick stop at the market, looking for some treats to bring to a friend's potluck. Chocolate has always been one of my favorite ways to shower others with affection, so my heart positively sank when I realized I couldn't afford even the small assortment I'd hoped to bring to the potluck that day. I could barely afford a single bar.

I was in my late twenties, had just completed my graduate program, and was working as a counselor in the mental health field. I was earning just enough money to afford my rent, utilities, student loan payments, and very little more. New clothes and dinner at restaurants were unattainable luxuries at this point in my life. While I was content foregoing most of those expenses, I really felt the pinch when I couldn't afford to buy chocolate to share with my friends. In that moment in the candy aisle, I felt an all-pervading sense of not-enoughness.

We all have our own triggers for experiencing enoughness: that peaceful, satisfied feeling where all is right with the world and you have everything you need to be happy, healthy, and whole. Many assume this feeling is directly related to how much money we have in the bank, so being plagued by not-enoughness is one of the most common reasons people seek out money work. While it's true that, sometimes, a few simple, external money practices can support more feelings of enoughness (like earning a bit more or even simply reviewing our income and expenses over a several-month period), more often, enoughness is a matter of the heart.

How can you tell if your feelings of not-enoughness go deeper than just dollars and cents? You may find yourself struggling with similar feelings of scarcity in areas of your life other than money: *"I just can't get enough sleep / When will I have enough clients to stay afloat? / He never pays enough attention to me."* Perhaps you have a hard time celebrating your accomplishments because they never feel like "enough," or maybe you find yourself compulsively saving every last tablespoon of leftover food. Lynne Twist, author of *The Soul of Money*, suggests Western cultures suffer from this lack of enoughness in a pervasive, soul-draining way that extends far beyond our pocketbooks:

> This mindset of scarcity lives at the very heart of our jealousies, our greed, our prejudice, and our arguments with life, and it is deeply embedded in our relationship to money. In the mind-set of scarcity, our relationship with money is an expression of fear; a fear that drives us in an endless and unfulfilling chase for more, or into compromises that promise a way out of the chase or discomfort around money. In the chase or in the compromises we break from our wholeness and natural integrity. We abandon our soul and grow more and more distant from our core values and highest commitments. We find ourselves trapped in a cycle of disconnection and dissatisfaction. We start to believe the

profit-driven commercial and cultural messages that suggest that money can buy happiness, and we begin to look outside of ourselves to be fulfilled. Intuitively, we know it isn't so, but the money culture shouts down the wiser inner voice, and we feel compelled to seek even the most transient relief and comforts money can buy.[10]

I'm not suggesting that you do inner emotional work *instead of* practical financial number-crunching and lifestyle design. You can cultivate enoughness by engaging with your numbers, by deepening your emotional and spiritual relationship with money, or through a combination of the two. Back when I couldn't afford those chocolate splurges for potlucks or other extras, I found enoughness by nourishing myself in ways that didn't cost a cent: long walks with friends by the creek, community music gatherings, and pausing to smell the lilacs in spring. We'll get to the practical, nitty-gritty side of things in the next phase of this book. Meanwhile, here are a few emotional and psychological practices to help you cultivate feelings of enoughness from the inside out.

1. GET CURIOUS ABOUT ENOUGHNESS IN YOUR BODY

Ask your body: what does not-enoughness feel like, physically? Where do you feel it most? Could you get a little brave and open up a dialogue with "not-enoughness," and see what it has to say to you?

Then, ask your body what enoughness feels like. Try your best to put words to the experience, so you can recall it later: does it feel warm, cool, relaxed, grounded, orange, violet, feather-light? Notice any ways in which it feels different than not-enough.

Finally, ask yourself what you really need to feel enoughness. Be open to anything that arises: it might be a quality of being, your kitten and favorite mug, or even "nothing at all." I realized years ago that having a big stash of toilet paper in the house always made me feel relaxed and provided-for. Silly, right? But it's an ultra-simple way for me to tap into enoughness.

---

10 Lynne Twist, *The Soul of Money: Reclaiming the Wealth of Our Inner Resources* (New York: W. W. Norton & Company, 2003), 45.

2. FILL YOURSELF UP WITH CHOICE

For many people, not-enoughness is associated with a lack of free-dom. *"I don't have enough money to go to that concert or buy that car—so I'm trapped here, doing nothing!"* There seems to be a bold dividing line between "enough" and "not-enough." If you find yourself in this black-or-white camp, you might have more choices than you real-ize. Sometimes, a few teensy shifts can transform "not-enough" into "enough-for-now."

Look for a few opportunities to exert your power of choice. If you're longing for new clothes but can't afford the pricey department store, you might give a consignment store a try or do a clothing swap with friends. If you're worried you can't afford the vacation you were so looking forward to, a small splurge like a bouquet of flowers might brighten your day just enough to help you realize you really *do* have what you need, for now. Perhaps you choose to sit on the porch and read one evening, instead of zoning out with a movie like you usually do. Get a little creative and leverage what power you *do* have. Even small choices like these can lead you to a sense of freedom, which grows your enoughness from the inside out.

3. PRACTICE GRATITUDE

Not-enoughness is often a self-perpetuating cycle: when we focus on what we don't have, we overlook what we *do* have (or could create), and feel even worse. But you can break this cycle by bringing your awareness to the present moment, accepting what is, and cultivating gratitude for what you have, right now.

When you're stuck in a not-enoughness loop, it can feel like you have *nothing* to be grateful for—but when you go looking, you will absolutely find things. Try making a list of big and small things you're grateful for, and don't stop until you find fifty: the roof over your head, the coffee in your mug, the man who smiled at you on the train this morning, etc. Or, you might make it a habit to name one thing you were grateful for, that day, when you get into bed at night.

Gratitude is one of those "simple-but-not-easy" practices, so you may need to be patient here. Keep in mind: impatience is the feeling of not-enough time, so give yourself the gift of patience. Trust your own timing, here.

Responsibility

In our secret, semiconscious dreams, we may imagine someone else swooping in, saving the day, and rescuing us from our money troubles. We might imagine someone gifting us millions of dollars, paying off that credit card bill for us, or handing us a winning lottery ticket. Or perhaps we dream that someone will simply "do" this money thing for us, so we don't have to learn to be literate and mature, here: a knight in shining armor or a kindly queen might file those tax returns for us, negotiate a better interest rate on our home, or set up a financial tracking system for us. Even if, on one level, we strive to become more responsible with money, there is often a deeper, shadow level at which we shun this burden and wish someone would take care of us, so we don't have to save ourselves. Yet, ultimately, this is up to us: money is a personal initiation, and we are the only ones who can step through it.

Cynthia, a mother of three, was coming face-to-face with financial responsibility for the first time in her life at the age of fifty-two. She and her husband had recently finalized their divorce, and she found herself in charge of household finances for herself and her three children. Until this point in her life, someone had always taken care of That Thing Called Money for Cynthia: first her parents, and then her husband, who had been the primary breadwinner during their marriage and taken care of the larger financial decisions. Now, Cynthia was faced with a steep financial learning curve to climb, and she needed to climb it fast. She had to learn to balance the checkbook, deal with the insurance companies, and tend to her retirement and investment accounts.

Cynthia's head was spinning: she was scared and overwhelmed by the amount of "money stuff" she needed to learn, and was also ashamed that she had never learned how to do it before. For a few days, she indulged in the fantasy of someone saving her from all this confusion and drudgery: maybe she could remarry quickly or find a good friend who could take this on for her. Soon, though, Cynthia worked through her resistance and began feeling a glimmer of excitement:

she was nervous about her new financial autonomy, but also felt like it had been an important, missing piece in her life. She was ready to take responsibility and get the financial education she had missed until then. Over the next year, Cynthia took some small (but mighty) steps forward: she found a class at her local library on personal finances, downloaded a personal spending app, and asked her family accountant to explain everything she needed to do to get ready for tax time. Even though it felt uncomfortable at first, Cynthia got more and more excited and empowered to embrace more responsibility in her money life: every small step she took emboldened her, and she soon found this confidence spilling into her work life, her parenting, and, eventually, her dating.

To work through this deeper theme of responsibility, Cynthia chose to let go of her dream of someone saving her, and instead saved herself. This concept is at the heart of Barbara Stanny's seminal book, *Prince Charming Isn't Coming*, whose purpose, she explains, is:

> . . . to urge you to accept financial responsibility as simply another part of life; to renounce the Prince and become personally accountable. Indeed, something wonderful happens when we stop searching for Prince Charming and start relying on ourselves.
>
> Prince Charming, in truth, is nothing more than a projection of our disowned selves. He rose out of the ashes of our perceived incompetence, out of our lack of self-trust. He is the self we refuse to see. So often we feel inadequate, or as one woman put it, "like there is something intrinsically wrong with me." We deny our potential power, project it onto a person or thing, real or imagined, which becomes the Prince who will save us. When we finally do recognize the "Prince" inside ourselves, we discover we have access to all those princely qualities we thought we lacked.[11]

---

11 Barbara Stanny, *Prince Charming Isn't Coming: How Women Get Smart About Money* (New York: Penguin Books, 1997), xv.

There are many ways you might embrace more and more financial responsibility in your life, whether you absolutely need to (like Cynthia did) or simply want to feel more autonomy, even if someone in your life is happy to do this for you. Depending on where you are in your inner (and outer) money journey, you might choose to:

- Take a class on money
- Educate yourself about money by reading a book, blog, or article every week
- Invite a financially savvy person in your life to coffee and ask them to *gently, patiently* talk with you about money questions. (Note, if this is a professional, they need to be paid because this is how they support themselves, but if it is just a friend, a cup of coffee and heartfelt thanks may work as payment.)
- Hire a bookkeeping trainer, financial coach, or financial therapist to support you with healing and practices

Whatever practices you take on to grow your financial responsibility, remember: this takes time, just like growing responsibility in any area of life. Keep hopeful, but don't shame yourself for not mastering this area of life lickety-split. Becoming responsible with money is a journey of small steps. And eventually, it may lead you to an even deeper theme: cultivating and claiming your *power.*

Power

Money is power. —*Way too many people*

While my parents were incredibly generous to me as a child and young adult, I was also keenly aware of the power my father wielded over me, especially around money. This was expressed in subtle, unspoken ways: for example, my parents generously paid for my college tuition, but made me manually track my expenses to the penny and send them a copy of this ledger every month. I experienced generosity, with strings attached. Money meant power, but it wasn't my *own* power: it was my father's. What's more, "power" meant "power over." It was synonymous with domination and subjugation.

During my undergrad years, I had the incredible opportunity to study abroad in Italy for one semester. Again, my parents generously helped me to pay for it, but it wasn't clear how much I could spend on extra things while I was there, like gelato and travel. Looking back, I have deep compassion for my parents and myself: we simply didn't know how to have open, honest conversations about money, and this set the stage for a difficult episode.

My college friends studying abroad with me often took little side trips during our semester in Italy: weekend getaways to the coast or longer trips to other countries. After a few months in Italy, I decided to join them for one of these: a week in France. But it didn't occur to me that I needed to run this by my parents, first. When I returned to Italy a week later and called my parents to gush about my French adventure, my father became furious. *How could you do this without telling us?* He instantly stopped sending me the money I relied on to pay for my food and other extras. But he never clarified with me why he was doing this. I had a few very scary weeks, there, eating on the cheap and trying to make my money stretch as far as I could. And, of course, I was profoundly grateful simply to be in Italy. Yet this was another episode where I felt dominated by my father and money. He was incredibly generous with me—yet without open lines of communication, our financial relationship felt deeply confusing. Again, money was power ... power *over* me.

In the years since, I have done volumes of inner work around power. Now, I can experience power as something more than power *over* or power *under* someone or something. I can relax, soften, and allow creative power to surge through me.

Power is a journey. It is made up of small moments where we take action in our best interest. It is built, brick by brick, from decisions and choices, insights and intentions. For many, this may include battling (or simply acknowledging) institutional or societal power structures—which are beyond the scope of this book (but see the Resources section for more). I have seen my community members claim and fortify their financial empowerment by simply getting brave and checking their credit score; choosing a bookkeeping system and learning how to use it; hiring a bookkeeper or financial planner; saying an elegant "No" when someone asks to "pick their brain" for free; having new, honest money conversations with their sweetie or child; spontaneously donating to a political or crowdfunding campaign that inspires them; learning to negotiate better, and on and on.

In my own life, feeling empowered with money has been more of a personal journey. It has meant forgiving my father for the sometimes harsh way he taught me lessons. It has meant choosing a husband who felt like my equal partner around money. It has meant creating work in the world that feels deeply meaningful to me, and sharing my gifts in ways that serve others. It has meant charging rates that feel good to me and creating business models that provide a sustainable, joyful lifestyle. It has meant honing and trusting my own financial competency more and more. It has meant finding my own truth and establishing boundaries to honor what's authentic and meaningful to me. Power has been a journey for me of softening, opening, releasing fears, and claiming my own value, more and more, in small ways and huge, every day.

Value

Value has nothing to do with money . . . and everything to do with money. Almost everyone has questions about value that they bring to money work:

> *What am I worth?*
> *How do I feel that worthiness, in my bones?*
> *What's the connection between value and money?*
> *If I "own" my value more, will I earn, spend, and save differently?*
> *On a daily basis, what can I do to grow, cultivate, and claim my value, more and more?*

Oh, these questions cut deep, fast. Value is paradoxical, subjective, and so much deeper than confidence or even trust: this is about your fundamental self-worth, as a human being. On the one hand, your value has nothing whatsoever to do with that number on your paycheck or bank statement. Value isn't something you earn; it's something you *are*. This is why we could never, ever put a number on your value. The idea that your value could be tallied or quantified is absurd. Your salary would need zeroes to infinity.

And yet, as intrinsic as our value is, in today's society we also need to find ways to monetize and quantify our value; we need to earn a sustainable income and price our products and services in ways that feel good. These are the external mirrors of our inner sense of value. In my experience, however, we must start with the internal, emotional work of growing our sense of value—only then will external practices (like negotiating a higher salary) bear fruit.

When we chronically earn less than we want, there may be many factors in play, from the societal to the deeply spiritual. As Underearners Anonymous, a twelve-step program similar to Alcoholics Anonymous explains,

> "Underearning" is many things, not all of which are about money. While the most visible consequence is the inability to provide for one's needs, including future needs, underearning is also about the inability to fully acknowledge and express our capabilities and competencies. It is about underachieving, or under-being, no matter how much money we make.[12]

Underearning is one of the clearest symptoms of not feeling (and claiming) your value, and it's not solely based on your income. You can have millions of dollars in the bank yet exhaust yourself at work every week and take on others' problems because you just can't say no: this is under-valuing yourself. On the other hand, you might earn under $20,000 per year, but live within your means, according to your values and desires, and lead a joyful, satisfied life: I wouldn't call that under-valuing or underearning.

Underearning can be about underselling, under-expressing,

---

12 "Home," *Underearners Anonymous*, accessed January 4, 2016, http://www.underearnersanonymous.org/.

under-loving. Over-giving, under-receiving. Under-no-ing, over-yes-ing. It has everything to do with your experience of self-worth—whether or not this is reflected in your salary or job description. Finding and claiming your sense of value is a lifelong process. It unfolds, over time and leaps and baby steps. It demands both internal and external work. We will delve into many of the external practices to claim and grow our value in the Money Practices and Money Maps phases of this book. For now, here are some of the practices my community and I have found most helpful in growing our sense of value and overcoming underearning from the inside out:

1 Healthy boundaries, boundaries, and more boundaries around what we deem vital, sacred, and solely ours. Practice the Art of the Elegant No.

2 Remember (and repeat as often as you need): "My job is to be myself. Nothing more, nothing less."

3 Know yourself, through and through. Know what you're great at and what you suck at.

4 Notice and delete all that negative self-talk (I'm not smart, I'm not good enough, I have nothing to say) and replace it with positive thought patterns: I'm smart. I'm capable. My voice needs to be heard.

5 Focus on your successes. Every little step you take is a victory. Celebrate everything. This is how huge change happens.

6 "Mistakes" are amazing. They are ripe learning opportunities, and often redirect us to our true gifts and the right route for us. Milk them. Keep fine-tuning.

7 Seek out the good in your life. Notice and appreciate it. Look for opportunities to be grateful.

8 Fill your cup. Self-care is amazing and 100 percent necessary.
   Make it a top priority, whatever it looks like, to you: hikes,
   morning tea, meditation, dancing, friends, community. Many
   of these gifts cost nothing and give so much.

9 Be willing to be uncomfortable. Author Barbara Stanny told
   me once that the number one prerequisite to making more
   money is this willingness to be uncomfortable. I would add
   that we feel uncomfortable when we're shifting any pattern.
   It's a good sign. Challenge yourself to stretch, dare to be
   brave. Stay with yourself through the discomfort.

10 Our value ripens with age. Time is on our side with this one.
   Trust and self-love are muscles. Work them, and they'll get
   stronger. Trust the timing of your life.

11 Summon the courage to love yourself. And then love yourself
   some more.

money practices

· · · · ·

Welcome to the second phase of our journey together.

This is the land of numbers and systems, nuts and bolts.

It's about gathering data and creating healthy habits.

Here, we learn the language of money.

We empower ourselves.

We take *action*.

We align our deepest values with our day-to-day.

We bridge heaven and earth.

We get help.

We take ourselves on nurturing Money Dates.

This is the yang to Money Healing's yin.

It doesn't have to be scary.

Step inside.

Let me show you how supportive
your Money Practice can be.

CHAPTER 7

money as a self-care practice

AT SOME POINT after beginning your Money Healing journey, you may find yourself ready to bridge the gap from inner exploration to outer actions, to roll up your sleeves and start working with your financial numbers in a nitty-gritty, practical, ongoing way. This is a *moment* in your money journey. Because I have seen it so many times, and because it is always so pivotal, I have named this moment: "Crossing the Bridge."

If you find yourself hesitating to cross the bridge into Money Practices, lingering in Money Healing before peeking at your numbers, take a moment and ask yourself: Is this truly because I need more inner healing work before I can continue? Or am I letting fear and resistance hold me back? If you're scared to dig into the practical aspects of your money and find yourself repeating any of the following ideas, I invite you to consider that sometimes, we need to ignite our discipline, focus our intention, and embrace some rigor:

I've tried doing this money stuff before and it didn't stick.

I'm honestly just not smart enough to do this.

YAWN. It's so booooooring!

Can't someone else do this for me?

I'd really rather just ignore this stuff.

I can't be bothered.

I don't have the time.

I don't make enough money to even track this stuff.

I make too much money to track this stuff.

My life is such that I could never have a traditional budget.

There's so much to do, I don't even know where to begin.

I can't do it on my own, and can't afford help, so I'm just stuck.

If we wait until we're completely ready to do something, we'll never do anything. Transforming our lives takes courage. It takes striving for what feels just a smidgen or two out of reach, over and over again. That's what makes this money work a practice.

Money Practices are where all those insights you uncovered in Money Healing come to life and start making real change in your life. Here, you apply your loving awareness to new, challenging situations. Here, you stretch and grow and reap rewards. If all of the ongoing steps and endless To Dos of money sound terrifyingly boring or un-sexy to you, take heart. You *can* do this. There are things you can do to make the experience more nurturing, less terrifying, and more creative than you ever thought possible. It all starts with redefining what a "money practice" is.

Money Practice, n.

Old definition: A terrifically tedious, stressful, and painful monstrosity that I *should* do, even though I hate it.

New definition: Everything I do, on an ongoing basis, to help bring more clarity, peace of mind, and success to my money relationship. Something that helps me maintain my money relationship as a steadfast and supportive part of my life. Something that is constantly evolving, uniquely mine, and deeply nourishing. Something that gives me continual feedback about how aligned I am with my values and intentions, and continues to refine my self-awareness, enhancing every moment and aspect of my life. I get the very best support for my Money Practice that I can, and in turn, it supports me and every area of my life.

So . . . What Exactly *Is* a Self-Care Practice?

If you came to visit my beautiful mountain town of Boulder, Colorado, you might hear people use the word "practice" surprisingly often, and in a slightly different way than you're used to. Here in the "Boulder Bubble," as we affectionately refer to it, people talk about all sorts of *practices*. A meditation practice. A yoga practice. A healthy eating practice. A conscious sex practice, a gardening practice, a journaling practice, or an authentic communication practice. While this might sound a little precious, it points to an important truth: we can take *any* area or habit in our lives, fill it up with intentionality, awareness, and compassionate discipline, and reap deep rewards.

Self-care practices like these aren't merely To Do–style chores: they are essential for keeping us happy, sane, and growing. When we take the time to love and replenish ourselves, we reconnect with our true nature and return to the world more capable of sharing our gifts. For me, self-care looks like a soothing lavender salt bath or a hike up my favorite mountain trail. For you, it might be dancing with friends, a massage, or something else entirely. Chances are, though, it doesn't look like hanging out with a calculator and a bookkeeping program.

But what if you could turn your "money stuff" into a decadent self-care practice? What if all that money drudgery could feel every bit as luxurious as that bubble bath (or whatever *your* version of that is)? What if you actually *looked forward to* your money practice because it made you so much happier, more alive, and mindful? What if it was founded in and reinforced your most cherished values? What if it connected you ever more deeply to yourself, the world around you, and even your spirituality (whatever that means to you)? This is truly possible when we approach our interactions with money as a self-care practice. So let's define exactly what we mean by this.

A self-care practice is something you do consciously, with intention, on a regular basis, to support and grow yourself. It's a healthy habit
that, over time, provides a cumulative benefit. Every self-care practice I
know of contains some version of the following three key ingredients.

First of all, a practice is something you do over and over again (and
ideally get better at, over time). One of my most cherished self-care
practices is my almost-daily hike up Mount Sanitas, near my home.
After many years, my legs have grown strong and my lungs aren't
intimidated by the thin mountain air. Repetition is your friend in a
self-care practice and reveals your progress to you.

Just like a daily hike, a true Money Practice is ongoing and consistent. Let's say you decide your Money Practice includes checking your
account balances once a week, on Monday evenings. At first, things
might feel awkward and shaky—as my legs did the first few times they
carried me up that mountain. But if you're consistent, this resistance
and awkwardness will dissipate. Over time, your nervous system will
relax into the reassuring repetition. If you keep showing up to your
practice, you will get better and better at it.

Secondly, every self-care practice is supportive and nurturing, in
some way. The benefits may be physical, emotional, mental, spiritual or
some combination thereof. My daily hike keeps me fit and strong, but
it also keeps me sane, calms me down, releases stress, and turbocharges
my creativity and spirituality. I get many of my best ideas on my daily
hikes. Like any good practice, my daily hike is conscious, compassionate, supportive, and enjoyable.

A regular Money Practice will do wonders for your financial
world, of course. By tracking your income, spending, and savings,
you can wield more conscious control over this area of your life and
align it ever more closely with your values. But the benefits don't stop
there. Engaging with your money regularly can help you bolster your
self-esteem, deepen your sense of safety, and strengthen your intimate
relationships.

Finally, the best self-care practices connect us ever more deeply to
ourselves, to each other, and to our spirituality. This is due, in large part,
to the repetitive nature of practices. Every day, I take the same path up

the mountain. The mileage is the same, and the steepness never varies. These constants provide a reliable measuring stick against which I can notice how *I* am showing up differently. On some days, I stumble more often, and realize I'm more anxious than I thought. On days when I seem to fly up the side of the mountain, swimming in the beauty of the ponderosa pines, foxes, and raptors, I *know* on a bone-deep level that I'm enjoying a particularly easeful moment in life, and I pause to celebrate. Our practices mirror back to us who we are, how we've grown, and who we're becoming. They connect us more deeply with ourselves, which in turn makes us more available to everyone and everything around us.

If you bring love and full awareness to your Money Practice, it will always bring you back to the present moment. If you do the same Money Practice over and over again, it will mirror back to you how you have grown and changed, over time. You may understand yourself better and better, and show up to your relationships with more peace of mind and playfulness. Your Money Practice, like any great self-care practice, can become a training ground where you deepen your emotional honesty, mindfulness, and compassion for yourself and others.

> We truly can bring all of our smarts, creativity,
> intuition, compassion, deep values, and playfulness
> to our relationship with money.
> In fact, we have to.

A successful Money Practice is a challenge you engage with consistently and regularly; it nurtures your finances but also much more than that; and it connects you ever more deeply with yourself, others, and the world around you. As important as *what* a Money Practice is, *how* we do it is perhaps even more paramount. There are a few elements—a few *hows*—that we can incorporate into our Money Practice to make it the most successful, fulfilling, and transformative as possible.

GOLDILOCKS IT UP!

An essential element in any self-care practice is finding the right amount of it: that sweet spot that's not too much, not too little, not too hot, not too cold, but just right. In a gardening practice, for example, you can't neglect watering your plants for too long, or they will wither; if you overwater them, they will drown, but if you find the just-right amount, they will flourish.

Likewise, in a Money Practice, you need to find the right amount of time and effort to devote to this area of your life. It is up to you to find the perfect amount of attention and energy to put into your Money Practice, so you enjoy the benefits without feeling neglectful, obsessive, or overworked.

RHYTHMS AND CYCLES

Once you land on your just-right amount of a practice, you will inevitably find yourself needing to shift it, as time goes on. This winter, I didn't do my daily hike for a solid month. I hadn't planned on this, but my family had been on the road for two weeks, and when we returned home, I was exhausted, it was cold, and I knew that the most nourishing thing I could do for myself was to relax into a deep, introspective winter phase. Rather than push myself to maintain a constant level of hiking practice, my body needed to slow down and rest. Four weeks later, as the snow began to melt, I felt ready and happy to return to my daily hike. Any practice will change like this over time, moving through ebbs and flows, ups and downs, rhythms and cycles.

When you begin a Money Practice, you may have buckets of enthusiasm, and devote an hour each day to it, only to find that, a few months later, you're craving a break. There may be phases in your life or periods in your year (like tax time) where your Money Practice needs more attention and love from you. Allow your Money Practice to ebb and flow: this is all normal, wonderful, and part of the process.

EXPERIMENTATION AND FINE-TUNING

Thinking you have to practice perfectly can keep you from practicing at all. People have told me they're terrified of picking a bookkeeping system because they fear they'll pick "the wrong one," and be locked into using it forever. Please take this pressure off of yourself and give yourself permission to experiment. You might begin tracking your expenses on beautiful, creatively designed spreadsheets you make yourself, only to decide six months later that you want to switch to an online tracking system. Rest assured, you are allowed (and even encouraged) to shift your tools and practices over time, as feels right to you.

In my own Money Practice, I did my own bookkeeping for many years. Over time, I learned the ins and outs of several software systems, learned to read and understand my financial reports, and studied the ups and downs of my business cash flow so I could craft more sustainable business models. After many years, I decided it was time to make a change: my business had grown to a point where I really needed more professional help with my books. I handed certain aspects of my Money Practice to a wonderful bookkeeper and have been thrilled with the results. I learned a huge amount during those years of managing my own books and sometimes miss it now that my personal Money Practice is less nitty-gritty expense tracking and more strategizing. Like any Money Practice, mine has shifted over time.

FOLLOW *YOUR* BLISS

My husband and I have completely different systems for tracking expenses. Forest is a techie guy and likes to do everything online. He uses iBank to reconcile his accounts and has even created a custom spreadsheet for cash flow forecasting. When he sits down to categorize his transactions, he treats the activity like a meditation, following the numbers as he would his breath while meditating. I'm more of an analog girl. For years, I carried around a vintage cigarette case, slipping my receipts into it after every purchase. Every few days, when my little case got full, I pulled out all the receipts on my desk, and placed them under a beautiful black granite rock. I lit my candles, opened my essential oils, and slowly entered my expenses into QuickBooks while nibbling dark chocolate. While my Money Practice looks different now that I work with a bookkeeper, those years of regular appointments—what I call Money Dates—with myself were a tremendous education, deepening my awareness about my spending. But I never would have stuck with them if I had tried to make them look like Forest's (or anyone else's, for that matter).

As different as our systems are, both Forest and I love how we track things, because our practices reflect our unique personalities. This is the difference between a *bearable* Money Practice and a *delightful* one. We will get into more specifics around Money Dates and infusing your values into your spending in the next chapters, but for now, I encourage you to be on the lookout for ways to make your Money Practice your own. Think about where and when to do your practice, what values you bring to it, and what materials and tools you like to use.

BANISH BEGINNER'S SHAME AND WELCOME GUIDANCE

There's always a learning curve when we begin a practice, and money is no exception. Please don't beat up on yourself for not knowing how to do everything perfectly on Day One (or even Day One Hundred and One). If you begin using a bookkeeping system or calling accountants for the first time and find yourself overwhelmed and in over your head, please take a breath, take a pause, and don't be afraid to ask for help. Take some time to dig into a tutorial or visit an online forum and ask questions. Remember to insert Body Check-Ins liberally and go as slowly as you need to, engaging with things in small, manageable chunks, with plenty of breaks to integrate and calm down.

Even if you're not a beginner and you think you should know how to do your practice by now, there is still no shame in asking for help. This spring, I decided to return to yoga after a hiatus of several years. I didn't roll out my mat at home and struggle through whatever I could remember; I went to a local studio and let an experienced teacher guide me. There is value in receiving expert guidance, even through familiar terrain.

If you find yourself struggling in your Money Practice, please know: there are people who can help you. You can hire a bookkeeping trainer to show you how to work with accounting software; you can work with a financial therapist to guide you through the emotional aspects of your money relationship; you can even hire a financial coach to help you create and stick to a spending plan. We all need a financial support team of some sort.

. . . . .

The Three Levels of a Money Practice

I find it helpful to divide a Money Practice into three levels: physical, emotional-psychological, and spiritual.

At the physical level, we get things done. We:

- Get online and check our balances
- Track expenses, spending, savings, and investing
- Review and reconcile our accounts
- Pay bills
- Work with our financial support team (friend, partner, bookkeepers, accountants, coaches, attorneys, consumer debt advocates, etc.)

At the emotional-psychological level, we practice being compassionately mindful of our moment-to-moment experiences with money. This is the realm of awareness, healing, understanding, and transformation:

- Practice the Body Check-In: notice any sensations, emotions, or patterns around your money
- Gently work through resistance
- Journal about feelings, memories, hopes, and dreams about money
- Work on forgiveness and Money Healing Rituals
- Do financial therapy

At the spiritual level, we explore the idea that money carries our deepest values and connects us with what matters most. This may include:

- Trust: Relax into the larger vision of your life, and know that you are taken care of
- Thriving: Deepen your experience of prosperity and abundance, whatever that means for you, in this phase of your life

- Generosity: Express your generosity and deep caring for others in ways that feel good, aligned, and sustainable for you. In some years, this might mean donating ten percent of your income to a charity; in leaner times, you might volunteer at a food bank once a month

We truly need to incorporate regular practices from each of these three levels to enjoy a sane, healthy, fulfilling relationship with money. If we only focus on practical matters, we may find ourselves held hostage by emotional resistance or unconscious patterns. If we only focus on our spiritual insights, we may find ourselves in deep financial trouble. A robust Money Practice attends to each of these three levels.

Invitations to Regular Practice

So what do you actually *do*, during a Money Practice? Here are a few suggestions for daily, weekly, monthly, and annual Money Practices. Each of these levels of practice builds upon the previous: your daily practice might take five minutes, while your weekly practice takes twenty to thirty minutes, and your monthly Money Date takes forty-five minutes or an hour.

Getting Started: Preliminary Steps

DAILY MONEY PRACTICE

You may choose to spend five to ten minutes per day (or every other day) interacting with your money in the following ways:

1. Save and track your expenses. Find a way to track your spending that feels good to you. Simply pausing and saying, "Yes, I'd like a receipt" at the register can bring a small breath of mindfulness to your money relationship. If keeping paper receipts feels too outdated for you, make it a regular practice to check your online balances to have a quick glance of where you're at and make sure everything looks accurate.

Then, every day or so, create a peaceful environment for yourself and sync your bank with your bookkeeping system or download your current transactions. If inputting your transactions manually feels better for you, go for it! Check the Resources section of this book for some suggested tracking systems and see chapter 11, "Your Financial Toolbox: Tracking Systems and Financial Support Teams" for help picking the right system for you.

2. Mini-Celebrations. Please be on the lookout for any opportunity to congratulate yourself for money work, large or small. Gift yourself a sweet *Huzzah!* each time you complete a round of entering your receipts or remember to do a Body Check-In. These simple acknowledgements reinforce your progress and keep you on track.

WEEKLY MONEY PRACTICE

I recommend taking yourself on a "Money Date" about once a week. We'll explore Money Dates in depth in chapter 9, "The Art of the Money Date," but to explain briefly, these can be on your own or with a partner and could last twenty or thirty minutes, depending on your pace and what steps you need to take. This is your time to do a "financial housecleaning": you'll survey your practical landscape, clean things up, and make small course corrections. These dates may entail things like:

1. Review Your Daily Steps. Think back over the previous week and take note of how many times you did your daily practices, how that felt to you, what supported or hindered your success, and anything you may want to shift. You may decide to lower your expectations one rung and aim for an every-other-day practice. Or, you might decide you really want to carve out a few minutes each day for this practice, and it's time to set firmer personal boundaries. Remember to be open and lighthearted here. This certainly doesn't need to be self-critical.

2. Get current with filing. Enter and file any remaining receipts from the week, check your balances, make deposits, and review your transactions for anything unusual or in error.

3. Pay your bills. You might mail checks, pay online, or set up automatic withdrawals.

4. Attend to other money-related matters. Send in health insurance claims, transfer monies between accounts, follow up on that fee waiver at the bank, etc. You might also check for any "money leaks"—expenses you are no longer using (like an old gym membership) and attend to these (more on that in the Money Maps phase, to follow).

MONTHLY MONEY PRACTICE

1. Love up your space. Take good care of yourself, first: do a Body Check-In, adjust your environment as needed, bring in some flowers or yummy snacks. Purge any clutter or mess in your physical space: get rid of files you no longer need; donate, gift, or trash items in your way. When we free up our space, we often access more energy, enthusiasm, and flow. Appreciate yourself for showing up.

2. Reconcile your accounts. Go through your monthly bank statements and make sure all of your transactions have been recorded in your tracking system. If you've been manually entering transactions, make sure you didn't forget one or lose a receipt—and if your tracking system automatically syncs with your bank, it's still a good idea to look at each transaction to catch any errors, recurring charges, or duplicates.

3. View, review, and refine. For the first few months of your Money Practice, simply track and witness your financial behavior and patterns without making changes to them. Even if it doesn't feel easy or right, give it a few months to see if you really need to tweak something or if you're just scared. Then, after you've tracked things for a good three to six months, go on to include this step.

This is where you get to see the concrete results of your intentions, goal-setting, and behaviors. Do a little reality check: make gentle, direct contact with your financial reports. Print them out or look at them onscreen in your tracking system.

Take a look at your income for the month. Is it steady, or has it changed? Do you notice any big patterns here? If you're an entrepreneur, review the numbers in each of your revenue streams. Notice how you feel about the numbers, and to what extent your work feels in alignment with your values. Celebrate your successes, and note what you'd like to change, moving forward.

Now, review your expense categories. What goals and intentions got attention (and funding) this month? Take a deep breath, and ask yourself which of your deep values you have honored in your spending, and which you'd like to spend more supporting. Again, celebrate your successes, and ever-so-gently inquire into any goals you didn't meet.

You may also choose to compare this month's data to the previous month's. Notice any change, any trends (increasing or decreasing numbers). Stay as compassionate as you can—this is a work in progress! The most important thing, especially at the beginning, is that you're taking the time to look at all of this, engage with it, and strengthen muscles of discipline.

Next, you may want to compare this month's data to the same month last year, if you have those numbers. Again, note what's changed and what's stayed the same. Are you spending more on childcare now, and less on clothes? See, notice, celebrate, and adjust if needed, with constant, heaping doses of self-compassion.

4. Refine your plan. Do you want to shift your income, expenses, savings, investing, or debt repayment goals? Where do you need to allocate more funds, and which areas could stand some defunding?

5. Celebrate! As always, please celebrate that you were willing to look at your numbers. Shower yourself with appreciation for your courage, discipline, and openness. Set your intention to stay current with your tracking and other practices, and set a date for your next monthly practice.

ANNUAL REVIEW

This is the Mount Kilimanjaro of Money Dates. Once a year (or every six months, if you prefer), you will gently and compassionately review the year that you just lived. In the Annual Review, you will follow the same process as the Monthly Practice, but instead of looking at just one month, you will review the entire year, at once.

Connect with what phase of life you are in, what is most important to you now, and where you are headed. Take stock of what the preceding year (or six month period) has been all about in the grand vision of your life, and do your best to set intentions for the year to come, knowing that you can't know everything that will happen. We'll explore this in much greater detail in the Money Maps section.

. . . . .

If all of this seems daunting or boring, please pause, take a deep breath, and remember: you only have to take one step at a time. Patience and gentleness are your dear friends on this journey. It will likely take you six months or more to feel really comfortable with this whole new Money Practice. That is OK and normal. Take your time.

When we begin any practice—whether it's a Money Practice or a get-to-bed-earlier practice—we have the opportunity to witness our relationship to discipline itself. For some people, discipline comes easily: they set an intention to jog every morning, and they simply do it, rain or shine, no grousing. Some have a harder time: the idea of committing to a regular practice, even if it's something they truly want, kicks up all sorts of resistance, struggles with authority, and self-sabotage. Most of us fall somewhere in the middle of this spectrum and have areas where discipline comes easily and areas that challenge us again and again.

If you find yourself kicking and screaming before every Money Date, check in with yourself—do you have this same pattern with exercise or other self-care practices? Are there other areas of your life where you rock it with discipline—and if so, what perspectives or tools can you bring from those areas into your Money Practice?

Your Money Practice is a golden opportunity to explore and hone compassionate discipline.

When beginning a Money Practice, it is incredibly helpful to rely on formality and structure. Schedule your weekly and monthly Money Dates in your calendar, always at the same time, for example. Set aside and devote a solid chunk of time to your Money Practice. This formality and structure help us carve a new groove where one did not exist and is a good foil for your resistance. After a while, when the whole idea of money practice is less daunting, you may find yourself loosening up your structure and taking advantage of a spare ten minutes before a meeting to reconcile a bank statement or make a money-related phone call. You may actually start looking forward to Money Practices, and even—gasp—doing them for fun. It has been known to happen.

Many people begin their Money Practice with a burning sense of urgency. They have a backlog of financial To Dos or have gotten into financial trouble and need to fix it right now. This urgency is common at the beginning and yet it is so helpful to slow things down a bit and remember that it will *not* feel like an emergency forever. You will complete tasks, get into a happy rhythm, overcome inertia, and teach your body and mind to look forward to dealing with money instead of being scared of it.

Any self-care practice is really about self-love and empowerment. Sara Avant Stover, an author, yoga teacher, and dear friend of mine, defines empowerment as "bringing the light of awareness and awakeness into *every* area of our lives. Choosing to open every closet. This is how we create the lives we want."

Warning: you may even fall in love with your Money Practice. This is the magic that can come from making this practice conscious, compassionate, and deep.

CHAPTER 8

the spiritual level of
a money practice

IF YOU CHOOSE to go deeply into money as a self-care practice, you may be shocked by just how deep these waters run. You may soon find yourself asking some profound, existential questions that go beyond the practical or even the emotional: questions about trust, gratitude, and generosity. This is the spiritual side of a money practice.

Devoted spiritual practitioners are sometimes surprised to hear that their contemplative or faith-based practices also can find a home in their money relationship. But as countless wisdom teachers from many traditions have explained, when we approach *any* aspect of our life with awareness, openness, and commitment to presence, it can become a genuine spiritual practice.

> "The true task of spiritual life is not found in faraway places or unusual states of consciousness: it is here in the present. It asks of us a welcoming spirit to greet all that life presents to us with a wise, respectful, and kindly heart." —*Jack Kornfield*[13]

---

13 Jack Kornfield, *After the Ecstasy, the Laundry: How the Heart Grows Wise on the Spiritual Path* (New York: Bantam Books, 2000), x.

"Cultivating the capacity to be fully present—awake, attentive, and responsive—in all the different circumstances of life is the essence of spiritual practice and realization." —*John Welwood*[14]

"'This very moment is the perfect teacher, and it's always with us' is really a most profound instruction. Just seeing what's going on—that's the teaching right there. We can be with what's happening and not dissociate. Awareness is found in our pleasure and our pain, our confusion and our wisdom, available in each moment of our weird, unfathomable, ordinary everyday lives." —*Pema Chödrön*[15]

"If we want to be spiritual, then, let us first of all live our lives. Let us not fear the responsibilities and the inevitable distractions of the work appointed for us . . . let us embrace reality and thus find ourselves immersed in the life-giving will and wisdom of God which surrounds us everywhere." —*Thomas Merton*[16]

"Whether we are traveling far, or just doing our daily tasks, all our actions can be sanctified by offering them to God." —*Rabbi Zalman Schachter-Shalomi*[17]

These are some of the thoughts and teachers of wisdom that guided me in my twenties and helped me along my personal path of bringing mindfulness into my daily life—or, as I like to call it, bridging heaven and earth. Through mindfulness and heart, washing the dishes becomes a meditation; gardening becomes a devotional practice; and even paying your bills or reconciling your accounts can become an intimate,

---

14 John Welwood, *Ordinary Magic: Everyday Life as Spiritual Practice* (Boston, Massachusetts: Shambhala Publications, 1992), xv.

15 Pema Chödrön, *When Things Fall Apart: Heart Advice for Difficult Times* (Boston, Massachusetts: Shambhala Publications, 1997), 21.

16 Thomas Merton, *Thoughts in Solitude* (New York: Farrar, Straus, and Giroux, 1956), 46.

17 Zalman Schachter-Shalomi, *Gate of the Heart: A Manual of Contemplative Jewish Practice* (Boulder, Colorado: Albion-Andalus, 2013), 26.

vulnerable practice of bringing your fullest, most essential self into the world.

You may not be interested in spiritual or contemplative practices of any sort—or you might reject the notion that they should intersect with your money practice. Perhaps you just want to get out of financial debt or deal with the mountain of bills. That works too. As always, I invite you to take what serves you in this chapter and leave the rest. And should you encounter something profound and unexpected later in your money journey, return to this chapter for some additional support.

Over the years, I've come to rely on four essential practices to support this deeper level of money work: Trust, Generosity, Thriving, and Thankfulness. Think of them as invitations to deeper inquiry, ways to honor what is already happening in your life, or simply interesting perspectives to consider and take to heart.

Trust

Many people find it incredibly challenging to trust themselves with their finances. They feel deeply unsafe with their money situation, and might mistrust the financial institutions they interact with, their own ability to effect change, or simply the possibility that *everything will be OK*. After several months of tracking your spending patterns and getting support with your taxes, you may gradually understand your financial world better and trust your own ability to navigate it. Yet you may also discover a profound substratum of mistrust—deeper than your mental worries or memories.

It helps me to think of trust as an ingredient that we can stir into our money work, right along with the practical and emotional stuff. Like most good things in life, we can actively work to cultivate trust.

Each time I go for a hike in the woods, for example, I grow my trust. I tune into my body, ask, and offer up my fear, anxiety, excitement, anger, and joy to the universe. You might experience and deepen your own sense of trust through gardening, playing with your grandchildren, watching the sunset, or volunteering at a soup kitchen. Some people practice meditation, prayer, or other devotional practices to cultivate trust, while others delve into great works of philosophy; you might even experience trust through dance or other movement practices. Find whatever brings you greater connection with yourself and a sense of faith-filled wellbeing. And know: this is deeply relevant to your money work.

Trust may be the most profound gift of money work as well as the most fundamental practice within it. There is a rhythmic, cyclical nature to life (and money). When we recognize this, we can relax into trust. We can *know*, with faith and certainty, that *everything* in life is transitory and ephemeral and even the most challenging moments will pass. Of course, some things in our money journey are excruciating and difficult: losing a home or receiving overwhelming medical bills, for example. Trust does not whitewash the pain or reality of these situations, but infuses the challenge with a little spaciousness and ease, so we can move through the difficult times. As Pema Chödrön writes,

> We think that the point is to pass the test or overcome the problem, but the truth is that things don't really get solved. They come together and they fall apart. Then they come together again and fall apart again. It's just like that. The healing comes from letting there be room for all of this to happen: room for grief, for relief, for misery, for joy.[18]

If you find yourself facing big challenges in your life or financial world, allow yourself to forgive, to conduct a Money Healing Ritual, or to rely on your expanding support network so you can gradually bring more and more trust into your relationship with money.

Generosity

In many religious and spiritual traditions, generosity and even tithing (giving ten percent of your income to your spiritual community) are encouraged. Though these practices are sometimes controversial, I think there is a beautiful teaching at the heart of them: we should be as generous as we can with our time, energy, and, yes, money. That "as we

---

18 Pema Chödrön, *When Things Fall Apart: Heart Advice for Difficult Times* (Boston, Massachusetts: Shambhala Publications, 1997), 10.

can" part is crucial. If your generosity toward others harms yourself, it is not true generosity.

Many years ago a young man came to my hospice office to talk about a lovely charitable organization that desperately needed our financial support. My colleagues and I listened to his heartbreaking stories for a full hour, and at the end of his presentation, he passed around a clipboard, requesting we each set up an ongoing donation, to be automatically withdrawn from our paychecks. As much as I wanted to support this worthy cause, I didn't contribute that day. At the time, I was making $11 per hour, and could barely make ends meet. I simply could not afford a financial contribution at that time.

In the years since that day, my ability to make financial contributions has waxed and waned and shifted along with my income, values, and priorities. For many years, I donated ten percent of my business income to a different charity each month. After my son was born and money was tight, I pulled back significantly and looked for non-monetary ways to give, often donating my time or services. These days, I'm experimenting with giving in more spontaneous ways: I give to crowdfunding campaigns for friends who are sick, a family who lost their home in a fire, or to good folks kickstarting their business dreams. I continuously fine-tune and experiment with how I can be most effective and where I feel both able and good putting resources, time, and energy.

Of course, donating money isn't the only or even primary way you can express your generosity. For many years, I donated support and mentorship to community members and gave free talks at an organization that helped lower-income women start their own businesses. My husband regularly volunteers his consulting services to creative entrepreneurs, and often donates his time driving a school bus to and from field trips at our son's school. Members of my community practice generosity in various and eclectic ways, from offering a compassionate ear to a friend in trouble to chauffeuring the elderly to and from doctor's visits or making sandwiches and giving them to the homeless. In a very real and tender way, the practice of generosity points us to the profound truth of our interconnection with others and the world in which we live.

We all need to find our own balance in generosity, depending upon how resourced we are at this moment in our lives. Self-awareness and self-compassion are essential elements of generosity. Be generous with others *and* yourself. You cannot pour from an empty cup. Regularly check in with yourself, your finances, and your connection with your concept of what is greater than yourself.

> "Attention is the rarest and purest form of generosity."
> —*Simone Weil*

Thriving

I'm not a huge fan of the word "abundance." Over the past twenty years or so, it has become a buzzword for anything having to do with money. I prefer the word "thriving" to describe that incredibly powerful and essential human experience marked by dignity, joy, and resilience.

There are so many facets, levels, and subjective aspects to thriving—and, as always, they include the financial numbers yet also go far beyond them. A 2010 Princeton study found that emotional well-being for Americans increased right along with income levels, but only up to a certain point: once individuals earned $75,000 per year, further income growth showed nominal or no increase in emotional well-being.[19] Of course, there are a multitude of factors at play, here, from the varying costs of living in different areas to the number of dependents to support networks and on and on. Few of us can thrive when we're worried about basic needs like food, shelter, healthcare, or surviving into old age. However, it's rarely that simple.

Thriving looks different to everyone, and our perceptions and ability to experience it change over the course of our lives, sometimes independent of our financial reality. Many people thrive in very simple, low-income lives, thanks to wonderful community connections, devotional religious practices, or fulfilling work. On the other hand, I've known more than a few millionaires who struggled to take a single satisfied breath.

---

19 Daniel Kahneman and Angus Deaton, "High Income Improves Evaluation of Life But Not Emotional Well-Being." Princeton: Princeton University Center for Health and Well-Being, 2010.

We all have our own pathways to thriving, including the practical, emotional, and spiritual. If you find yourself longing to thrive more, it's worth taking this inquiry seriously. Tune into yourself and ask: What do *I* need to thrive? Be open to the answers that come. You may discover that you truly need to increase your income or save up an emergency fund of a certain amount. You might be able to utterly shift your sense of well-being, at least for a time, by splurging on a great meal or dancing alone in your kitchen. We can also deepen our capacity for thriving by recognizing the gifts we already have, living within our means, and taking time to enjoy the small pleasures in life. Be on the lookout for your personal gateways into greater thriving, however small or surprising they may be.

Thankfulness

Ah, gratitude. It is so beautiful, so life-changing, and sometimes *so* challenging. Life and money can feel—and *be*—so hard. Yet even on our toughest days—perhaps especially on our toughest days—we can take a few moments, take a few breaths, and shift our focus to what we are grateful for. It might be that savings fund you saved so hard for—or it might simply be this moment, sipping a cup of tea, listening to the robins chirp.

Sometimes, we can get so goal-focused, we lose sight of the beauty that's right here, before us. Or, we can achieve one milestone (raising your credit score or paying off that debt), only to move directly into the next project, without pause. No matter how much or how little you have in the bank, please: take the time, take a moment, take a breath, and be grateful for all that you have, all that you've done, and all that you are.

· · · · ·

Slow down.

Bring loving attention to this precious moment.

Relax into the rhythms and cycles of life . . . and money.

Honor yourself.

Bring your fullest self to your money work.

Tap into your essence, beneath the worry and mental chatter.

Cultivate your connection with truth, beauty, and goodness.

Seek opportunities for gratitude.

Feel the fullness of this moment.

Let trust in.

the art of the money date

I BROKE OFF a small square of my favorite dark chocolate, admired the flickering candlelight, and made myself just a little cozier in my overstuffed chair. I turned toward my computer, noticing a little flutter of excitement and anxiety in my solar plexus. A memory surfaced of my mother paying bills at the dining room table when I was a child. I took one more deep breath and I clicked open the software. A goofy smile spread across my lips. This program was my new favorite toy. And this little ritual—which I practiced every few days or so—was shockingly fun. The program was QuickBooks: a heavy-duty accounting software. And while I didn't call them that then, these sweet little evenings with my finances would eventually turn into what I now call "Money Dates." And trust me when I say: *They change everything*.

I learned about QuickBooks from a cowboy hat-wearing, sustainable home-building contractor named Jeff. When I mentioned my budding interest in accounting to him at a party, he lit up: "I'll teach you how to use QuickBooks!" A few weeks later, I met Jeff at his office, where he guided me through the ins and outs of the software. This program is the industry standard for accounting software, and has a steep learning curve. But his reassuring guidance (combined with my burgeoning enthusiasm for all things bookkeeping) kept me engaged and excited. Within a few days, Jeff hired me to do his business bookkeeping, and I also started using QuickBooks for my own business and personal finances.

What really knocked my socks off about QuickBooks was that I could actually *do* it. (Which is why I know that you can, too, if you like!) The gleeful breakthroughs were fast and furious at the beginning, and over the next few weeks, I was pinching myself in happy disbelief. "Holy cow: I can *see* what my numbers are!" I fell head-over-heels in love with bookkeeping, not just the clarity and peace of mind it gave me but, most surprisingly, the actual *process* of sitting down, entering my income and expenses, and reviewing my patterns. It became a fascinating, empowering ritual.

From that point on, for many, many years, I sat down with QuickBooks every few days and manually entered my income and expenses. There was always dark chocolate, of course, and whatever other "creature comforts" I needed to get into my little zone. Once a month, I treated myself to a slightly longer "Money Date," when I reconciled all of my accounts, reviewed my income and expenses, and noted patterns. Those early days with QuickBooks were the beginning of my personal money practice. My Money Dates have changed significantly over the years—evolved, expanded, simplified, and refined—but during those evenings spent with my numbers, I built an incredible foundation of financial understanding and know-how.

The Money Date: What *IS* it?

A Money Date is simply a time and space for you to connect with your money relationship. This is the regular, ongoing practice that breathes life into a money relationship. It's where we build healthy habits—on daily, weekly, monthly, and annual bases—to get more honest, clear, and empowered in this area of our lives. This sort of "date" might not seem as exciting as your other dates—at first. But it's more fun than "Doing My Budget" or "Paying the F-ing Bills" or "Keeping My Head in the Sand."

Money Dates can be gentle, sacred, playful, minimalist, or comprehensive; solo or with your honey, business partner, or friend; spontaneous or scheduled, quick or luxuriously long. Any time you set aside to look at your money relationship could be called a "Money Date."

POST-ITS, ZAFUS, AND SPREADSHEETS

My husband's Money Dates are different from my own. For the first few years of our relationship, he wanted absolutely nothing to do with money: he *hated* looking at his numbers. While I was at my desk, working on QuickBooks with my chocolate and candles, Forest would go outside with a Post-It note and list four expenses: Rent, Food, Gas, Health Insurance. Next to that, he wrote Income, and did a little quick math to see if he could make ends meet. "I was in barely-surviving mode," he recalls, "so my budgets and projections were very simple. It wasn't a 'date' at all. It was more like looking at a fuel gauge and seeing if I could eke out enough fumes to make it another few weeks. I always waited until the last possible minute to do it."

After years of practice, Forest has ditched the Post-It notes and now uses a combination of sleek online tracking systems and his own, customized spreadsheets. While I needed someone to hold my hand and teach me QuickBooks, he actually enjoyed teaching himself the ins and outs of different bookkeeping software systems. During his Money Dates, he sits with a straight spine at his desk and focuses on his breath. Just as during meditation, he notes any thoughts that arise and lets them float on by, like clouds out of the sky. He makes it a practice to bring himself back to his breath, back to categorizing and reconciling, back to his true self beneath the money resistance. "Everything changed for me the day I realized I could make bookkeeping a meditation practice," he explains. "I went from hating it—it was boring, mind-numbing, and the software always made me angry—to realizing the resistance was just another phenomenon happening in my mind. I could just sit and watch it arise and pass away."

While Forest's Money Dates evolved into a more complex and even spiritual practice over time, other people choose to simplify and de-ritualize their Money Dates the more experienced they become with them. Geoffrey, an architect in his mid-forties, loved the idea of sacred, elaborate Money Dates. For the first few months, he brought every spiritual practice he could think of into his Money Dates: a meaningful opening chant, candles, bowing to the four directions, and on and on. While these early Money Dates were incredibly helpful in melting Geoffrey's money resistance and wounding, he soon found his enthusiasm waning: each Money Date took multiple hours and a *lot* of energy. What he *really* needed, he decided, was to simply look at his real-deal numbers and attend to his financial To Do list. So Geoffrey dramatically streamlined his Money Dates, keeping only a few simple elements to make it meaningful to him: his special candles and some soothing music.

Some people prefer elaborate, ritualized Money Dates, with prayers and music. One of my community members insists on putting on sexy tango shoes and ruby-red lipstick before she sits down for a Money Date. Another woman burns sacred *palo santo* wood, sprinkles purifying salt water over her desk, and lights incense and wafts it with an eagle feather. Some couples sip liqueurs in bed together, play classical music, and share childhood memories about money. Other couples open all the windows, kick things off with a funky dance to New Orleans brass band tunes, and then plan their income and expenses for the next month. All of this variation is wonderful and utterly necessary to keep you engaged and excited about your own money practice.

How to Take Yourself on a Money Date

As with any good date, taking a little time to get prepared can make your Money Date all the more effective, meaningful, and fun.

What can you do to create a beautiful little space for your Money Date? You might want to clear off your desk, light a candle, bring in fresh flowers, or play a little music. Perhaps you'd like to take a few slow, mindful breaths or blast music.

Once you're ready to get started, consider the three basic levels of a Money Date:

1. THE PRACTICAL LEVEL

What do you need to do regularly to have a better sense of where you are with your money? You might log into your online banking, check your balances, and pay bills, if they're due. You could organize your receipts and add up your income and expenses for the month. Maybe you need to call up a new accountant and interview him. It might be time to zoom out and set or review your yearly goals and intentions around money.

Consider what bookkeeping system you'd like to use. Check the Resources section for suggestions, but remember, it all comes down to what works for you. You might even create your own spreadsheet system—or use a beautifully illustrated ledger. Don't get too stuck trying to pick the perfect bookkeeping system. Stick with the same system for at least six months, though, so you can tell if it's really working for you.

2. THE EMOTIONAL LEVEL

Remember: the practical, nitty-gritty, number-crunching of your money relationship is emotional, too! Be gentle and patient with yourself, here. Do a Body Check-In before diving in, when you're finished, and anytime you're feeling stressed or stuck.

3. THE PSYCHO-SPIRITUAL LEVEL

What truly matters to you? Perhaps rename those boring budget categories to remind yourself of what you value. "Mortgage" might become "Home" or "Sanctuary," for example. (Much more on this in the next chapter.)

Make some time for the deeper aspects of your money relationship on your Money Dates. You might want to pull out a journal and contemplate larger concepts like value, success, trust, and safety, as they relate to your money relationship.

· · · · ·

Money Dates with a Partner

For the first seven years of our relationship, Forest and I kept our finances and our Money Dates separate: me with my dark chocolate, him with his Post-Its. We made sure every expense was split evenly, down to the penny. When I became pregnant, we made the decision to fully merge our finances. We opened a joint checking account, began filing joint taxes, and began making more spending decisions together.

We were no longer two separate boats, sailing next to each other: we were in the same boat, co-navigating. The emotional side of merging our finances was far more meaningful than the practicalities: this was a big, big move for us.

There is no definitive right path for whether you should make separate or individual financial decisions. Couples in my parents' and grandparents' generations traditionally merged their finances when they married: this was the social norm, and few people questioned it. However, this often entailed some dark drawbacks, including a dynamic where one person wielded more understanding and power over finances than the other. Over the years, I have worked with many women who have had to learn about money for the first time as they were getting a divorce, after their spouse died, or as their partner became unable to continue managing the finances. This can be shocking and challenging—but it can also be a powerful initiation.

Marie and Jeff, a postal worker and butcher from a small town, merged their finances as soon as they married. Eighteen years later, they decided to separate their finances in order to feel more in control as individuals. This separation made them feel more autonomous *and* intimate. Paula and Maggie, owners of a rustic B&B, kept separate accounts for twenty years of domestic partnership, but merged their finances as they ended their relationship to solidify their commitment to transparency in their joint business venture. Tim and Jacquie, a librarian and stay-at-home mother, merged their finances at the very start of their relationship without giving it much conscious thought. Now, ten years into their marriage, they are keeping their finances merged but finding other ways to bring more honesty and equality to their money dynamics through open communication and regular Money Dates.

When my husband and I merged our finances, our Money Dates took on a whole new level of meaning and complexity. We had to find ways to come together in this area that felt good for us both. Sometimes, that meant scheduling a sexy night out at a favorite restaurant to discuss Big Vision future plans and what we wanted our money to help us accomplish in the upcoming weeks, months, and years. Other times, we sat on our couch with our laptops, me with my chocolate and him with his sparkling water and lime. Often, we'd have what I call "quickies in the kitchen": short, spontaneous check-ins about how we were doing with money. We also had ongoing discussions about what roles we each wanted, in our financial life: I kept up the bookkeeping for many years, until one day my husband announced he would love to take it over. We both also continued to do money work on our own, outside the relationship, noticing our own patterns around money.

Whether or not you merge your finances with your partner, and no matter what sort of roles each of you take on in the financial realm, you can have wonderfully successful Money Dates with each other. Sure, it matters *what* you do: those bills need to be paid and someone needs to talk to the accountant. But what matters even more than *what* you do is *how* you do it.

BE PATIENT. EXPECT MESSES AND CLEAN THEM UP

So many couples are terrified to even *begin* having Money Dates together: they can't imagine that having good, intimate, enjoyable conversations about money is even *possible*, given their history of fighting about money (or avoiding the topic altogether). Many couples have only ever talked about money in heated or crisis moments: right before bed when they're exhausted or when the credit card statement arrives and one of them is shocked at how the other spent money that month.

This bears repeating: Money Dates with your honey will take practice. Most of us were simply never taught how to have safe, compassionate, and playful money conversations with our partners, so it takes some time to open up lines of communication around money and make these conversations feel safe and good. At first, this may be uncomfortable, but over time, tension dissolves and is replaced by compassion, intimacy, and understanding. I have seen this over and over and over. Trust the process, stick with it, and be patient.

My husband and I have had serious fights about money. We've locked horns about spending decisions. We've had to cut Money Dates short so we could each go to our respective corners, cool off, and do some introspecting about why we were so triggered.

Sometimes, things get messy. Emotions get stirred up. This is normal and part of the process of learning how to talk about money with your honey. Things will not go perfectly all the time. That does not mean you're doing things wrong, or that you can't get better at this practice. Embrace the process, do the best you can, and accept the messiness with as much spaciousness and love as you can muster. You may even want to close your Money Dates by each sharing one thing you appreciate about your partner, so you end on a sweet note.

CREATE A SAFE SPACE

It's crucial to set an intention, before every Money Date, not to shame or blame each other. Agree to hold space for each other's stories, vulnerability, emotions, and desires. You may start by taking turns talking for fifteen minutes, the other simply listening. Set some intentions for *how* you are going to communicate in this Money Date. "I want to talk honestly and calmly about money with you for twenty minutes." "I'm scared to talk to you about this month's bills, but we need to have this conversation. Please be gentle with me as I share some of the practicals with you, as well as how I'm feeling about it. I want us to make a plan, together."

START WITH A CHECK-IN

It's also a wonderful idea to check in with each other at the start of a Money Date. If it's a more spontaneous Money Date, ask your partner, "Is this a good time to talk about money with you? Do you have the time and emotional capacity to have a Money Date with me right now?" If you schedule Money Dates, take a moment to "arrive" at the task together: simply voice how you're feeling, what's on your mind, how your day was. If you're feeling scared or hesitant, that doesn't mean you need to cancel the Money Date. (If you wait until you're in the perfect mood for a Money Date, you might never have one.) But do make a little time and space to become aware and compassionate of where you both are, emotionally. And know: these dates *will* get easier, if you keep showing up for them.

SHOW SOME R-E-S-P-E-C-T

Because money is such a charged emotional issue, passions can run high and sometimes, respect can fly out the window. If you find yourself getting agitated, take a moment, take a breath, and tune back into how much you love and respect your partner. Even though you might not see eye-to-eye on how you should "do" money (together or separate), speak to each other with the respect you want your partner to have for you.

HONOR YOUR EMOTIONS

Be sure to track your emotions right along with the practical stuff. You may want to share how you're feeling at the beginning and end of the Money Date, and even throughout the process. If you find yourself or your partner getting resistant, shut-down, angry, or sad, acknowledge the feelings and then continue the conversation. This is part of the work.

TALK ABOUT VALUES

Money is always intertwined with our values, so know that when you and your partner disagree about a money decision, it may be because you need to have a conversation about the value *behind* the decision, not just what the numbers say or which one of you is right or wrong. Come to an agreement about what values you want this decision to reflect and then continue the conversation from there.

KEEP IT PLAYFUL

During tight times, Forest and I created a playful "code word" for a financial crunch, and would announce it with a little smile whenever it arrived: "Maximum Lockdown, honey!" Money can start to feel like a very heavy topic, very quickly. Without making light of financial realities (this *is* important stuff, after all), try to break the tension every so often with an inside joke, funny face, or goofy dance. Remember, laughter is a wonderful antidote to stress.

Dreamkeeping

Michael and Lucie, a business consultant and acupuncturist, were pros at compartmentalizing their "money stuff." Despite merging their finances immediately when they came together, Lucie was the only

....

MONEY TIME WITH YOUR HONEY: 4 PHASES

1. STORYTIME

Carve out a special time and place to share your Money Story with one another. You can focus on what you learned as a child about money, what lessons have stayed with you, or any other aspect that makes sense to the two of you. Let one person speak while the other just listens. Then switch.

This isn't anything like normal conversation: if you're in the listening role, your only job is to listen. Let your partner talk for five, ten, or fifteen minutes with no interruption. Simply take them in. Then switch, and speak until there's nothing left to say.

Money Storytelling and deep listening help you explore some of that deep, emotional territory of money with each other: where you come from, what your parents taught you about money, why you "freak out" about certain things, what you feel shame about, why you spend or save the way you do, or simply what your feelings are (even if you don't completely understand them, yet).

You might ask each other questions, such as: What's your mother's relationship to money? How has your ethnicity, religion, or spirituality impacted your relationship with money? When you were a child, what was your role in the family, when it came to money?

You might just tell stories for the entirety of your first few Money Dates. Or you might begin each Money Date with a short story.

2. ALIGN AND COMPARE YOUR VALUES

I'll say it again: Every money conversation is also a values conversation. Take the time to clarify what your own values are and to share them, as a couple. Wires get crossed and issues get muddled when we don't recognize what our values are and share them honestly with each other. Celebrate the values you share

....

and work on cultivating compassion, curiosity, and respect for those you don't.

Let these values and deeper intentions guide your decisions. If you find yourselves getting upset or lost in the Money Date jungle, always return to the question: What are you needing and wanting, as a couple, in the present moment? Let your answers to these questions guide you to your "best right now" decision.

3. DOWN TO BRASS TACKS

Once you have the emotional foundation of shared reality *and* have aligned your values as best you can, it's time for some practical stuff. If you haven't already done so, take some time to discuss and agree upon:

- **Merged accounts, separate, or both?** There is no wrong answer, here, only the sweet spot that fits your relationship. Remember: that spot will likely shift, over time.
- **What tracking system will you use?** There's no perfect system: they all have upsides and downsides. The key, here: pick one, and attend to it regularly.
- **Who does what?** Make *conscious* agreements, here, to minimize resentment and disempowerment. Discuss and agree upon who will do the bookkeeping and other financial tasks. Get on the same team and figure out who's on first, second, and third.

4. MAKE THE TIME + CREATE THE SPACE

Money Dates are about creating regular, healthy, ongoing habits with money and with each other. Staying current with all of this and with each other is the result of ongoing practices, big and small:

- **Quickies in the Kitchen:** These are the short, casual, ongoing money chats you have about cash flow and other money matters.

continued

- **Weekly Money Dates:** I highly recommend scheduling regular weekly dates with your partner to reconcile your finances and attend to whatever needs your attention. You can use this time to check in with each other, reconcile your accounts, or make financial decisions. Or, you can use this time to share stories, feelings, or insights about money. Especially in the beginning, you need more time here as you find your "sea legs," so actively work on cultivating compassion and understanding toward yourselves and each other.
- **Deep Dives:** Monthly, set aside a little extra time for a more comprehensive review: what money flowed in, and where did it go from there? What worked and what didn't? Where were you in or out of alignment with your values? Your annual review might take several hours and involve looking back over the past year and setting intentions for the upcoming one.

Whenever you do a Money Date with your honey, do what you can to make it pleasant. Light candles, get treats, dress up. Go slow. Breathe. Make a safe space for you to both get vulnerable and share what's coming up for you. Remind one another how much you care.

. . . .

one who paid the bills and tracked their finances. After eighteen years of marriage, they had conscious practices in every single other area of their lives—their intimate relationship, their parenting, their gardening, their careers—except money. When it came to money, they both kept their heads in the sand as much as possible, only emerging to yell at each other about it.

Michael and Lucie took to Money Dates like fish to healing waters. They called their dates "Dreamkeeping" to remind themselves that their real purpose was to nurture their dreams and bring them into reality. After a year of this work, they held a celebration to acknowledge how much more clarity they had around their finances. For the first time in their lives, they had a whole year of records of their income and expenses to review and they felt closer than ever before. As Michael told me recently, "The money practices, for us, were less about emphasizing the future and more on working to maintain our present-moment focus."

Money Dates: Not Just for the Lovers

Fran, an administrator and single mother of two, scrunched up her nose at the calendar. Her daughter's prom was only two weeks away, and she had begged Fran for a formal gown. The year before, Fran had splurged on a dress for her daughter's homecoming dance, charged it to her credit card, and been stressed for months about the debt. This year, she was determined to make better choices with her money, which for her meant using her credit cards only in emergencies.

Fran called her daughter into the kitchen, poured two glasses of orange juice, and took a deep breath, reminding herself of her intentions: to speak clearly, honestly, and with love to her daughter and also to not spend money they didn't have. Fran gently told her daughter she wanted to have a quick money conversation. She explained that this year, she was focused on making better money choices, which meant she wouldn't be charging a new dress to her credit card like she had the previous year. She then clearly told her daughter how much she felt comfortable spending on her prom outfit.

To Fran's surprise, her daughter appreciated the conversation, and was excited by the challenge of finding a gorgeous dress within her budget. Over the next week, she visited the mall and a few vintage stores, and found a beautiful teal dress, *with* shoes, for well within her mother's budget. Her daughter was proud of her resourcefulness and Fran was proud of herself for modeling good money choices. Most of all, she felt grateful for the opportunity to get a little closer to her daughter this way.

We can and should have honest Money Dates with other people in our lives—not just our romantic partners. In fact, any honest and important conversation about money could be called a "Money Date," whether it is a heart-to-heart with your parents or a serious meeting with your business partner. Even an afternoon in a coffee shop counts if you're sitting with a friend to cheer each other on while you take the leap and check your credit scores.

Money Dates for Creative Entrepreneurs

Thirteen years into our marriage and seven years after merging our finances, my husband and I decided to merge our business endeavors, as well. Forest became the Chief Operating Officer of my business. From that point on, we have been husband-and-wife, coparents, and business partners.

Money is the lifeblood of a business. Yet a shocking number of the business owners I've worked with over the years were afraid to even peek at their numbers. At some point, no matter how fastidiously you've shoved your "money stuff" under that rug, running a business will drag it *all* out into the open. That's why, as an entrepreneur, it is nothing short of essential that you look at and understand your numbers on a regular, ongoing basis. Having regular Money Dates becomes part of your job description.

Now, my COO and I talk extensively about our business financials. Sometimes, we have Money Dates just for our personal finances; other times, we talk about business stuff, exclusively; and we also have a third kind where we look at it all, smooshed together, seeing how every aspect of our money lives impacts the others. We still apply copious Body Check-Ins, deep breaths, and treats as needed. We check in with the numbers, project cash flow, and strategize on weekly, monthly, quarterly, and annual bases. We track our numbers, but also our emotions and values, making decisions about hiring, marketing, and products based on what feels most true and good to us. We watch the nitty-gritty details of our finances *and* the big picture of where our business currently is and where it's heading. All of this is great for our money relationship—and it's also a smart, savvy, and necessary business practice.

Some solopreneurs may choose to have Money Dates that encompass both personal and business finances; others might feel better separating the two, and have mini-Money Dates for each. And, of course, there are levels of complexity going on up from solopreneurs to small business owners to CEOs of large companies.

Tea, Credit Scores, and Cheerleading

Margaret, a therapist in her late thirties, returned from the counter with two piping hot cups of Earl Grey. She set them down on the cafe table, where her friend Beth, a health coach in her twenties, was pointing excitedly at her laptop: she had just figured out how to create an annual "profit and loss" report with her bookkeeping software, so she could see exactly how much money her business had made that year and the previous two years.

Normally, Beth wouldn't feel comfortable sharing her finances this way, but Margaret wasn't an ordinary friend, and this wasn't a typical day at a cafe. Beth and Margaret were both solo creative entrepreneurs who had agreed to meet regularly to cheer on each other's money work. Some of their Money Dates focused on sharing stories about early money memories and what their parents taught them about money. Sometimes, they celebrated little money victories—from paying off a credit card to finally calling that accountant—and showered each other with un-shaming compassion when things got tough. Their plan for this particular Money Date was to check in on their business finances and make some decisions about strategies for the next quarter.

Margaret looked through Beth's recent invoices and noticed two clients who hired her on a regular basis for health coaching. Margaret suggested putting them on a retainer agreement, and listed what the benefits to Beth might be if they agreed. Beth thought it was a great idea, and made a note to email her clients later that day.

Unlike Beth, Margaret was already fastidious about tracking her income—what her business finances needed was a shot of creativity and a way to make more money. Margaret was looking for advice on whether to raise her rates and Beth felt comfortable enough with Margaret to help her consider a number of factors involved in this decision: the average rates for therapists in their area, how much value her clients got from their work with her, how much income she needed to bring in over the next three months, and how much she *really* wanted to charge for the work she did. As it turned out, Margaret didn't really *want* to raise her rates—she loved making her work affordable for lower-income folks, and her lower pricepoint wasn't false humility or resistance. So Beth suggested a few alternatives: she could offer a group therapy program at an even lower rate and *still* make more money for the time she put into it. She also suggested Margaret turn some of her writings into a $5 ebook for sale on her website so she could earn some passive income as well. Beth showed Margaret where to get free ebook templates and promised to help her set up all the techie stuff. Stories like this one show the massive power of a little Money Date. When we talk openly and honestly about money, it can truly not only help us financially, but it can also bring us closer to others.

In my own Money Dates about my business over the years, I have constantly tweaked and refined things. I have expanded my business, pared it back down, welcomed a team, and moved my offerings from in-person to online. I have experimented with different business models to find what feels right and good and sustainable to me—and allows me to serve the most people in the best ways. I have identified what I'm good at and what I'm not-so-good at and I've expanded my support team. I have tracked my numbers, projected my income, relaxed into the present moment, celebrated successes, and visioned the future. All of these things could be aspects of entrepreneurial Money Dates.

Merging our businesses has meant my husband and I now have *huge* Money Dates, where we can talk about everything financial in our lives in an integrated way. The decision to offer a new product from our website might be tied into what taxes we owe for that year or a dream to build a home in the future. We may need to discuss emotions around paying our team members more or reassign which one of us does what, in the world of our business finances. This doesn't necessarily mean that all of our Money Dates are epic, lengthy events: we still have "quickies in the kitchen," too. But, over time, our Money Dates have allowed us to relax into money being an ever-present and welcome thread in our lives. We're not *always* talking about money, but we can do so at the drop of a hat, without tons of angst and resistance. This is the beauty of ongoing, regular Money Dates, whether you're an individual, a couple, or an entrepreneur.

values-based bookkeeping

IN THE LATE summer of 2003, while living in Sebastopol, I had one of the most vivid, paradigm-shifting dreams of my life. It had been two weeks since my first money mentor, Tamara Slayton, passed away. In accordance with her wishes, her community had gathered at her home for several days after her death, remembering, telling stories, and honoring the impact she had had on our lives over the years. I spent many hours reflecting and journaling on our friendship and the legacy she was leaving.

I had been privileged to spend the last two years of Tamara's life with her, soaking up her philosophy on money. She had been my teacher, my mentor, and my friend. When I had just started my first business doing bookkeeping for creative professionals, she was one of my first clients. We spent countless hours together reviewing her numbers, setting her goals and intentions, and having brilliant conversations about her own philosophy on money, life's work, and value.

In my dream two weeks after her death, a curious package arrived at my door. I ran my fingers over the brown kraft paper and through the butcher's twine looped around it. Something about it felt sacred and otherworldly. I tore open the brown paper to see a stunning, scarlet-red book, and instantly knew: Tamara had made this book and sent it to me. She had felted the creamy white paper, hand-sewn the edges, and bound it all in red vellum. Inside I found a ledger of every single moment of Tamara's life, every idea she had concocted and shared, every piece of artwork, and every activity—and next to each one was a monetary value. Line after line, page after page were meticulously inscribed in Tamara's swirly, flourish-filled handwriting. This red book was Tamara's Book of Life: an honoring, a remembering—*and* a financial accounting!

I awoke confused. Wasn't it somehow sacrilegious to assign a monetary value to these moments and creations in Tamara's life? My mind couldn't fully wrap itself around this strange concept, yet my heart knew this was as far from sacrilegious as you could get. This Life Chart of Accounts was the full integration of Tamara's esoteric vision and financial teachings. It elevated money matters to the realm of the sublime and the sacred. Here was the bridge I had been searching for, for so long between heaven and earth, between heart and money, between deep values and tangible moments.

While it took me a few years to fully unpack the message contained in this vision-like dream, it forever and instantly changed my relationship with bookkeeping—both in my own life and in my work as a financial therapist. In that red book, I glimpsed a radical new way of interacting with financial numbers: one that not only reflects our deepest values in the world, but honors them, strengthens them, and brings them to life in a tangible way.

Values-Based Bookkeeping: A Sacred Vessel

That dream eventually evolved into the practice I call Values-Based Bookkeeping. In this realm, we translate intrinsic values into extrinsic actions and transform boring budgeting into a powerful vehicle for carrying our dreams into reality.

Even before I had the dream about Tamara's book, I knew that I wanted to find a way to make dry, dusty "bookkeeping" more creative and meaningful, both for myself and for my creative, mindful clients. So many of us affirm our commitment to values like creativity, sustainability, intimacy, or personal growth. Yet so often, we assume that money is somehow separate from these crucial values that make our lives our own. We relegate money (and *especially* the nitty-gritty practice of bookkeeping) to some shadowy, cobwebby room in the attic. We rarely visit, and when we do, we check our values and dreams at the door.

Values-Based Bookkeeping reimagines money practices entirely. Instead of separating money from our deepest values (or aligning them in some hodgepodge, hit-or-miss fashion), here, we make money a vessel that contains and nourishes that which matters most to us. Values-Based Bookkeeping is a practice where we pull down our visions and birth them into day-to-day reality. Tracking our spending, earning, saving, and investing becomes a way to gently track how aligned our intentions are with our daily life.

Many years ago, I stumbled across this passage from Gloria Steinem:

> What if one day, as I was crossing the street, I got hit by a Mack truck? Temporarily stunned, I'd lie on the ground, and a crowd would gather to help. No one would know my name, what I did for a living, or what I believed in. But if one of them picked up my checkbook (thrown from my purse by the impact), what would she see? Would those check stubs reveal the kind of person I was? Would they know what mattered to me, based on where I spent my money?[20]

When I read this little passage back in my twenties, it opened my eyes to a different way to "do" money. It challenged me to bring more mindfulness and sovereignty—and more of *myself*—into those bank statements and check stubs and moments at the cash register.

One of the simplest, most profound and playful ways I've found to bring our values into our money world is through the simple practice of renaming the categories within our tracking systems. (If you don't use a tracking system yet, don't fret: the next chapter focuses on the emotional *and* practical considerations of choosing one.) If you feel even the slightest hint of resistance about beginning a bookkeeping practice (or continuing the one you already have), this concept of renaming just might have you singing a far happier tune.

---

20 Gloria Steinem, *Moving Beyond Words* (New York: Simon & Schuster, 1994), 204.

"To be a wise and good steward of money is simply to save, spend, and invest it in ways that align with my truest desires and deepest values. It's that simple (and that hard sometimes, too)."
—*Lisa Byrne*

Your Chart of Accounts: The Non-Scary Version

Before you start renaming your expenses, however, it's helpful to know the "traditional" names and categories that people use for keeping track of money. That way, you'll know what kind of categories might need naming or renaming in the first place.

The first step in understanding how your values and money intersect is to demystify the idea of a Chart of Accounts. When I first heard the term "Chart of Accounts," I froze like a deer before headlights, and an icy shiver bolted up my spine. I couldn't even parse those three words: it just sounded like one big, scary, inscrutable beast: *chartofaccounts.* Thankfully, it is *way* less boring and intimidating than it sounds. In fact, it is pretty simple and can actually be profoundly interesting.

A Chart of Accounts is a list of all of your accounts (whether for you, as an individual, or for your business, if you're an entrepreneur). "Account," here, has a slightly broader definition than you might be used to. It doesn't only refer to checking, savings, and credit card accounts, but also includes other things, like property, debts you owe, and even income you're expecting. A Chart of Accounts is an inclusive, bird's eye view of your entire financial reality. It is beautifully comprehensive, yet also simple enough to be the very first thing I usually teach when introducing people to bookkeeping. If you're itching for a little more clarity about your financial reality, creating your Chart of Accounts is a huge, helpful step in that direction.

The wonderful news is: there are only five big categories inside a Chart of Accounts. I think of these as the five "bones" of the main structure of your bookkeeping system. These five areas constitute the entire big picture framework of your bookkeeping—whether you're using QuickBooks, a DIY spreadsheet, or the back of an envelope. This is the structure of your bookkeeping system (or *sacred vessel*, if you prefer).

Even if you're not ready to set up your tracking system with these areas, yet, I encourage you to read the following descriptions of these five "bones." Knowing their (truly simple) definitions will bolster your financial confidence—and the deeper alternative descriptions I love using with them just may open your eyes to another level of your financial reality. Each of these five "bones" can be fleshed out with subcategories, but for now, let's keep things simple.

The Five "Bones" of a Chart of Accounts

1. ASSETS

Classical definition: Everything you own or control that contains (or could be converted into) positive economic value. Your checking and savings accounts; investment and retirement funds; real estate, vehicles, and personal property. Even that cash you have stashed under the mattress.

Businesses may also include inventory and equipment, accounts receivable (invoices that haven't been paid yet), and even less tangible things like intellectual property (copyrights, patents, trademarks).

Alternative, creative, meaningful considerations: Everything above is an *extrinsic* asset. I believe it's also incredibly important to list out our *intrinsic* assets: who you are, deep, deep down, and what gifts you bring to the world. Intrinsic assets may include your health, creativity, intellect, empathy, ability to create beauty, and on and on. I strongly encourage you to take a few moments and list out at least ten of these. No, really: stick with it until you get to ten. Some people find this exercise very challenging—I believe that's an indicator of just how crucial it is. (Note: all of these alternative definitions are wonderful exercises for your personal growth, not to share with your accountant.)

2. LIABILITIES

Classical definition: Everything you owe. Your debts, credit card balances, utility bills, mortgages, student and auto loans, money you borrowed from friends and family members, etc. You might divide this into "current liabilities," which must be paid off within the next year, and "long-term liabilities," which you can take longer to pay off.

Businesses may also include payroll (because you want to set aside a certain amount for this), taxes, and accounts payable (money you owe other people or businesses but haven't paid yet).

Alternative, creative, meaningful considerations: My first money mentor, Tamara Slayton, often said to me, "Sometimes liabilities are hidden assets." On one level, she was referring to those student loans you took out that you *know* will translate to greater earning potential, over time—or those business startup costs you put on a credit card that you hope will bring you a big return on your investment. Yet there's an even deeper level to plumb here.

In a long life, there will be seasons and cycles, ups and downs, happiness and grief, growing and letting go. Sometimes, we encounter a death cycle (literal or metaphorical), a health crisis, or a huge life transition. Sometimes, we fall apart. And in these moments, we need resources. We may dip into our savings, cash out our retirement accounts, go into debt, or borrow money from friends and family. These times in life can stretch us to our limits—especially when we add the weight of money guilt or shame on our shoulders. If you are or have ever been in one of these phases and watched it affect your finances, I hope you will take this to heart: trust in these moments, as much as you can. There are hidden assets within certain liabilities: they may multiply your compassion for others, teach you invaluable life lessons, or hone skills that you will rejoice in, later on. It may take months or even years for these to reveal themselves, but I encourage you to trust that they *will* appear, if you show up fully for them.

3. EQUITY

Classical definition: Simply put, your assets minus your liabilities equals your equity, or "net worth." Or: what you own minus what you owe is your net worth. This number is calculated as a snapshot, at any given moment, and many bookkeeping systems will do this math for you.

Alternative, creative, meaningful considerations: Please always remember: your "net worth" is NOT your "true worth." Period.

4. INCOME

Classical definition: How you bring in money. This might include your salary, dividends from investments, and even gift income. Businesses may have just one or many different income streams (coaching income, product income, referral fees, and so on). It's up to you to determine whether listing these out individually is helpful to you or not. It usually is.

Alternative, creative, meaningful considerations: However we choose to see money—as fuel, as energy, as compensation for how we bring our gifts and "superpowers" to the marketplace—it flows in and out of our lives. Income is simply a measure of all the ways and amounts in which it flows into your sphere of influence.

5. EXPENSES

Classical definition: What you spend money on. You might have ten, twenty, fifty, or a hundred categories here, including your rent, groceries, utilities, garden supplies, bike gear, gifts, and doodads.

Alternative, creative, meaningful considerations: We're conditioned to believe that "income = good; expenses = bad." Please shake yourself loose from this constricted view. You may choose to track and control your expenses carefully—yet, never forget, these really represent different areas of life you get to enjoy. Just as money flows into your life, it also flows out; the beauty of bookkeeping is bringing awareness and empowered choice to all directions of this flow.

. . . . .

That's it! Hooray. Now you understand what a Chart of Accounts is, and all five of the main "bones" of this system.

If you choose to create your own Chart of Accounts, you can do so within your bookkeeping software (depending on its features), or you may choose to list everything out on your own, back-of-an-envelope style. You might keep things ultra-simple, or you may include elaborately long lists of subcategories under each of these five areas. You might keep these simple, classical names, or you might choose to make up your own, creative names, as well.

As with all things bookkeeping, please insert Body Check-Ins before, during, and after this exploration. You're learning the language of money, and soon you'll find yourself feeling more and more comfortable here.

What's in a Name?

Sandra, an attorney in her early fifties, felt like she had a mountain of credit card debt weighing down on her. To say she was "resistant" about it would be an understatement. She absolutely couldn't get herself to make those monthly payments, and felt utterly drained by the entire situation. Every time she received her monthly bill (always with late fees and interest charges) or considered mailing a check, she became paralyzed by anger, shame, and a total lack of energy around this debt.

I asked Sandra, "Where did the majority of this debt come from? What did you buy with this card?" As it turned out, Sandra originally ran up this credit card debt on a big trip to Italy she'd taken years before. That experience was far more than a vacation: it was a turning-point, profoundly impacting Sandra's physical, emotional, and even spiritual levels for the better. Yet the accumulation of years and the snowballing interest fees had gradually obscured her debt's "origin story," completely disconnecting it from the pivotal experience it had made possible.

Once Sandra realized the beautiful origin of this debt, she decided it deserved a new name in her bookkeeping system: instead of "credit card," she called that line item, "My Italian Experience." Immediately, she noticed a huge shift: she created a plan to pay it back quickly (without stretching herself too far), and began making her monthly payments on time. Her resistance melted away and was replaced with gratitude, enthusiasm, and a deep honoring of what this money had allowed her to create in her life.

Even if your debt comes from dealing with something more negative (a loss, a health crisis), naming what you are really paying for is critical. The simple act of renaming our budget categories can be transformative. It's a small thing, and might even seem petty or silly, but renaming can connect us with the personal value of our expenses. No longer are "my life" and "those cold, dusty numbers" living in separate rooms: your bookkeeping system reveals and strengthens their intimate connection and reminds you of it on a regular basis.

Taxes and Community Contribution

A few years ago, my husband and I found ourselves with a huge financial resistance connected to taxes. While we've always been good about setting aside money for annual or quarterly taxes, we started noticing a big resistance to actually mailing those checks. We'd often wait until the very last extension deadlines were upon us and we would throw real grown-up tantrums, kicking and screaming our way to the post office. The resistance was draining us far more than the actual expense, so at a certain point, we decided we really needed to shift our relationship to paying taxes.

We started by talking openly about all of the ways our tax money is used. We named the things our tax money pays for that we don't agree with, and processed our feelings about this. Then, we turned our attention to the wonderful, positive things our tax dollars pay for, like the courageous relief efforts of the National Guard during a recent, devastating flood in our mountain town, our beautiful national parks, and the smooth, safe roads we travel on. We decided to focus on these positive uses of our tax dollars, and based on this, renamed our "taxes" spending category, "Community Contribution." From that day forward, every time we set aside monies into that category, we felt grateful for our beautiful community. And when it came time to send off those tax returns, while we didn't exactly hop-skip-and-jump to the mailbox, we felt far, far better about where our money was going than ever before.

Imagine looking over your budget for the month. Your expense categories might include: Mortgage, Student Loan Debt, Car Payment, Groceries. Now, consider these categories, instead: Home Sweet Home, Fabulous Education, Wheels, Nourishment. Might that inspire you to feel just a little more engaged with your finances? Renaming our categories is one of the simplest and easiest of Money Practices—and a lot can happen when you shift your words.

Creativity and a Big, Fat Zero

Kat, a twenty-nine-year-old administrative officer for an investment company in San Francisco, took a long, hard look at the printouts before her, convinced she was reading them wrong. Six months prior, she had written a list of her top ten values—the things that mattered most to her—and turned those into spending categories for the month. She then tracked her expenses—for the first time in her life—for six months.

Kat had listed "creativity" in her top five values and created an expense category to track it because she was craving more creativity in her life. She was so determined to experience more creativity, she even listed subcategories under "creativity" with planned purchases such as dance and theater classes. She'd always wanted to perform onstage in front of an audience, and she hoped that by putting creativity right into her budget, she'd take some steps toward this dream.

Six months later, she looked at her budget and realized she hadn't spent a *single penny* on creativity. The expense line item on her budget was a big fat zero. Kat realized that if a stranger saw her bank statements, they would have no clue how important creativity was to her. More importantly, she'd disappointed herself. The numbers revealed the truth: she wasn't living in alignment with her values.

Kat resolved to make a big change. She was ready to graduate from simply tracking her expenses to consciously directing them toward the life she'd wanted for so long. Within a few weeks, she had signed up for a theater class and a dance fitness instructor training. Thankfully, Kat's job paid her well enough that she did not have to scrimp in other, vital areas of her life to afford these expenses: instead, the work for her was to value herself enough to spend money on something as "frivolous" as creativity. Soon, she auditioned for a local play and got a part. Within six months, she landed a bigger role in another play. She completed her dance fitness instructor training, got certified, and began teaching classes. When we last spoke, Kat was gearing up for a performance in New York—and, most importantly, felt vital and satisfied with all of the creative outlets in her life. Finally, her values and outer life were in alignment, and she attributed this big change in her life, in large part, to this simple practice of renaming (and tracking) her spending categories.

> Get clear about your values. Track how much you really spend on
> them. And take action to bring them to life.

Of course, it's not always necessary or possible to spend *more* money to bring your values more to life. If creativity is a core value for you, for example, there are plenty of free ways you might support this. Perhaps what you need more than more money is more time. Often, living your values means spending *less* money on certain things: only buying new clothes you know were made in a fair and sustainable way (or bought secondhand), choosing to take your bike or public transportation instead of your car to reduce your carbon footprint, or cutting back on drive-through dinners to spend more time cooking and enjoying healthy food with your family.

Perhaps one of the reasons many of us are afraid to inventory our values and track our spending is that we know our inner and outer worlds are out of sync and we don't think there's anything we can do about it. Yet as Kat's story illustrates, getting honest about your current reality is the first step toward creating the life you want. When your inner clarity fuels your money practices, a "budget" really does transform into something far more like a map for where you want your life to go.

Anything you want to do or create can go in your spending plan. Even "attracting a life partner" (or "finding my dream woman"), if it's an important intention, could be included in your Values-Based

Budget—maybe even with subcategories like dating site memberships, drinks at the local watering hole, or splurging on a new haircut.

We can also use Values-Based Bookkeeping to make sure that other areas of our financial life are aligned with our values, beyond just spending: our earning, saving, investing, and gifting are all opportunities to express what matters most to us. Jack, a tax lawyer in his early sixties, was quick to list environmental sustainability as one of his core values. Yet when he compared his values list to his Chart of Accounts, he had to face the cold, hard truth: part of his income this year had come from an investment in a large oil and gas company, whose practices he felt deeply misaligned with. Even though Jack made regular contributions to environmental organizations, he couldn't bear the misalignment between his values and his financial life. He took a deep breath, checked in with himself, and knew: it was time to move his investments to companies that reflected his values—even if that meant enjoying less *financial* return on his investment, it would make all the difference to his conscience and heart.

Remember, though: it is up to each of us to discern the best decisions, for us, for this particular moment in our lives. Values-Based Bookkeeping need not be some "holier-than-thou" tool for shaming ourselves or others, but rather a loving mirror, and an invitation into ever-deepening intimacy with yourself, your values, and the truth of your life at this moment.

Champagne and Organic Blueberries

Cindy, a single New Yorker in her sixties, had just taken a huge leap in her life. After years as working as a therapist, she had jumped tracks in her career and started her own business as a financial consultant. As a newbie entrepreneur, she felt a constant swirl of excitement and terror, anxiety and glee. Inspired by the concept that "fear is excitement without breath," Cindy set an intention to focus as much as she could on the positive, exciting feelings of this time of her life. She resolved to take herself out to a celebratory lunch every Friday afternoon as part of this commitment—and always have a glass of champagne. Sometimes she took a friend or two, sometimes she went out on her own, but

CREATE YOUR OWN VALUES-BASED BOOKKEEPING CHART OF ACCOUNTS

Create a calm, quiet, beautiful space for yourself (whatever that looks like, for you).

1. WHAT ARE YOUR VALUES?

What is most important to you, at this phase in your life? Remember: these answers are yours, and yours alone. They come from within yourself—not from your parents or anyone else. And you can change your mind, over time.

2. WHAT ARE YOUR MONTHLY EXPENSES?

Depending on how much time, energy, and enthusiasm you have, you may go through several months' worth of bank statements for these numbers . . . or you might make some back-of-the-envelope estimates.

3. COMPARE YOUR LISTS.

How do your heart-based values and reality-based expenses line up?

Hand on heart. Do you need a break, here? Honor any needs you have before moving forward.

4. REFRAME, RENAME, AND REIMAGINE YOUR EXPENSE CATEGORIES AT WILL.

This is the fun part! A few suggestions:

- You might start by looking at your expenses and asking yourself if you couldn't find a more meaningful, playful name for any of them. For example, you might not list "Sanctuary" on your values list, but realize when you see "Rent" on your expenses just how important that is to you.
- Or, you could look at your values list first, and see what expenses already fit under those values. For instance, if

continued

"Community" is a core value, do your travel, phone, internet, and dinner parties with friends belong there?

- You don't need to rename everything at this point—if "Mortgage" feels OK to you, leave it for now, but be sure to try on, at least as a thought exercise, what it would feel like if you saw "Love Shack" or something like it in your monthly bookkeeping reports instead of "Mortgage."
- Your expenses are the main place to use values-based renaming, but feel free to play with this in other money areas: your income, investing, savings, gifting, etc.
- The style of categories will reflect you. You might prefer short, Zen-like names . . . or whole, flowery sentences.
- Keep it simple. If all of your names, categories, and subcategories start getting complex, slow down, do a Body Check-In, and simplify.
- Feel free to start with a rough or incomplete draft, then let it "simmer" for a few days before finalizing it.
- Be creative, keep it playful . . . and have fun!

5. CELEBRATE THIS HUGE STEP YOU JUST TOOK.
Truly: don't skip this part. Treat yourself to a bubble bath or glass of wine or movie—whatever feels celebratory to you. Celebrations are *so* important.

SAMPLE VALUES-BASED CHART OF ACCOUNTS

Use this sample chart to spark your creative process, but keep in mind: the magic, here, is naming things exactly as *you* want. Also, know that many subcategories could fit under several different main categories: "Travel" might fit under "New Perspectives," "Community Building," or "Networking," while "Clothing" could just as easily fit under "Self-Expression" as "Beauty." Feel your own way through these grey areas, and know: the only "right answer" is the one that makes sense to you.

EXPENSES:

- Home, Sanctuary or Love Shack (rent or mortgage)
- Stylin' Wheels, Batmobile, or Freedom to Ride (car payment)
- Nourishment or Healthy Food (groceries)
- Self-Care, Self-Love, or Radiant Health (healthcare, health insurance, massages, etc.)
- Happy Fun Time / Joy (spontaneous splurges, movies, etc.)
- Personal Growth or Creativity (therapy, workshops, art supplies, etc.)
- Beauty or Self-Expression (clothing, lotions, makeup, etc.)
- Community or Connection (travel, potlucks, events, etc.)
- Generosity, Giving Back, or Community Contribution (charitable donations, gifts, etc.)
- Adventure, Family Fun Times, or Arts and Culture (travel, museums, etc.)
- Financial Support Team (bookkeeper, accountant, etc.)
- Peace of Mind (life insurance)
- Furry Friends (pets, food, veterinarian)
- Quality Education or Mind-Expansion (school tuition or student loans)
- Whoops! or Life Happens (late fees, speeding tickets, etc.)

SAVINGS ACCOUNTS:

- Peace of Mind or Breathing Room or Curveball Preparedness (cash flow savings)
- Travel Adventures or Fancy New Wheels (specific savings goals)
- Happy Golden Years (retirement)

DEBT REPAYMENT:

- My Big Italian Experience
- Expert Medical Care or Healing Adventure (medical debt)
- My Big Transition or Life Pivot (a career change, divorce, move, etc.)

for several months, she made a point to never miss a Friday champagne lunch. This ritual reinforced all the reasons and dreams that had spurred Cindy to start her business in the first place. She decided that it was so important to her new life as an entrepreneur that she created a budget category, "Business Celebration," and made sure to schedule it, track it, and honor it, each and every week.

Even though Cindy was already taking herself on those lunches, calling the expense "Business Celebration" as opposed to "Restaurants" or "Food" honored her intention behind the ritual, and reinforced the benefits she got from it. We all have things that we already spend money on, each and every month. By shifting their names to reflect our core values, we remind ourselves the real reasons they're meaningful to us.

Road Bikes and Acupuncture

If you budget and work out financial categories as a couple, then this renaming will ensure that you have deep and challenging conversations about your shared values and you will see where they diverge. On the surface, my husband and I are in 100 percent agreement about many of our values and expenses. We both prioritize the healthiest food we can afford for our little family and excellent childcare and schools for our son. And we have had tough conversations over the years about what expenses to cut to afford these things: for example, we put off buying a house for many years so we could afford sending our son to a wonderful Montessori school.

Yet there are naturally places where our values—and spending priorities—diverge. A few years ago, my husband wanted a new bike. He's an avid cyclist and had done a lot of research into which bike would best fit his needs. When he ran the numbers by me, and I saw how much it would actually cost, I was gobsmacked: "You want to spend *what* on *that?*" Because Forest knows me so well, he quickly recognized that we weren't just in a numbers conversation, we were in a values conversation. So he explained to me why that new road bike was so important to him. His cycling practice had done wonders for keeping his Lyme disease in check over the previous couple years. Not only did he feel significantly better when he kept up with his cycling, he also saved money on expensive medications and doctor's visits. Plus, he *loves* the experience of riding: the wind against his face, the mountain roads pitching up to the sky in front of him, even all the techie gadgetry and tracking his training progress—it all excites and enlivens him to no end. Once he had clarified for me just why this expense was so important to him, I realized: it's equally important to me, too, because I want all of those things for him. I got completely on board with the values behind the expense, and thus the expense, itself.

Toward the end of this particular Money Date, my husband ran a report comparing what I spent the past year on self-care practices he doesn't indulge in. While his self-care and healthcare was the price of owning and maintaining a road bike, mine includes visits to the acupuncturist and chiropractor and (free) daily hikes. Over the span of a few years, Forest and I end up spending about the same amount on our different forms of self-care, though in very different ways.

This entire Money Date turned out to be a revealing conversation for us. Because we had the numbers, instead of getting lost in blaming each other, we got honest about what things added to our happiness. By having the conversation about *values*, not just *things and numbers*, we were able to understand the other's reasons for spending as they did and support them when it made sense.

You may find that while on the surface your values are utterly aligned with your partner's, when you dig into how those values translate into financial choices, there are more differences than you thought. Sometimes, negotiations need to happen, and it's important to truly hear each other, not just about the numbers (the reality and constraints of your financial situation) but also about the values and desires at stake. Spending money on one thing often means cutting back in other areas, and the decisions can get tough quickly. If this happens, proceed slowly and respectfully. This may be challenging work, but if you take the time to listen to each other with curiosity and compassion, you just might find yourself closer (and more in love) than ever.

A Few Final Considerations

"NONE OF YOUR EFFING BUSINESS"

Some people get really stuck trying to figure out how (or even *if*) to track their cash expenditures. Don't let this decision hold you back from starting: simply do what feels good and makes the most sense to you, right now, knowing that you can shift this, over time. Some people love tracking every single expense, but others prefer creating a simple "Cash" or "Spontaneous Splurges" category, where they track expenses they don't want to itemize yet. One of my early students created a "None of Your Effing Business" category—this was his playful way of honoring his resistance to tracking every single penny he spent.

MAKE IT YOUR OWN

I don't curse a lot, but I *love* the previous example because it's so playful and personal—and these are two *essentials* for creating an enjoyable, workable Values-Based Chart of Accounts. For so many of us, money is a heavy, onerous thing and Values-Based Bookkeeping is a wonderful place to introduce some levity to money and infuse it with much-needed fun and personality.

Oopsies and Life Happens

Sometimes, we create glorious, idealized versions of monthly spending plans (with all those twinkle-toed, values-based categories) . . . and then life doesn't go according to plan. You get a speeding ticket, the cat needs to go to the vet, or you incur some late fees. You probably didn't create any categories for such expenses, because you didn't *want* to spend money this way. You may choose to add a category called "Life Lessons" or "Curveballs" to track little surprises like this. Remember: your Money Practice should invite you into the future you want, all while honestly honoring the reality you're living, right now.

Big Life Transitions

Some surprise expenses are a little bigger and more challenging than an "oopsie": health crises, career changes, a death in the family, or a divorce. These big life transitions are, well, a big deal: we will honor and discuss them in much more depth in the Money Maps phase of this book. In the meantime, simply consider whether you are entering, exiting, or in the thick of a major shift that deserves its very own expense category—and name it in a way that feels meaningful and good, to you.

Values-Based Bookkeeping is one powerful way to breathe life into your hopes and live your way into your dreams—day by day, baby step by baby step. It's one small (but mighty) way to start creating your very own red Book of Life in your heart, in your days, and in your check register.

CHAPTER 11

your financial toolbox: tracking systems and financial support teams

RUTHIE'S SMILE WAS so big, I could practically hear it over the phone. A classical cellist in her early thirties, Ruthie had just reached a major milestone in her money journey. She had written me,

> Bari, I just had my first ever meeting with an accountant! I can't believe it: I didn't cry once (thank you, Body Check-Ins), everything was so easy and fun and clear. Plus, I can't believe how much we got done in two hours: we walked through all three years of tax returns I still need to file. She saved me over a thousand dollars, and pointed out a couple of mistakes that would have gotten me audited, for sure. We've already set up another meeting to talk strategies about what I need to be doing, now, to save money on taxes next year. I don't know why I put this off for so long—getting help was the absolute best thing I could have done! I'm so proud of myself, I feel like I could go out and tame a lion or fly on a trapeze or something.

I often talk to students like Ruthie who, after doing some Money Healing, delve into Money Practices and are astonished by how much they are able to accomplish, quickly. Going on Money Dates with yourself, tracking your income and expenses, and attending to all of the other practical aspects of your money relationship can be overwhelming—especially if you have never done it before. The three most important elements I suggest to help work through this overwhelm are:

- Learn some best practices
- Get some help
- Go as gently and patiently as you can.

Ruthie was successful in her Money Practices because she incorporated all of these elements—but also because she spent over a year working on her money relationship before calling up that accountant. She spent time gently examining her emotional patterns around money, bringing loving awareness to them. She practiced Body Check-Ins regularly. She wrote in her journal about money. She had vulnerable conversations about money with her family, and got support from her friends. Over time, Ruthie could feel her trust and resilience around money growing.

Yet no matter how much deep emotional work Ruthie did on her money relationship, she knew she could never generate the kind of financial clarity, empowerment, and intimacy she longed for until she rolled up her sleeves and began interacting with her numbers on a regular basis. She started this process by setting up a financial tracking system and having regular Money Dates to enter her income and expenses and reconcile her tracking system with her accounts. Because her musician lifestyle meant her income and expenses were often unpredictable, this practice was especially powerful for her. Her tracking system helped her see how much money she needed to bring in immediately and midterm, where it was all going, places she could tighten her financial belt, and how much of a savings cushion she could rely on when paying gigs got scarce. "Now, anytime I start feeling a little ungrounded in my life, doubting a decision or something," Ruthie said, "I now ask myself: Do I know what's going on with my money? Simply sitting down for five or ten minutes to reconcile my accounts *always* gives me some clarity. Even if I see some numbers I'm not thrilled about, simply getting in touch with reality makes me feel better. Every single time."

Over time, Ruthie got brave, got smart, and grew her financial tool-box. In this chapter, I will share a few of the practices she used, which many of my students have found helpful, too: tracking systems and having financial support teams. Please keep in mind, however: these are only two categories of financial tools and practices you may want to put in your own toolbox. Many of my students reach this point in their money journey and feel ready and excited (if a little nervous, still) to learn more about money management strategies, from the best way to pay down credit card debt to investing in the stock market or saving for retirement. The nitty-gritty specifics of those practices are beyond the scope of this book, but please see the Resources section for more on this: there are so many books, tools, and people who can support you with these things, and I hope the big picture ideas in this book will help make that experience more easeful and clear.

Systems and Software and Spreadsheets, Oh My!

Ruthie's initial experiences with a tracking system weren't exactly bliss-ful. Her boyfriend, a seasoned freelance web developer, shared his homemade Excel spreadsheets for tracking income and expenses with her. While they suited *his* needs, personality, and aesthetics, they drove Ruthie utterly bonkers. She would spend hours staring at them, a many-tentacled ball of anxiety in her stomach growing, until she gave up.

Thankfully, Ruthie didn't give up for good, but instead did a little research on other tracking systems. With a little experimenting and patience, she found the software app for her. It had the features she wanted and, once she learned the ropes, it made sense to her. She has now used this system for two full years, and recently admitted to me (with a little blushing) that she's positively in love with it.

Setting up a tracking system can be a huge milestone. Many people reach this stage of Money Practices having never tracked their income and expenses before, at all; others have tried to track, with various sys-tems, only to drop them like a failed diet at a donut shop. Setting up—and sticking to—a financial tracking system generates an enormous amount of intimacy, clarity, and savvy about your financial reality. Yet it can also spark anxiety, self-doubt, or shame. Many people linger in "decision paralysis" around a tracking system for a long time: they get so overwhelmed by the multitude of options in tracking systems that they never begin using one, or they feel the need to compulsively try every single system and app out there, their heads spinning with the conflicting pros and cons, unable to commit to a single one.

Let's go back to basics for a moment. What, exactly, is a tracking system?

A financial tracking system (also known as a bookkeeping or accounting system, software, or app) is simply a tool to track, project, and/or review your income, expenses, assets, and liabilities. This is where you collect the raw data about your financial reality, so you can see, learn from, and understand your numbers. And, as with everything in your money relationship, setting up and sticking with a tracking system contains both emotional and practical considerations.

CHOOSING A TRACKING SYSTEM

The Emotional Side

That's right: this is emotional work, too. There will be a learning curve to choosing, setting up, and using any tracking system. Take your time. Many of us need someone to hold our hand and offer us tissues or chocolate as we go. Give yourself permission to feel your feelings and take your time—but also know that, sometimes, it's time to fire up your commitment and courage and keep moving forward, even when it's uncomfortable.

First, ask yourself what works best for you when making decisions. Do you like doing a ton of research, first? Prefer picking intuitively? Crave crowd-sourced answers? Delighted to just dive in and see how it goes?

Next, remember: this is hugely subjective territory. Your best friend's favorite system might be your personal hell realm. Your needs, personality, and preferences will mesh differently with each system's features and frameworks. Follow your head *and* heart.

The best bookkeeping system is the one you will use and even enjoy. I have seen people swoon over Mint and get giggly about YNAB. Some of these people began the process kicking and screaming, convinced they would surely die of boredom or confusion.

Remember, this isn't a life sentence. You can *always* change your mind down the road. And: there is no such thing as a perfect tracking system. Give yourself permission to find the best system, for you, for now.

The Practical Side

New systems become available all the time. And their features are ever-changing and updating.

There are two main ways to track your numbers. Some tracking systems are geared better for one kind or the other—and some systems allow you to choose either option.

1 **Automatic Syncing:** Some tracking systems automatically sync with your bank, downloading all of your transactions for you. This can work beautifully for people who don't do many cash transactions, use traditional banks (some of these systems don't play well with co-ops or credit unions), and don't want to spend a lot of time manually entering transactions.

2 **Manual Entry:** Other tracking systems require you to manually enter every transaction into the software and to make sure everything reconciles, yourself. While tracking in this way takes more time, it can also help you generate an incredible amount of awareness, intimacy, and mindfulness about how and where your money flows in and out. I often recommend people who have never tracked their finances before to start with this method.

Consider:

- Do you want a system that handles personal finances, business, or both?
- If you need business tracking, will you use the same system for your personal finances, or choose a different system for each?

- Do you need to be able to create and name custom categories that reflect your values, or are you happy using preset categories?
- Do you need billing, invoicing, and payroll features?
- Do you want desktop-only software, or must it be cloud-based and sync with your phone, as well? (Some people prefer paper systems over digital—that's OK, too.)
- Do you want cash flow planning and budgeting features, too?
- Would you like to track your tax deductions and investments here?
- What sorts of reports do you want to be able to pull?
- How much are you willing and able to invest in a system?
- Does it need to be aesthetically pleasing?

See the Resources Section for some of my recommended tracking systems.

Let the Real Fun Begin: Pulling Financial Reports

It often takes people a month or two to choose, set up, and feel comfortable with a financial tracking system. I also recommend that most people stick to simply tracking income and expenses for a few months. In this initial phase, you treat your financial tracking system like a bucket: it's where you collect and sort the raw data of your financial world. Once you're comfortable with this practice, you get to take this raw data and *do* things with it. This is where the fun of pulling financial reports begins. Here, you take all of those numbers you have so fastidiously collected or downloaded, analyze and interpret them, and use them to support a greater understanding of your financial world.

Depending on the tracking system you're using, you can generate a number of different reports. These range from broad to specific, complex to simple. I recommend becoming familiar with three basic reports. Think of these as three different lenses through which to view your financial landscape, at any given time. Again, wait to create these reports until you have at least a few months of just tracking your expenses under your belt.

1. INCOME AND EXPENSES (ALSO KNOWN AS "PROFIT AND LOSS" OR "P & L")

This is the most basic, beginner-friendly bookkeeping report you can pull. This report shows your income (how much money flowed in—and from where) and your expenses (how much money flowed out—and to where) for any period of time. These reports are most commonly generated on a monthly basis, though you could easily look at a shorter or longer duration, too.

2. THE PRESENT VS. THE PAST

It can sometimes be helpful to compare your Income and Expense report for two slices of time: this month vs. last month, for example, or this November vs. last November. Perhaps you're curious how much that new insulation is saving you on winter heating costs or wondering if you usually have a "dry spell" for your business over the summer. Comparing two (or even more) different snapshots of your financial reality can put your mind at ease or shine a light on things you'd like to shift.

3. INTENTIONS VS. REALITY

You may choose to periodically do a side-by-side comparison of your intended expenses and your real expenses. If you're an entrepreneur, add your intended and real *income* as well. If your intentions and reality are very similar, it's celebration time. If they don't line up, this is an empowering moment for you to decide whether to shift your intentions, your behavior, or both. (More on how to work with these numbers in the Money Maps chapters to come.)

Many people notice immense, painful amounts of judgment when they look at these reports—especially the first few times. I've had hundreds of clients, from single working people to double-income no-kid couples, who have admitted to me that their jaws dropped when they saw (perhaps for the first time) how much they spent on groceries each month. They immediately criticized themselves for spending "too much." Yet the vast majority of them also had *no* reference point for how much other people spend on groceries and many of them would say sustenance and nourishment for themselves and their families were high priorities. Know that you will likely experience judgments as you go, here. This is where your foundational Money Healing work gets even more real, relevant, and profound. Be gentle and patient with yourself, and do your best to notice your feelings, reactions, and thoughts. Feel them, honor them, and when you're ready, move forward.

Growing Your Financial Support Team

After religiously tracking her income and expenses for six months, Ruthie knew more than she ever had about the money flowing in and out of her life, her income and spending patterns, and had become more and more and peaceful in her money relationship. But then, tax time rolled around. (*Dun, dun, dun!*) Ruthie now knew she was capable of learning about money and tackling To Dos that once seemed impossible. But she also felt ready to reach out for some professional support.

Unfortunately, many people don't allow themselves to welcome support in their financial world. As a culture, we judge ourselves harshly for not somehow, intuitively, knowing how to properly file our taxes or set up Quicken or find creative cost-cutting solutions. We don't apply this logic to other areas of life, however: if you want to get in better shape, and are scared of retriggering an old knee injury, going to a group class or hiring a personal trainer seems perfectly acceptable—smart, even. Your trainer or workout buddies won't exercise *for* you, but they will educate you, keep you safe and accountable, and help you work to the appropriate edges of your capacity. In the same way, working with a financial support person (or whole team) is not for the lazy or uninformed; it is often an incredibly savvy and empowering move.

> You do not have to know everything. You can ask for help, here. Sometimes, getting support is the strongest, bravest thing you can do.

Many people don't realize what kinds of financial professionals exist, let alone what each of them does, and how to know if you need one or the other. Here, we will break down some of the main financial players you can add to your support team: bookkeeper, bookkeeping trainer, accountant, financial coach, financial planner, and financial therapist. But first, a few general guidelines when choosing *any* member of your financial support team:

1 Start your search with friends and colleagues. Their referrals are often the best way to find a great match. However, this is also a very personal choice: your best friend might adore her accountant, but he might rub you the wrong way. Give yourself permission to find the right person for you. (See the Resources section for other places to start looking.)

2 Check credentials. How long have they been doing this? What type of training and experience do they have? Are you satisfied they know their stuff?

3 Include Body Check-Ins galore. Do you feel safe, comfortable, and trusting in their presence? Do you like their personality and attitude? Ask them what they *love* about this work, and see how the answer sits with you.

4 Consider values. It might be important to you that your financial support team share similar worldviews and priorities as you.

5 Talk money. Don't be shy about asking how much they charge and how. (Hourly? Set fee? Retainer?) You might even ask them about their own relationship to money. After all, you're here to talk with them about money.

Remember: if you lined up ten accountants, money coaches, or financial planners and asked each of them these questions, you would get ten different sets of answers. As with any kind of financial professional, do your own research, ask for referrals, and move forward with the person who feels like the best fit for you.

BOOKKEEPER

What They Do

Bookkeepers do all of that financial tracking for you. They set up a system for you, create categories, and track and organize all the ins and outs of your income and expenses, savings, credit card transactions, investments, and more—on a daily, weekly, monthly, quarterly, and yearly basis. They also reconcile all of your accounts and produce those wonderful financial reports (mentioned previously) for you: income and expense reports; current year vs. previous year reports; projected vs. actual income and expenses. These reports are wonderful for you and incredibly helpful for doing your taxes (whether you do them yourself or hire a tax professional). Some bookkeepers will even pay your bills and invoice clients for you, if those are things you'd like to delegate.

Additional Considerations

Bookkeepers have widely varying levels of experience, training, and rates. Some will simply set up your systems and run reports—but others will sit down with you, review your numbers, and help you plan a bit.

Not Everyone Needs A Bookkeeper

You might choose to do your own bookkeeping (because you want to get more intimate with your numbers, because your finances are quite simple, or simply because you do not wish to spend the money on a bookkeeper). As I've mentioned, I did all of my own bookkeeping for twelve years, and it was a priceless education about money and business. At a certain point, however, my business grew large enough that I knew it was time to graduate to an outside bookkeeper.

Questions to Ask a Potential Bookkeeper

Consider the general questions listed above (ask about their credentials, rates, length of experience, what they love about this work, and more). Additionally, you might ask:

1 Do you have any suggestions to help me decide whether I should hire a bookkeeper or do my own books?

2 How do we do this? Do you prefer to do all of the bookkeeping for me? Or do you want me to jump in for parts?

3 Do you offer virtual bookkeeping, or will we work together in my home or your office?

4 If you offer virtual bookkeeping, how do you get my information?

5 What type of bookkeeping software do you like to use?

6 Will you send me monthly reports and teach me how to read them?

7 Are you open to teaching me how to use a bookkeeping system and pull, read, and understand financial reports? (If you want this.)

8 Do you offer both personal and business bookkeeping? (If you need both.)

9 Do you work with a lot of people in my profession/age range/lifestyle?

10 Can I have three references from current clients?

BOOKKEEPING TRAINER

What They Do

Let's say you've decided you want to keep your own books, but you're tired of pulling your hair out trying to teach yourself a tracking system. You may be able to find courses to help you learn the system (online or locally, sometimes low-cost or even free). However, you can also hire a bookkeeping trainer, which can be incredibly empowering.

Additional Considerations

Bookkeeping trainers often charge a higher rate than bookkeepers, but over time this is usually less than working with a bookkeeper on an ongoing, monthly basis. More than anything, a bookkeeping trainer must be a good teacher, able to sit down, hold your hand (figuratively), and show you how to navigate a system.

Questions to Ask a Potential Bookkeeping Trainer

In addition to the general questions listed above, you might ask:

1 What bookkeeping systems do you teach? Just one, or many different ones?

2 Are you able to help me choose the best bookkeeping system for my needs?

3 Why do you feel you're a great teacher? Do you think you're good at patiently and clearly explaining concepts that are new and complex to me?

ACCOUNTANT OR TAX PREPARER

What They Do

Accountants and tax preparers are the people who are thrilled to no end when you show up with all of your numbers and data all neat, organized, and categorized according to standard tax deductions (thanks to your bookkeeper, even if that bookkeeper is yourself). They typically ask you some additional questions, then take all of that data and file your taxes for you. They study accounting rules and tax law, and keep up on all of its rules (which change slightly each year). Some accountants are even hip to the laws that will change in the next few years, so you're really covered.

Additional Considerations

I think it's wonderful to meet with an accountant a few times a year. Not only do they file your taxes for you, they can help you with your tax strategy as well. Should your business be a Sole Proprietorship, LLC, S-Corp, or C-Corp? Some specialize in business consulting, others specialize in real estate or other areas.

Whatever their specialty, accountants take all of that great data you have from your bookkeeping and find as many legal tax deductions as possible, so you're paying the right amount of taxes (not too much, not too little).

Questions to Ask a Potential Accountant or Tax Preparer

In addition to the general questions above, you will want to ask:

1   Do you work with a lot of people in my profession/age range/lifestyle? Do you have a tax specialty or preferred area of work?

2   How do you charge? Can you give me a range or estimation of your fees? Do you charge for phone calls and email support?

3   Do you handle my case personally, or outsource it? Will I deal directly with you, or a variety of people in your office?

4   Do you consider yourself conservative or aggressive with deductions? And can you help me determine what strategy might be best for me?

5   What would you advise me to do if my tax situation was in a "gray area"?

6   How do you handle audits? Can you represent me in front of the IRS?

7 How can you help me get the information you will need from me?

8 Do you like to teach and educate your clients? Or do you prefer to just do things for me?

9 Do you have a preference of what bookkeeping system I use? Are you cool if I choose a different one?

10 Will you meet with me twice per year to discuss my Chart of Accounts and advise me on how to get the most deductions throughout the year? If so, how do you charge for this?

11 If you are an entrepreneur: will you help me determine the best business entity structure and set up any new entities I may need?

12 How long is your turnaround time?

FINANCIAL COACH AND MONEY COACH

What They Do

A financial coach will help you become aware of your spending habits, create and maintain a budget, and better manage your cash flow. These folks tend to get ultra-practical, dig the numbers with you, and help you decide: What do I want to spend on each category, each month? How much should I save, what pace should I pay down my debt, and what can I put toward an investment? Which categories are negotiable, and which are absolute musts? Some financial coaches (depending on their training and focus) can also support you with the emotional and psychological aspects of money and help you incorporate your goals and values into financial planning.

The term "money coach" has recently gained in popularity and encompasses all of the practical financial coaching listed above and, often, more behavioral and emotional support, as well. Specifically, a *Certified Money Coach* specializes in helping people understand and change their money patterns and behaviors, drawing from extensive training in neurodynamics, behavioral modification, and more.

Additional Considerations

You can find a financial coach or money coach who specializes in personal or business finances or both; others specialize in working with women, creative entrepreneurs, or couples. These coaches are fabulous at creating short to mid-term goals and plans for the next six months, year, or even five years. They can be a precursor to working with a financial planner, whose job is to think more long-term.

Questions to Ask a Potential Money Coach

In addition to the general questions above, you may want to ask:

1 Do you specialize in personal, couple, or business finances?

2 Do you address financial behavior in addition to the practical aspects of money?

3 Do you have a strict, one-size-fits-all philosophy about debt, savings, or other money areas? Or will you guide me into the best choices for me, personally?

4 What if I get overwhelmed, anxious, or upset as we're working together? Can you hold space for a bit of the emotional side of money, too?

5 Do you specialize in working with people of my income level/goals/profession?

6 Do you tend to do a single session with clients, several, or work over longer timespans?

7 Are you open to collaborating with my accountant or financial planner?

FINANCIAL PLANNER AND FINANCIAL ADVISOR

What They Do

These folks specialize in investments and long-term visioning. Thinking about retirement planning, long-term savings, paying for your toddler's college? This is who you want. They love thinking about the big picture, and where you can be in five, ten, twenty, thirty, or even fifty years. Many will help you choose the right investments. Should you invest in the stock market, based on your risk levels, values, and life goals? If so, where? How about real estate, startups, or microfinance loan funds?

Typically, a financial planner will help you examine your whole financial life in a holistic way, including your budgeting, savings strategy, tax and estate planning, and more. A financial advisor, on the other hand, might do some financial planning but focuses much more on managing investments, typically a portfolio of marketable securities, but also community development, private debt, and equity opportunities.

Additional Considerations

If you inherited money from your family, you may have inherited a family financial planner along with it. For some people, this works beautifully—and for others, they reach a point where they need to find their own financial planner who better understands their values. Socially Responsible Investing (SRI) is a growing field that explicitly specializes in values-based investing. Make sure you find a financial planner who will honor the investment values you hold, and will work within the parameters that matter so deeply to you.

Questions to Ask a Potential Financial Planner or Financial Advisor

In addition to the general questions above, you will want to ask:

1 Are you a Financial Planner or a Financial Advisor?

2 What range of services do you offer? Will you only advise me on investments, or do you offer more comprehensive planning, including retirement, insurance, and estate planning?

3 What is your investment approach? Do you consider yourself conservative or high-risk/high-reward? What kind of market volatility can you handle?

4 Do you specialize in Socially Responsible Investing (SRI)? If so, what does that mean to you?

5 How do you charge? By the hour, initial fee only, annually (including a set number of consultations), or by percentage of investment/assets under management? (This is a particularly important question to ask of a financial planner or advisor. Some earn money by selling you specific products, which may create a conflict of interest. Not only should you know how much the service will cost you, but you should determine whether they have an incentive to sell you things, and if so, if you are comfortable with that.)

6 How much contact do you have with your clients?

7 Could you share one or two clients I could talk to?

FINANCIAL THERAPIST

What They Do

While all of the financial professionals on this list may offer a smidgen of emotional support, most of them aren't trained explicitly for this. Financial therapists are the exception. They will go deep with you into all of the inner, emotional "money stuff"—*and* they are trained in the practical, nitty-gritty aspects of money, as well.

Financial therapy is a relatively new (though growing) field, and does not have one clear definition. When I began calling myself a Financial Therapist in 2001, only one other person was using this title; now, many more professionals have joined the field. As a Financial Therapist, myself, I describe this work as integrating deep psychotherapeutic training with practical skills, tools, and financial training.

This very book is my personal financial therapy methodology, including Money Healing, Money Practices, and Money Maps. In 2010, the Financial Therapy Association was founded, and they define financial therapy as involving "the integration of cognitive, emotional, behavioral, and economic aspects that influence financial well-being, and ultimately, quality of life."

Additional Considerations

Some financial therapists have a primarily therapeutic background, later receiving financial training; others start out as accountants or financial planners and get additional training in counseling to become financial therapists. Both sides of this equation are very important in a financial therapist.

Many financial therapists work with both individuals and couples. Some specialize in small businesses and creative entrepreneurship.

Questions to Ask a Potential Financial Therapist

In addition to the general questions above, you will want to ask:

1 What is your therapeutic background/training? What is your financial background/training? How have you combined the two?

2 How do *you* define financial therapy? Do you focus more on the emotional side, the practical side, or a balanced combination?

3 Have you done your own "money work"? What is *your* relationship to money like?

4 Who do you love working with? What aspects of this work do you particularly enjoy or feel skilled at?

5 What does a typical session look like? Will we simply talk, or will you look at my financials with me?

BONUS PLAYERS

One of my favorite aspects of my own work and teaching model is getting to collaborate with a wide variety of financial professionals. So believe me when I say: there are so many types of people you can draft onto your financial support team!

Beyond the main financial professionals listed in this chapter, you may also consider adding to your team an estate planner, an attorney, a consumer debt advocate, or an insurance professional. I also consider a somatic therapist an important addition to your financial support team.

. . . . .

Please remember: you do not have to add all of these people to your team at once. You may start with just one. Check in with yourself once or twice a year; as your situation, needs, and financial savvy shift you may choose to add or subtract members from your financial support team. If you are just starting out, you may consider adding a trusted, willing friend or family member to talk with you about money matters. This is *your* journey, and you are the captain of this ship and crew. Feel your way into the right timing and the right alignment for you, for now.

PHASE THREE

money maps

· · · · ·

Welcome to the final phase of our journey.

These are the deep waters of visioning and life mission.

Here, we dare to dream.

We strategize by moonlight.

We zoom out to the wide, wider, widest views of our ever
unfolding and evolving life-and-money journey.

We honor its rhythms, cycles, and phases.

We learn to dance with it all.

Inhale, exhale, trusting ever deeper.

Here, we attune to our legacy.

We light our paths by our guiding stars.

We align dreams, goals, and numbers.

We marry grand meanings and feet-on-the-ground practicality.

Welcome to a sacred space where you craft your own
integration of deep values and the everyday.

Spontaneous dance breaks and radical
self-love are encouraged, as always.

Grab your scuba gear.

Let's go deep-soul diving.

the three-tier money map

JOYCE PULLED THE gauzy afghan a little more snugly around herself as she peered out of her new kitchen window. Her gaze cascaded past cherry blossoms, then her cozy Victorian neighborhood, and finally the snow-graced peak of Mount Hood, barely visible through the Portland fog. She warmed her hands around a cup of tea, deeply inhaling the floral steam.

This was a rare moment of tranquility for Joyce, the first respite she'd had after a whirlwind of transition over the previous six months: logistical turnarounds, job changes, and a cross-country move. Finally, she and her dear wife Samantha were settling into a beautiful new rental house. They were beginning to feel at home in their little house and new town, and the accumulated stress was slowly working its way out of her body. Joyce could see herself being happy here for quite some time. She had a loving partner, a beautiful home, and a growing online business as a life coach that felt fulfilling to her *and* truly helped others. She ate well, slept well, and played well.

Yet Joyce was anxious about money. She was waiting for her fledgling online business to pick up steam; she and Samantha, a software engineer, were dreaming of finally owning a house instead of renting, and Joyce longed for an even deeper sense of stability in her health and lifestyle. The specter of money loomed like a dark cloud over her hopes. She and Samantha had just enough money to maintain their present lifestyle, which was far from extravagant, but Joyce had no idea how they would be able to make their big picture dreams come true and stop "treading water" financially. All of those big life dreams and goals seemed so very far away—and money felt like the immovable road-block between her and the life she most wanted.

This financial worry wasn't new. I'd worked with Joyce for a few years and she had worked hard to shift her money relationship. She had reexamined her old, semi-conscious beliefs about money, unraveled her shame about her credit card debt, and even created her own money healing ritual to release some childhood wounding around financial enoughness. She had a pleasing software app to track her expenses. She and Samantha were also having regular Money Dates together, and while she certainly still had moments of "money freakout," she was beginning to remember, more often and more quickly, to do a Body Check-In when things got tough.

But Joyce was ready for something bigger, deeper, and wider. A grander integration of her money and her Big Life Goals. She was ready to direct her funds more discerningly, to start living her way into her big, longer-term dreams. And she'd had just enough success with money work already that she was open to the idea that money could possibly *not* hold her back from her big dreams, but might even help her bring them into reality. It was time to take all of that Money Healing and apply it to a grander view of her life. This is the work of Money Mapping.

Budget Baggage

If Joyce had gone to a traditional financial advisor at this point with questions about how money could help her accomplish her longer term goals, she likely would have been instructed to create a strict budget and stick to it, no questions asked.

I don't know about you, but I can feel my jaw tighten just looking at that dreadful word. *Budget.*

Almost every person I've ever worked with has had resistance to budgets. (You might call it "budget baggage.") And with good rea-son: many of the reasons people (like Joyce) dislike budgets are the very reasons they fail, over and over again. If you have resistance to budgeting, please do not try to strong-arm yourself into overcoming it. Instead, let's look at that resistance, uncover the wisdom within it, and use what we learn to create a fresh way to consciously direct our money—one that includes all of the wisdom of this resistance, and none of the yuckiness.

Here are some of the most common types of budget resistance I have seen in my community, along with the useful little gems they contain:

BUDGET BAGGAGE #1.

IT'S ALL ABOUT DEPRIVATION

Many people think of a "budget" as a rigid, constrictive regimen that harshly limits their spending. "OK, only $50 per week on groceries— that's *it!*" "No, I can't go to the movies with you, because it's not in my budget. *Sad trombone.*"

Like a fiercely restrictive diet where one counts calories and weighs out portions, this kind of spending plan is almost always doomed to fail. Just as strict diets march us irresistibly toward guilt-ridden binge- ing, overly strict budgets lead to rebellious over-spending.

This first kind of budget resistance held me in its throes for many years: I simply couldn't stomach the idea of feeling deprived or limited in my lifestyle, and a budget felt like an unkind authority figure wag- ging his finger at me, telling me what I could or could not do, *young lady.* The funny thing was, my income was low enough at that time in my life that I *was* limited in what I could spend, whether or not I made a spending plan. Yet the idea of sitting down and creating categories and monthly spending limits made it all too real for me. Instead, I dunked my head firmly in the sand, relying on "magical bookkeeping" for years, just hoping things would somehow work out.

Of course, some people respond beautifully to firm financial bound- aries. Depending on your personality and what phase of life you're in, this approach may work well for you. But remember: discipline needn't feel like punishment, and an income and spending plan needn't feel harsh to be smart. The more compassionate we can be with ourselves, here, the more sustainable our systems will be. As you will see, there *is* a way to create a plan that brings intention and focus to your income and expenses without feeling limiting or restrictive.

BUDGET BAGGAGE #2.

IT'S BASED ON NUMBERS, AND NUMBERS ONLY

Years ago, I worked with a successful corporate accountant named Amy. Despite earning many hundreds of thousands of dollars per year, Amy still found herself sinking farther and farther into debt. Because she worked as a corporate accountant, planning and directing cash flow for large corporations, she *knew* how to budget, and even enjoyed it— yet, like so many financial professionals, she couldn't use those skills for herself. She even hired a financial planner, who put her on a strict budget—then watched, gobsmacked, as Amy "cheated on" and finally abandoned her spending plan.

Delving into some deeper money work, Amy quickly discovered the gaping disconnect between her finances and her inner world. She didn't have a budgeting problem; she simply didn't know how to integrate her values and her numbers. Once she learned about Values-Based Bookkeeping, renamed her income and expense categories to better reflect what truly mattered to her, and did the deep inner emotional work of Money Healing, everything shifted for her. The heavy fog of resistance lifted, and she suddenly had energy (and even enthusiasm) for crafting and shaping her Money Map. She began setting significant savings and debt-repayment goals, and got excited as she watched herself make progress. Suddenly, she was in the driver's seat on her financial journey, and her progress was fueled by a boundless inner wellspring of her true passions: achieving peace of mind, creating a sustainable and happy lifestyle, freedom from debt, and generously supporting causes that mattered to her.

Many approaches to budgeting skip this crucial inner work, and simply look at the *external* practicalities: a list of income and expenses. But as Amy learned, any financial plan *must* remain connected to our deep, inner values, goals, purpose, and dreams for it to succeed.

BUDGET BAGGAGE #3.

SIX FIGURES OR BUST!

A large portion of budgeting plans tout overblown, wealth-obsessed goals: "The Five-Step Plan to Retire as a Millionaire!" or, "How to Earn

Six Figures in One Year!" While I am committed to lovingly supporting everyone in achieving a comfortable lifestyle as long as it's not at
the expense of themselves or others, I also know just how short-sighted
and ultimately ineffective these wealth-building strategies and systems
can be when they neglect what *should* be the ultimate driving force: creating a deeply meaningful, satisfying, growthful, and generous life. In
short, they don't direct you to create a happy life, whatever that means
to *you*.

Many years ago, when I was a newbie entrepreneur, I brought
my financial projections for the next two years to Christopher Peck,
a financial planner (who has since become one of my dearest financial
colleagues). I had stayed up all night visioning: dreaming up coaching packages and group programs to sell, imagining how my revenue streams might grow and shift. I proudly walked him through my
detailed reports, excitedly pointing out how quickly my business could
grow over the next year. After listening quietly for a few moments,
Christopher paused, gently interrupted me, and said, "This is great,
Bari, but will this be a *good life*, for you?" His question stopped me in
my tracks (and I adored him for asking it). I had not considered just
how much time and work my business plan would require and even if
it was truly what I wanted for the next several years. While that plan
ended up working well for me, after all (I was young, not yet a mother,
and enthusiastic enough about my work to put in long hours), a few
years later, I needed to pare down my business model to allow for my
daily hikes, time with my family, and rest.

The *true* litmus test of a great Money Map is whether it is leading
you toward a happy life. And *you* are the only one qualified to define
what a happy life looks like, for you—and what steps you're willing to
take toward it. For some people, a happy, successful Money Map may
mean earning more money, spending less, or aggressively paying down
debt. For others, it might actually mean working a little less, so they can
enjoy time with a new baby or recoup from a health crisis. A spending
plan should guide you to a life *you* want to live. It takes a little inner
inventorying to determine whether that *actually* means earning six figures or slashing your expenses to the nubs. Money Mapping is about

discerning what's important to you in life (knowing there are rhythms and cycles to this), and relying on money to reverse-engineer a lifestyle that supports *your* version of happiness. This is an incredibly personal endeavor, and it will shift and evolve over time, right along with you.

Your Money Map: A Clarion Call for Conscious Earning and Spending

Money Mapping is far gentler, more sustainable, and meaningful than traditional budgeting. It is about giving attention and loving intention to our finances so that we can harness the power of money to help us shape our lifestyle over time. Whether you're living paycheck-to-paycheck or have hundreds of thousands of dollars in the bank, everyone can benefit from consciously directing the inflow and outflow of money. One of my favorite ways to do this is the Three-Tier Money Map.

A Three-Tier Money Map is a heart-crafted, savvy tool for tracking your income and expenses and aligning them with the intentions and goals you have for your one precious life. It emerges from inside of you: it's your own, personal creation and reflects what is dear to you now, at this stage of your life.

The Three-Tier Money Map

Most traditional approaches to budgeting have us list out a single, Master Plan version of our income and expenses for the month. And while this may be helpful for some people as an initial money practice, it ignores the richness and complexity of our money relationship as something that is always unfolding, shifting, and evolving, over time. The Three-Tier Money Map is the antidote for this over-simplification. Here is its basic framework:

1. THE BASIC NEEDS LEVEL.

These are the bare bones, bottom-line needs for your life. And only *you* decide what that means. Is it just groceries, rent, and utilities? Does it include a particular kind of food? Is a daily coffee a must for you to function? Does it include savings and debt repayment? You're the boss here.

2. THE COMFORTABLE LIFESTYLE LEVEL.

Here, introduce some more comfort into your lifestyle. What's the next level up from Basic Needs, for you? What's included? How much? Does this mean a monthly (or even weekly) massage or pedicure? Some disposable income for movies, restaurant dinners, or the latest electronic gadgets? The ability to gift a little money to friends and family?

3. THE ULTIMATE LIFESTYLE LEVEL.

Here we progress another step. Imagine having sufficient income to live out the *fullest* expression of your desires. All your intentions are funded. Does this look like millions of dollars in the bank, jet-setting from Tokyo to Buenos Aires to Paris, anytime you like? Or is it a surprisingly simple lifestyle, living debt-free on a rural sheep farm? Take the time to clarify what this means *for you.*

Everyone defines their Three-Tier Money Map differently: one person's Comfortable tier is closer to another person's Basic Needs or even Ultimate tier. I know this in part because every year, I send an anonymous survey to the participants in my year-long Art of Money program. Among other questions, I ask them whether they would describe themselves as currently living at their Basic Needs, Comfortable, or Ultimate lifestyle levels. Each time I ask this question, I get a completely even split between the three levels: one third of our community is at each level. However, there's no direct correlation between annual income and lifestyle tier. Our definitions and dreams for each of these levels are as unique as we are, involving not only different *types* of expenses, but also vastly different *amounts.*

This Three-Tier framework is supportive and illuminating no matter what your income level or expenses are. Anyone can get out of control with their spending habits, bury their head in the sand about their income or debt, or lose focus of their priorities. And no matter how much or how little money you have, directing it with intention is *always* a pathway to greater clarity, connection, and empowerment.

Feelings, Things, Numbers: Creating Your Three-Tier Money Map

What distinguishes the Three-Tier Money Map from a traditional budget isn't just the multi-leveled framework—it's also the specific *process* for creating it. We're not simply going to throw numbers into a spreadsheet and hope we can willpower ourselves into following them. A Money Map begins with some internal mapping.

As with any Money Date, take a moment to prepare and set the scene: gather anything you need to feel prepared and comfortable. Grab your financial tracking data (if you have it) or recent bank statements and income and expense reports. Pull out a journal and pen or open a fresh document on your computer. Pour yourself a favorite beverage, light a candle, play music, nibble chocolate, and place your phone on "Do Not Disturb"—do whatever you need to feel ready and wonderful.

1. FEELINGS FIRST: FREEWRITE

First, write about each of the Three Tiers of your Money Map: Basic Needs, Comfortable, and Ultimate. Don't include any numbers, yet. Turn within and get a *felt sense* of what each of these levels means to you. Write out your *personal* definitions for each tier, what you associate with them, how you imagine them making you feel day-to-day and month-to-month. This is completely subjective, and there are no wrong answers.

As always, do whatever feels good to make this process your own including renaming the tiers. While I usually refer to the three tiers as "Basic Needs," "Comfortable," and "Ultimate" Lifestyles, I've heard all sorts of names over the years for these. Some refer to these levels as "Needs, Wants, and Desires." Others use "Bottom Line, Lovely, and Luxurious." Some people even rename the whole shebang, calling it a "Map of Intention" or "Money Mojo Plan" instead of a "Three-Tier Money Map."

2. THINGS SECOND: WHAT'S INCLUDED?

Once you have a felt-sense description of each of your three tiers, it's time to look at what items are included at each level. What expenditures do you need to be able to afford to create the *feelings* you identified for each level? Does your "Basic Needs" tier include rent, groceries, health care, transportation to and from work, and that's it? Does a daily coffee or monthly movie feel like a Comfortable expenditure, or do these expenses feel like Basic Needs to you? Does your Comfortable lifestyle include cable television, a cell phone, and books? Does an annual vacation to visit your family go under Basic Needs, Comfortable, or Ultimate, for you, at this phase of your life?

3. NUMBERS THIRD: GET SPECIFIC

Now take all of that prioritizing and bring in the real numbers. On three separate sheets of paper (or three separate spreadsheets), list out all of your monthly expense categories, for each lifestyle tier. Apply numbers to every expense item. If you've already tracked your expenses for several months, you may be able to look at recent averages to help you or you may do some quick, back-of-the-envelope estimates. Don't forget those big ticket and rainy day expenses that happen less frequently, like insurance premiums, car repairs, dental bills, etc. Divide annual expenses by twelve to calculate average monthly expenses. Also include savings, debt repayment, and investments in any tier those fit into, for you.

Remember, your "Comfortable Lifestyle" will include all of the expenses from your "Basic Needs" tier, plus any additional expenses that come into play for you at this level; likewise, the Ultimate level will include everything from your Comfortable Lifestyle, along with additional items. (Debt repayment is a bit of an exception to this basic rule: perhaps your vision of an Ultimate Lifestyle includes living debt-free, while your Comfortable tier, today, means aggressively paying down your debt. If you have debt, find your own best way to account for it in your plan.)

Keep referring back to the feelings, definitions, and included items you came up with a few moments ago. Consider what additional expenses you'll include at each level, and do your best to estimate what they might be.

Use whatever format you like, here. Pull out the old-fashioned pen and paper or create your own Excel spreadsheet. Do what feels grand for you. Once you've listed everything out, total up your expenses for each of the three tiers, and calculate your average monthly expense.

4. COMPARE INCOME AND EXPENSES

Once you have expense totals for each lifestyle tier before you, it's time to calculate your monthly income. Some people have a set, predictable salary each month, which makes this calculation delightfully simple. However, if your income fluctuates over the course of the year (whether you're a freelancer, a new business owner, wait tables, or shift income streams periodically), just use your best estimates. Remember: there are pros and cons associated with both steady income and more flexible income sources. Relax as much as you can into an open-minded fact-finding mission here. Take a breath, take your time, and do your best with what information you have.

5. GET HONEST: WHAT LEVEL ARE YOU LIVING?

Now that you have your average monthly income, compare it to the numbers for your Three-Tier Money Map. Is your planned income enough to meet your Basic Needs level? If so, wonderful! Are you actually living at your Comfortable or even Ultimate level?

Some people don't like what they see when they compare their income and Three-Tier Money Map. You might find that your current income doesn't cover your Basic Needs expenses, or that you're light years away from living your Ultimate lifestyle. It is very easy to feel discouraged here. Remind yourself that you're looking at these numbers so you can start making positive changes. Honor any feelings that arise with as much compassion as possible.

6. CELEBRATE!

Once you have all of your numbers in front of you, do a Body Check-In. Hug yourself. Celebrate: you have just taken a *huge* step. It is a *really big deal* to look squarely at your numbers in this way. Now, with numbers on paper, it's time for a little reflection.

· · · · ·

When Joyce compared her income to her three tiers, she felt a little discouraged: she was barely living above her definition of Basic Needs, and her Comfortable lifestyle felt a little too far away for, well, comfort. In a flash of inspiration, she decided to add an additional tier, "Basic-Plus," as an intermediary step between her Basic Needs and Comfortable Lifestyle levels. Once she calculated her expenses for this level, she felt relieved: it was a stretch from her current reality, but one that felt *doable* over the next six months. Eventually, Joyce added two more tiers to her plan, for a total of six. While some people would prefer a simpler plan, seeing things laid out meticulously galvanized Joyce's enthusiasm, and encouraged her with short-term income goals she felt were a bit more within reach.

Some people create their first two lifestyle tiers and find themselves ready to stop, right there; it's simply too challenging for them to plot out their Ultimate lifestyle at this moment. While I always encourage people to list out all three tiers if at all possible, just to see the largest view of their financial landscape as possible, *always* take your time and honor your limits. Some people plot out their Basic Needs and Comfortable tiers, then come back to add their Ultimate in a few days, weeks, or even months, when they feel ready for it.

Stretch Your Edge . . . Gently

I know how challenging looking at your Ultimate lifestyle can be—especially when it feels painfully far away. Indeed, for the first few years I taught the Money Map (in small group settings), I would walk people through the first two tiers, then ask them to complete their Ultimate tier after class, at home. Likewise, if you find yourself cringing at the idea of plotting your Ultimate lifestyle, don't fret. Simply leave it, for now, and know that you can come back to it whenever you like.

However, if it feels at all possible for you to look at your Ultimate lifestyle tier, I encourage you to dip your toes in those visioning waters. The simple act of visioning like this can gently push through limited beliefs we carry about ourselves. Even plotting your Basic Needs level can be utterly empowering: *look how resilient I can be*! So, be gentle here.

Listen to your resistance, and find the right balance, *for you*, of working with and through it. And, if you notice that you have less resistance around this now than several weeks or months (or years) ago, by all means, celebrate that.

Most of all, remember that everyone defines each of these three tiers in different ways, reflecting what truly matters most to them at this phase in their life. Joyce discovered that at each successive lifestyle tier, she wanted to donate more and more to her two favorite charities; generosity is one of her core values, and additional money represents a way to give back, in her world. Other people find themselves able to take care of family members or adding in more and more self-care and pampering at each successive tier, while still others dream of more travel and adventure or even starting a business venture. By allowing yourself to dream in big ways, you will transform what might have been a dry, dusty budget into a pathway for greater self-awareness and connection with your values. Give yourself the gifts of curiosity, wonder, and joy as you play with your Money Map.

Stepping into Ultimate

Sometimes, the hardest news to share is the good stuff. After creating her Three-Tier Money Map, Monica, a forest ranger in her mid-forties, saw that she was just on the cusp of stepping out of her Comfortable into her Ultimate lifestyle tier. She had a steady, well-paying job, no debt, and a savings account just shy of $100,000. Yet she readily admitted that *her* definition of "Ultimate" might not be someone else's. She and her husband lived in a rural outpost at the far northern reach of Canada. They had no running water and no electricity. In the winter, they had to brave temperatures 40 degrees Fahrenheit below zero to go outside to use the outhouse. Monica felt secure and even abundant financially—though she *did* dream of an indoor bathroom, someday.

When Monica shared her good news with others, she was surprised to find that many of her friends had similar stories of financial well-being and gratitude. As the responses poured in and people described their almost-Ultimate lifestyles, there were some common themes: a focus on experiences over possessions, daily gratitude practices, trust, faith, and hope. Yet there were also big differences in the numbers people shared. Some people had hundreds of thousands of dollars saved in retirement accounts, yet still considered themselves at only a "Comfortable" lifestyle tier, while others had much smaller savings or, like Monica, lived in homes without electricity, yet were confident they were approaching their Ultimate tier.

As she reviewed her Three-Tier Money Map, Monica could see she still had some creative visioning to do before she could even *define* what an Ultimate lifestyle meant to her, let alone breathe it to life. Did she truly want to buy that house with a cozy indoor toilet? Or would she rather pour her rare disposable money into a real vacation, somewhere warm? Should she forget about both of those big expenses, and instead focus on directing more money into her savings account? She considered hiring a financial therapist to help her sift through some childhood "money stuff," and was excited to begin working with a financial planner to help her prepare for retirement.

Monica had a firm foundation in Money Healing that helped her celebrate her abundance and all that she had accomplished. Thanks to the deep inner work she had already done around her money relationship, she was able to engage with her Money Mapping with a clear head: she felt confident defining her three lifestyle tiers on her own terms, recognized where she was holding herself back, and stepped bravely through her own barriers.

Return to Money Healing and Money Practices as Needed

If you find yourself panicked, overwhelmed, or rebellious as you plot out your Three-Tier Money Map, I invite you to turn within and ask yourself if there are some old chapters of your Money Story that need attention. Many of us have a difficult time discerning between "needs," which might go on our Basic Needs tier, and "wants," which might belong on our Comfortable or Ultimate tiers. Sometimes, this difficulty goes back to childhood, when we did not get our physical or emotional needs met. As adults, all kinds of irrational money choices, from addictive shopping to hoarding to an inability to receive or appreciate wealth can stem from an unconscious attempt to fulfill those missing pieces from our childhood. By revisiting the practices of Money Healing, we have an opportunity to soothe old wounds and honor our deepest needs.

Dorothy, a dental hygienist, had a world of resistance about plotting out her Ultimate lifestyle level. When she did a Body Check-In and allowed herself to simply notice her resistance with compassion and curiosity, she found its source. "I was afraid to make more money because I didn't feel like I had the capacity to track it, use it well, and make good choices. I realized that when I get into more money than I can track well in my head, I feel floaty and ungrounded."

Indeed, while many people *say* they want more money, it can be a little scary to even imagine this if you don't trust yourself to know what to do with it. The more money practices Dorothy put in place, and the more regularly she stuck to her Money Dates, the more confidence she had that she could consciously direct additional income. This is why a good foundation in Money Practices is key before moving on to Money Mapping.

Balance Hope and Gratitude

When Joyce, the life coach who had just moved to Portland, totaled the monthly expenses for her Ultimate lifestyle, she wasn't sure she'd ever make it a reality. While articulating but not reaching your Ultimate lifestyle can bring up hopelessness or despair, it's also an opportunity for growth.

We all go through many different phases in life, moving sometimes fluidly, sometimes jerkily through ups and downs, transitions and breakthroughs. The work of Money Maps is not only about goal setting, but also honoring these rhythms and cycles of life. It is up to us to strike a conscious balance between planning for the future and finding acceptance and gratitude for our present circumstances. The opportunity for mindful practice, here, is to recognize and honor both sides of this equation: striving toward our goals *and* resting in gratitude for what we have, right now.

Some people naturally tend toward one side of this equation: they are more apt to mind-jump into the future. These people might naturally save more, dream bigger, or get anxious about things to come. If this describes you (whether in general or simply in this moment), your Money Map work may focus on increasing your awareness of reasons to feel satisfied and abundant right in the present moment.

Other people find it easier to rest in the present moment, yet are challenged thinking about the future. They might prioritize spending money on fun things, like dinners and vacations, but have a harder time saving for retirement or strategizing about a long-term career jump. If this sounds like you, your Money Map can provide some very helpful guidance as you start thinking about the future you want to create for yourself.

Joyce tried to balance hope and gratitude, planning and present-moment satisfaction in her Money Mapping. For her, this looked like plotting her next, "Basic-Plus" lifestyle tier—while also taking some time to slow down, pet her cat, and gaze appreciatively at her beautiful home.

Money Mapping as a Couple

Once Joyce finished her Three-Tier Money Map, she excitedly told her partner, Samantha, that she'd love to discuss it with her on a Money Date. A few days later, Samantha and Joyce sat down with steaming mugs of hot chocolate to look at Joyce's Money Map. They set an intention: to share in a spirit of openness, curiosity, respect, and love about where they were in agreement *and* the ways they might be envisioning the future differently.

Like most couples, Joyce and Samantha saw eye-to-eye on many of the categories in each lifestyle tier, but not all of them. Samantha was surprised to see the monthly housekeeper they employed listed under Joyce's Basic Needs tier, as she felt this expense was a splurge that belonged in the Comfortable tier, if not the Ultimate. This sparked a conversation between them about their differing energy levels and work commitments. By the end of their Money Date, Samantha understood better just how exhausted and busy Joyce was, while Joyce got a greater appreciation for how independent and self-sufficient her wife was. As they talked through each tier and category, they celebrated both their similarities and their differences.

If you have a partner, you may decide that it works best for you to map out your Three-Tier Money Map on your own, first, as Joyce did, and only share it with your partner when you feel it's complete. This allows you the opportunity to tune into your personal definitions for each tier before considering your partner's opinions (and perhaps getting influenced or derailed by them). Then, you may get a lot from sharing this map with your partner (and seeing your partner's map as well) and figuring out where they overlap and diverge. Other couples enjoy the process of creating a Three-Tier Money Map together, right from the start.

Rose and Matthew, a kindergarten teacher and personal chef in their twenties, chose to make their own, separate Three-Tier Money Maps but to do the exercise at the same time, in the same room, and to compare notes as soon as they were finished. They were living together and sharing many expenses, but were far from fully merging their finances. After almost an hour of visioning and calculating, they finally took a peek at each other's spreadsheets. What they saw was a little shocking: Matthew's "Ultimate" lifestyle tier was significantly lower than Rose's "Comfortable" level. This led to a deep and challenging conversation about their upbringings, their work histories, and their ultimate goals.

Three months later, Matthew revisited his Three-Tier Money Map. To his surprise, he found his original numbers for Comfortable and Ultimate lifestyles far lower than his current numbers. In the three months since creating his Money Map, his new private chef business had taken some big steps forward, and he was earning more money than ever before. He had also spent a significant chunk of time journaling about his relationship to money and all of the beliefs about it he had inherited from his childhood. He suddenly found himself more excited and inspired to dream a little bigger about his future and envision what an "Ultimate Lifestyle" might look like. He had also reexamined where he was, at the moment, and realized he was ready for a greater level of financial ease: his definition of "Comfortable" had shifted, as well. As with everything else in our money relationships, the Three-Tier Money Map will change and evolve over time, right along with us.

. . . . .

One of the toughest aspects of creating a Three-Tier Money Map for Joyce was figuring out how to factor in the income and expenses for her business. Joyce was committed to creating a business that truly shared her gifts with the world in a big, direct way. To that end, she had recently created a website for her life-coaching services, offering a free blog, private guidance, and small group offerings. She was excited about this new entrepreneurial venture, and poured loving work into it every single day; yet, it was new enough that she wasn't earning very much money from it yet. Joyce knew it would take some time to grow her audience and earn any reliable income from her business. She felt confident this was the right work for her and was happy to be patient, yet this uncertainty about how, when, and how large her income could grow made it challenging to create her Three-Tier Money Map.

Entrepreneurs like Joyce often find it difficult to plan their finances. Many tell me, "My cash flow is so unpredictable—there's no way I can create a realistic budget!" While it's true that Money Mapping with unpredictable incomes is more challenging, there are absolutely ways to work within this complexity. In fact, when cash flow is uncertain, it's often all the more crucial to track, plan, and consciously direct financial influx and outflow.

The first question I recommend entrepreneurs ask themselves is: Do I need to create separate Money Maps for my business and personal finances—or roll them into one?

Because Joyce's business was so new, and represented such a small slice of her income and expenses, she decided to create one master Money Map, which included both personal and entrepreneurial finances. Six months later, her business had grown into a new, bigger phase, and had enough financial volume and complexity that it made sense to her to create a separate Money Map for her business.

Buckle Up Your Dancing Shoes

The Three-Tier Money Map isn't a one-off exercise. It is an essential practice that I recommend returning to again and again, over time, as you, your life, and your financial landscape shift and grow.

Perhaps the most important idea of Money Mapping is that your finances can, should, and will shift and evolve, right along with you, throughout your life. Creating a Three-Tier Money Map is a ginormous first step in this dance—but it is only the first step. What happens when Big Life Stuff happens, and everything changes? What if you lose your job, launch a career, have a baby, have a serious illness, or decide you want to buy a house? These questions require further exploration into how you can converse with, play with, and dance with your Money Map.

dancing with your money map

THE TANGLED WHITE sheets surrounded me with weird nooks and surreal rabbit tunnels. Sunlight streamed through the white curtains, pausing on a few particles of dust in the air before landing on the crumpled mess of linen and pillows: the bed that had been my home for the past two weeks.

I rolled ever-so-gingerly to my side, wracked with pain, careful not to split the stitches still holding my belly together. For a disorienting moment, I couldn't remember if this was sunrise or sunset—the days and hours blurred together in a hyperreal haze. My disorientation switched off instantly the moment my bleary-eyed gaze returned to *him*: my beautiful baby boy, sleeping peacefully beside me. The pain in my body, the stacks of dirty dishes I *knew* were cluttering the kitchen, the pain meds working their way out of my bloodstream—none of it mattered. All I cared about was right here in the bed: those perfect fingers, those impossibly tiny toes, and the otherworldly blue eyes of my newborn son.

It had been two weeks since my husband and I had brought our son home to that bed. During labor, I had felt something was terribly wrong and demanded we go to the hospital instead of continuing with our planned home birth. Just thirty minutes after we arrived at the hospital, I began hemorrhaging from a ruptured placenta and went into an emergency C-section in the nick of time. I was grateful beyond words that we all made it through, but my son and I had so much recovery to do, it was a full-time job. For many weeks, neither of us slept more than two hours at a time. At the same time, my husband had recently been diagnosed with Lyme disease, so he was ravaged and worn-out from an epic health battle of his own.

Thankfully, we had a large and generous community who supported us through this intense transition, and I will be forever grateful to these wonderful healers and helpers. With their support, and emboldened by the crazy-powerful mama love that surged through me, I found the strength to keep putting one foot after the next during that recovery period. But, truth be told, I was out-of-my-mind exhausted. I knew, deep in those mama-strong bones, that it was time to dramatically shift my life, my work in the world, and my money.

Noah was born mere months before my fortieth birthday. Up until the month he was born, I worked forty to fifty hours per week in my business as a financial therapist. I offered private financial therapy to individuals and couples, mentorship to creative professionals, and taught a number of group programs. Additionally, my business partner and I oversaw a wide, eclectic, and busy team of financial coaches and bookkeeping trainers. I loved collaborating with these incredible money professionals. Our team had been together for almost four years, and each passing year was bigger, busier, and more profitable. I loved my work, I adored my team, and the energy of expansion was electric. During my pregnancy, I had planned on returning to business as usual after Noah was born. Yet once he arrived, as I spent those weeks in an intense healing crisis with him in that bed, the truth sank in: I simply couldn't (and didn't want to) return to my previous pace and my complex business model. Life had become exquisitely simple: love him, feed him, sing to him, sleep, eat, bathe, love him more, sleep. All of my attention was on Noah, and that's the only place I wanted it to be. I needed to find a new way to work, one that aligned with mamahood. This was my "money koan" (or riddle): how do I earn money *and* serve others *while* honoring my need for rest, family, and simplicity? I wrestled with this question for weeks, pondering everything from logistics to life purpose. Eventually, I got clarity.

I lovingly ended my relationship with my business partner. I parted ways from my wonderful team. And after a four-month maternity leave, I returned to work as a one-woman show. I shifted from a predominantly local business to a one hundred percent online business, which allowed me to forgo fancy, professional clothes and leaving the house to teach. Because our recovery was prolonged and challenging (neither my son nor I slept much, those first few years), I could only work about ten hours per week that first year. This was as much as I could do . . . and it felt good and right.

This moment in my little family's life was many things, not the least of which was a big financial decision: cutting back my hours and shifting my business model meant a drastic reduction in our income, just when our expenses were higher than ever. Plus, Forest had just been let go from his full-time job and was starting up his own freelance web design business, which was nowhere near financially stable, yet. Thankfully, Forest and I had some savings to carry us through this transitional time, along with the loving support of friends and family. I am incredibly grateful that we were able to make this big leap—yet it was far from an easy decision, especially given our culture's bias toward "more, bigger, better" as a definition of success. Our little family had to make big changes to accommodate this precious time. "Simple" became our mantra, our way of life, and our saving grace.

This is how life is: in some years we expand and grow, while in other years we intentionally pare down and simplify. Nothing is static in this world. Progress sometimes looks like downsizing. This is why the traditional advice most "money gurus" implicitly espouse—that we should earn more and more and more each year—simply doesn't work.

In order to truly support your best life, your money relationship must reflect these natural rhythms and cycles. It must shift, slow down, or speed up, right along with you, as you move through phases of expansion and simplification, growth and transition. Through all the ups and downs of life, we can strive to remain as lovingly present as possible within this shifting, twirling world.

The essential work of Money Maps is to bring this dance into our money relationships, recognizing and honoring how things change. To stay in an ongoing conversation with our money and ourselves, we ask:

What phase of life am I in, and how can money best support that? What has changed over the past month, six months, year, five years? What are the themes of this present moment in my life, and how can money support them? Once you have created your Three-Tier Money Map, these are the sorts of questions you can ask, as you work with it.

Perhaps, after creating your Three-Tier Money Map, you notice that you're living at your Comfortable Lifestyle level, and would love to someday reach that Ultimate level. Yet right now, your energy levels are depleted, and working more hours is unthinkable. You might find creative ways to decrease your expenses so you can enjoy more rest and quality time with your loved ones. Or perhaps you realize it's time to shift your business model so you can earn more money in less time. Or maybe you feel drained by those monthly credit card payments, and the idea of tightening your belt to aggressively pay them off for six months makes you excited as heck. There is a near-endless array of financial strategies and tactics that can support you, depending on what your values and goals are, at the moment.

Just as there is no such thing as a "one size fits all" approach to money, there is also no such thing as a "one size fits you forever" approach to money. The attitudes, practices, and tools that serve your money life best in your twenties will be vastly different from what you need in your sixties. How we relate to money can and must change over the course of our lives—and it is up to us, as conscious, caring, evolving people, to discern exactly how we must shift over the course of our lives. I call this process of discernment Dancing with your Money Map.

Like any good dance, Money Mapping is interactive—an ongoing give-and-take between you and your money. Let's say you aggressively pay down your credit card debt for six months; in return, your credit score soars, and you end up qualifying for a car loan. You take action, your money responds, and the dance continues. If you keep dancing, you will start to recognize and celebrate how things change. You may even relax when things feel hard, trusting the rhythms and cycles of your life.

In life, things change. Including money.

Learning to Dance: The Five Money Areas

Ellie, an artist and businesswoman in her early twenties, was at a critical choice point in her business and money life. She had just been presented an opportunity to expand her art studio (and make a lot more money) by taking over the fur coat shop next door. The fur trade felt misaligned with her ethics, so she was very hesitant to earn money this way long-term. Yet she also recognized that running the fur shop for six months or a year would bring in a large amount of money, which she could use to expand her art outreach programs and serve more people in her community.

Her question was one I hear often, especially from people trying to engage with their Money Map and discern the best ways to fine-tune it: "How do I align my ethics and my earnings, and do they *always* need to be aligned?" To answer that question, it's helpful to tease out the five main "money areas" in life:

1 Earning and income
2 Spending and expenses
3 Saving
4 Debt repayment
5 Investing

You might notice that these "money areas" are similar to the main categories in a Chart of Accounts—here, though, we will be looking at them through a Money Mapping lens instead of a bookkeeping lens. Also, there are some other forms of money exchange—like borrowing, lending, and gifting—but for now let's focus on these five biggies.

Simply put, these are the five main ways you can interact with money. It's usually not possible or even ideal to focus on all five of these money areas all the time. When we're working on our financial strategy or even doing the emotional work around our "money stuff," most people tend to focus on just one or two of these areas, while placing the others on the back burner. That is fine and normal. But it's even better when we make those choices to prioritize or back-burner an area of our finances consciously and intentionally.

As Ellie was deciding whether or not to take on this second business, she needed to think about which of these five areas she most wanted to work on at that time. Did she want to focus on expanding her earning potential? If so, did it feel more important to do this purpose-based work, aligning her income with her ethics? Or, was she at a point where she simply needed an influx of cash, whatever the means? Perhaps this was a moment in which her ability to give back to the world (the investing area) actually mattered more to her than having money—if so, she thought she might prefer finding new, creative ways to give back to her community that didn't require that additional income.

A few weeks after reviewing these five money areas, Ellie made her decision. She was too excited by what she could accomplish with additional income to let the fur shop opportunity slip by, so she took on this additional revenue stream. However, she switched the fur shop to a used, vintage, and consignment business model: that way, even though she was selling furs, she wasn't contributing to the demand for new ones. Within a year, she had earned enough additional income from the fur shop to afford the renovations she needed to expand her art studio. She tore down the wall between her old space and the fur shop and created a thriving community center, offering paid and donation-based arts, theater, yoga, and dance programs. By focusing on expanding her earning potential for a focused period of time, Ellie was then able to expand her capacity to invest and give back to her community. She had shifted her focus from one money area to another. Let's go into each of these five money areas in more detail to help you identify which area most needs your loving attention, right now.

MONEY AREA #1.

INCOME AND EARNING

Some people seem to have an innate gift for earning: it has always been easy for them to bring in as much money as they need (or even more than they need), and their "money work" is more around reining in their spending or aligning their values with their choices. I firmly believe that we *all* have strengths around money, some intrinsic and some hard-won, and they should all be celebrated. If earning is one of your strengths, please celebrate this! However, if you struggle with earning money, whether this means achieving your Basic Needs, Comfortable, or Ultimate lifestyle tier, please know you are not alone.

Before starting my own business, I struggled to earn money. Fresh out of graduate school, I was earning just over minimum wage, working in a hospice and the mental health field. I couldn't afford to buy the organic food I wanted, let alone splurge on massages or dark chocolate treats. I was ashamed that I couldn't earn more money and angry that our culture didn't value the important caregiving work I did enough to pay more for it. I tried to keep the faith that somehow, someday, I could do incredible work in the world *and* earn plenty of money—yet at the time, this felt impossible.

I now have the words for my conundrum: I was trapped beneath a "money ceiling." I desperately needed to break the $11 per hour barrier, if only so I could feel for myself that it was possible. So I took on a second job, working in an accounting department for $13 per hour. That small raise of $2 per hour felt utterly life-changing. Within a year, I started my own bookkeeping business and raised my fees—then shifted into work as a financial therapist and earned even more. Thanks to these shifts, I was able to break through money ceiling after money ceiling: past that $11 per hour, then past $25 and $100 per hour, and eventually past the annual income I had set as my goal.

Over the years, I have continued to make different and creative choices to break through money ceilings. While it worked well for me to take on a second (and eventually third) job in my twenties to stretch my earning capacity, in the years since then, I have broken through money ceilings differently, depending on what phase of life I was in and what my resulting priorities were. Sometimes, this meant raising my fees, while other times it mean *lowering* my fees to welcome a larger number of participants to group programs. Today, I focus on finding balanced, sustainable ways to integrate my income and lifestyle: I have continually tweaked and fine-tuned my business model and offerings so that I can enjoy the rest and family time that light me up while also earning an income that feels sustainable and good to me.

Money Ceilings

What is your real money ceiling? Name it. Because it needs to be named. What's the amount of money that you've not been able to make more than? What is the most you have made hourly? Or monthly? What's the most you have made over a quarter or a year? Brainstorm creative options for bringing in more money. Even if the options feel totally "out there" or not possible, just let your creativity flow here. Get out your journal and write. Let your rational mind relax and simply write out some options.

Please know: there are so many options and resources to support you in earning more money, if that is what feels essential to you right now. I've had clients negotiate raises, take on a second job, rent out their spare rooms on Airbnb, teach guitar lessons, or sell antiques online. Many of the creative entrepreneurs I know have fine-tuned their business models over the years to come up with new income streams and/ or better leverage their time so they can earn more money without working more hours. Countless others have chosen to turn within to address their underearning. If earning more is a priority for you right now, please know that it *is* possible. This is multifaceted work, so draw on tools from Money Healing, Money Practices, and Money Maps to do the inner work of cultivating and claiming your value and the outer work of pricing, business models, and income streams. With determination, compassion, and patience, you *can* stretch your earning capacity.

MONEY AREA #2.
SPENDING AND EXPENSES

Money Cleanses

A few years ago, I decided it was time to put myself on a food cleanse. I was *so* ready to release the remaining pregnancy weight I had been carrying for years and perk up my energy, and I had an intuition that eliminating certain foods for awhile could help me reset my system and renew my relationship with my body. So I eliminated grains, coffee, sugar, and dairy from my diet for one month. Normally, I am not a fan of restrictive diets—and I know "cleanses" can be a slippery slope for so many of us, leading into emotionally wacky territory, riddled with negative willpower, scarcity, and just plain not-fun-ness. But I decided to treat this cleanse as a special phase: an experiment, a dance of temporary simplicity, a special period of loving myself in a new way and giving myself what my body was craving. It ended up being a truly lovely experience: by the end of the month, I had lost a little weight and my energy levels were higher than ever (though I was extremely ready for some dark chocolate). But the most surprising benefit I received from my little experiment was a fresh way to think about spending.

Inspired by my food cleanse, one of my clients decided to do a "money cleanse." Just as I had felt weighed down by the baby weight, she felt drained and weighed down by her debt. She urgently wanted to pay off these debts, and knew she would need to eliminate some excess spending to do so—yet she was also clear that she wanted this process to feel graceful and loving, not like some harsh, punishing "money diet." She began looking for ways to cut back on her spending, but in a very intentional, self-loving way.

I thought this was brilliant. I shared her idea with others, and we all brainstormed ways to bring more consciousness to spending during a "money cleanse." Some people chose to scale back to their "Basic Needs" Money Map tier, only spending what they absolutely needed to for a set amount of time. They set specific intentions for what they would do with any extra money at the end of the month—and practiced saying "no" from a place of empowerment, clarity, and love. One woman decided to stop using debit or credit cards for a month, and only used cash: actually touching the green stuff made her feel more present and intimate with the money flowing in and out of her life. Another person cancelled all of his automatic payments and set up reminders for himself to manually pay each bill: this made him far more intentional about his spending, and even reminded him of a "money leak," an old gym membership he was ready to eliminate altogether. Of course, there are as many versions and protocols for a "money cleanse" as there are for food cleanses: that is to say, the possibilities are endless. These temporary simplifications can be as structured or intuitive, as rigid or lavish, as you wish.

Maximum Lockdown Mode

As you might recall, my husband and I created our own playful term for "money cleanses" in the early years of our relationship when it was a necessity: "Maximum Lockdown Mode." The first time I heard my husband decree "Maximum Lockdown Mode, Bari!" I got a little scared: it sounded so harsh, and I hated feeling deprived. Yet over time, as we practiced, this phrase became infused with bucketfuls of playfulness and humor. It helped us shift what could easily have been very intense, heavy times into a lighthearted game: How well could we live, without spending much? And, perhaps most importantly, using this phrase reminded us both that this was a temporary phase; things *would* shift again, soon enough.

Over the years, we have returned to "Maximum Lockdown Mode" a number of times—yet exactly what this entails has shifted along with our business and lifestyle. Whereas in the first few years of our marriage, "Maximum Lockdown Mode" might have meant beans and rice for two weeks, now it might mean holding off on our weekly restaurant dates for a while. This kind of evolution is all wonderful and good—and part of the ever-changing dance of Money Mapping.

Conscious Splurging

Of course, not everyone's "growing edge" with spending is spending less. For some people, what's most difficult is to spend money on themselves without feeling guilty or transgressive.

A few months ago, one of my dear students posted a photo in our private Facebook group: she was grinning ear to ear in her new work outfit. Once she completed her Three-Tier Money Map, she realized that, according to her own definitions, she was living at least at her "Comfortable" lifestyle tier (and soon moving into her "Ultimate" tier). Yet she had not allowed herself to buy new clothes for many years, because she had so much anxiety around spending too much money. She realized that her *real* work in the spending area was releasing some of this old worry, so she took herself out to buy a chic new pantsuit for work. Even though it wasn't very expensive (and she desperately needed new clothes for her job), this felt like a huge splurge and massive step forward for her. Even bigger, she did so with a huge smile on her face, without feeling guilty or worried.

"I know this will seem backward," she confessed, "but this work is teaching me how to *spend* money, not save it!" I reassured her that there was no such thing as "backward" in this money work, as long as we are being present and loving. We all have our different strengths and challenges around money; some of us need to learn to save more, others need to spend with less worry. And, perhaps most importantly, we need to recognize just where we are, in the grand scheme of our lives. For this particular woman, in that particular moment, the most evolutionary and healing thing she could do was splurge a little. (And we all helped her celebrate, of course.)

MONEY AREA #3.
SAVINGS

Over the years, I've collaborated with hundreds of financial experts, planners, and coaches, and when the subject of savings comes up, it is as if they're all singing in some operatic chorus, using (almost exactly) the same words. The refrain goes something like this:

Savings is a muscle. You have to strengthen it. Practice setting aside money, every single week. Even if it's only one dollar. Over time, this adds up—and so does your capacity to save. It's a discipline, and you'll only get better at it if you start now. What are you waiting for?

While I do see the wisdom in this stance on savings, I also know that, frankly, things aren't that simple. The core recognition of Money Mapping—that our lives shift and evolve over time, and our relationship with money shifts too—brings more subtlety to this money area. Surely, savings is a muscle we can strengthen over time. Yet sometimes we need to focus on other muscles.

In those first two years after our son was born, my husband and I didn't save a single penny. In fact, we dipped into the savings we had spent years accumulating. We made this decision consciously, intentionally, and lovingly, because spending time with our boy trumped flexing some "savings muscle." A few years later, when our son was old enough to go to a play-school several days a week and we were rested enough to work (and earn) more, we returned to our practice of regular saving. Our relationship to setting aside money has shifted over the years, and rarely in a linear fashion. Saving has followed the ups, downs, and transitions of our lives. This is exactly as it should be for us.

It is up to each of us to determine what our right relationship to savings is, at any moment. For some people, this means choosing a certain percentage or dollar amount to set aside once a week or once a month. Some people love creating separate savings accounts for specific savings goals, like a vacation or new car. I know many entrepreneurs who create "cash flow savings" accounts to cover payroll and other expenses when their income hits an inevitable dip. One woman I know has a very specific "bottom line" savings number. If that account drops below $100,000, she panics. While this number might seem extravagantly high to many people, it is what she needs to feel secure after an impoverished childhood. Over the years, I have worked with people who have incredibly strong savings muscles. Some of them find a greater sense of ease and freedom when they learn to relax their focus on saving for the future and instead enjoy splurging a bit more or practicing generous giving.

Savings Shame

Arianna and her husband, Mauricio, a young couple living in Mexico, sat down for a hard talk: it was finally time for them to discuss their "savings problem." Since getting married and merging their finances, their income had fluctuated a good deal, and saving, in particular, was a constant struggle. During cash flow dips, they often relied on their savings to cover basic expenses like rent and groceries. "It was basically a checking account with a savings account costume on," Arianna remembers. When their income stabilized, they would sock away money again, only to dip back into it a few months later when things got tough. This cycle had them both feeling exhausted and ashamed, though for different reasons.

Each time Arianna saw their dwindling (or empty) savings account, she felt a red-hot flush of shame and failure. Her whole life, she had been coached to put a certain percentage of her money in a "safe place": first it was her childhood piggy bank, then a savings account, and eventually a retirement fund. "I grew up with the understanding that saving money is simply what responsible, successful adults do—no ifs, ands, or buts about it. When our savings dwindled, I felt that cloud of shame looming over me; I was terrified of my family seeing the long row of zeroes in my account."

Arianna's husband, Mauricio, had an equal yet opposite kind of savings shame: every dollar they put into their savings account only *added* to his sense of failure. He had learned, from childhood on up, that any money left over after basic expenses should be shared with family. This was simply how things were done in his native Uruguay. Tucking away money for a "rainy day" or emergency, or even a retirement account, was synonymous with greed, stinginess, and egomania.

Once Mauricio and Arianna were able to name and understand their different flavors of "savings shame" and articulate them to each other, they realized that they didn't have a "savings problem." They had a communications challenge and a deep healing opportunity. They began practicing Body Check-Ins when those feelings of shame began to swell. They also made time to regularly check in with each other about their Three-Tier Money Map, savings goals, and financial gifts to family members. After several months of focused money work together, Arianna realized, "those old jaw-clenching, grit-your-teeth fights about money weren't so much about how much we disagreed about money. Rather, they were a symptom of the fact that we didn't have a process for sharing our perspectives and making financial decisions that both of us could feel good about." Ultimately, they struck a balance of spending, saving, and gifting that they could both feel good about, and one they knew they could change over time.

Emergency Fund Anxiety

Sophia, a branding consultant in her early thirties, scrunched her nose as she looked at her laptop screen. She had a savings account that was holding steady for the first time in her life, even climbing slightly every month, and yet her money anxiety was only growing, right along with her savings. What was going on here?

Reviewing her Value-Based Bookkeeping system, Sophia realized precisely what the problem was. She was tracking her savings account in a category called "Emergency Fund." As this number grew (past $500 and then $1000), Sophia found herself imagining bigger and more dramatic catastrophes. On a semi-conscious level, she was worrying about the question, "What *emergency* is going to cost me that much money?" Each month, as her savings grew, that tragedy swelled to more and more dire dimensions.

Sophia remembered: she had the power to rename this category in her tracking system to *anything* she wanted. She did a Body Check-In, reflected for a moment, and typed: "Peace of Mind Fund." She instantly noticed her shoulders relax and a contented smile spread across her face. This is Values-Based Bookkeeping in action, and it's lovely—but what Sophia did next took this realization into Money Maps territory.

You see, the name "Emergency Fund" used to work well for Sophia. For several years, she truly was worried about some emergency arising—her mother falling ill, for example, necessitating a quick, cross-country flight back to her hometown; a sudden cash flow dip in her consulting business or an angry landlord who could evict her if she didn't have rent on time. However, Sophia had recently moved back to her hometown, and was living rent-free with a dear friend—plus, her income had stabilized thanks to a long-term consulting project. An "emergency" at this point in her life would be something *utterly* catastrophic. She realized that her growing anxiety at seeing "Emergency Fund" was actually a signal that she had shifted into a different phase of her financial life, one in which she actually felt more secure than ever before. As soon as she changed her savings category to "Peace of Mind Fund," she noticed a swell of excitement and pride each time she saw that number grow. She still needed and appreciated what this savings offered her, but during this new chapter of her life, it represented something slightly different than before. Changing the name helped her understand and celebrate this shift, within herself and her money relationship.

MONEY AREA #4.
DEBT REPAYMENT

Most financial gurus have a very strict view of debt. "All debt is bad! You cannot be truly free and be in debt," they often proclaim.

Understandably, the people hearing their message who do have debt feel like failures.

As with almost everything money-related, my experience has given me a far less rigid outlook on debt. Granted, some people do have unhealthy relationships with debt: they may spend compulsively or become addicted to the experience of being in debt, and these people can and should seek help to support them. However, except in these cases, taking on and repaying debt is a much more nuanced creature, and needs to be taken on a person-to-person, phase of life-to-phase of life basis.

I do believe that borrowing money can be incredibly supportive (and sometimes utterly necessary) at certain phases of our lives—especially during tough transitions. Also, it bears repeating, sometimes liabilities can actually be hidden assets. This is readily apparent with debt incurred to earn a degree or certification, start a business, or buy a car. Yet even less "positive" debts can sometimes offer subtle rewards, when we look deep enough: life lessons learned, marriages saved (or avoided), and so on.

Just as we must discern the right moments to take on debt in our lives, we can also discern the right timing for paying it back. As with savings or any other of the five money areas, debt repayment can be done in a way and at a pace that aligns with our situation and values. Some months and years, it feels wonderful and right to aggressively pay down debt as quickly as possible; at other times, we may need to slow down or even stop this repayment in order to focus on other priorities.

Dealing with debt almost always necessitates some Money Healing: working with any shame around the debt and even renaming it something that energizes you to repay it with enthusiasm and appreciation. For example, you might rename "student loan debt" "amazing education" or repay your "lifesaving health help" instead of "medical bills."

Debt repayment also requires smart Money Practices: tracking your debt carefully, making on-time payments to avoid late fees, watching those interest rates (consolidating or working with a debt advocate if needed), and exercising as much financial savvy as you can about how much and what kind of debt you choose to take on at this point in your life. Be smart, take baby steps, and above all else, be gentle with yourself when it comes to debt.

MONEY AREA #5.

INVESTING

Please don't skip this section because you don't think you have enough money for investment. If you think "investing" is just about stocks and bonds and cold, hard cash; if you think it's something you couldn't possibly do until you have a ton more money; if you think you've got way more pressing priorities in life and money right now . . . then I respectfully disagree.

All of these sentiments grow out of a faulty, far too narrow, and sadly widespread definition of "investing." My financial colleague Christopher Peck recently opened my eyes to just how deeply meaningful the concept of investing can really be. He put words to something I had always felt, deep down, about life, money and investing— and it goes far beyond cash. In *The Resilient Investor*, Christopher and his partners Michael Kramer and Hal Brill write:

> Rather than wrinkling up one's nose and doing "investing" the way we have been taught, we are asking people to take a step back and really think about what a powerful and creative role this activity could play in their lives. This begins with expanding our notion about what investing truly is, so try this on for size: investing is something that we all do by directing our time, attention, energy or money in ways that move us toward our future dreams, using a diverse range of strategies. We think investing is really cool. A focal activity where people make decisions that change their lives and the world.[21]

The authors go on to explain that "resilient investment" is a cultivation of several different types of assets: personal (learning, health,

---

21 Hal Brill, Michael Kramer, and Christopher Peck. *The Resilient Investor: A Plan for Your Life, Not Just Your Money* (Oakland, California: Berrett-Koehler Publishers, 2015), 7.

spiritual growth), tangible (home, food, ecosystem), and finally financial (stocks, bonds, and savings). Plus, they remind us that time is our most precious resource and that we "can and should bring this to the investing table by being thoughtful about the ways we focus our attention and channel our energy."

I love this broader, deeper understanding of investing. It takes that old, narrow definition of investing, limited to trading stocks and strategizing investment portfolios, and weaves it back into the entirety of our lives. From this vantage point, we can recognize and honor countless more ways we are already investing, each day: from our daily walks to a few moments spent in meditation to money spent at a farmer's market to cleaning our homes to, yes, buying stocks or socking away savings. We can invest in ourselves, our family, our health, our business, our education, our retirement fund, and our peace of mind.

Whenever we spend time, energy, or money, we are making an investment. Recognizing this fact awakens us to the truth: we always have a choice about what investments we make. It's up to us to consider the best ways to invest our time, energy, and money in accordance with our values, our dreams, and what phase of life we're in.

When it comes to cash investments, we also have enormous choice at our fingertips, including many opportunities for Socially Responsible Investing, which allows investments to be made with your values in mind. (See the Resources section for a few worthwhile suggestions.)

Ultimately, this final area of Money Mapping is all about deciding where you want to put your money, time, and energy: for now and for the future. Investing is an opportunity for you to tune into yourself, listen to your life, and consciously direct your precious resources the very best way you can.

Striking Your Perfect Balance

If you are committed to finding *your* right balance of these five areas and yet feel yourself longing for a smart, simple framework to start with, one of my favorites comes from Elizabeth Warren's book, *All Your Worth*. Elizabeth suggests splitting your after-tax income like this:

50 percent for Basic Needs

This might be your "Basic Lifestyle Tier," and includes the bare essentials: rent/mortgage, groceries, utilities, minimum loan payments, etc.

30 percent for Wants

These are life's "nice-to-haves," and might include vacations, entertainment, clothes, eating out, gifts, etc.

20 percent for Savings, Debt Repayment, and Investing

If you have debt, Elizabeth considers your minimum monthly payments "basic needs," but anything beyond that falls under this final category—as do retirement savings and any other investments.[22]

Not everyone will want to use a framework—you might even rebel against one. But if you do want to experiment with some rules of thumb, Ms. Warren's guidelines are a good place to start. This structure came out of her twenty-plus years of research on women and bankruptcy, and helps make sure you strike a sane balance between saving for the future and enjoying your income, today.

As you consider this 50/30/20 framework, you might notice that you need to increase your income (or decrease your expenses) to keep your basic needs below fifty percent of your after-tax income. Or, you may realize that your income is high enough that you can easily put more money into savings without surpassing that twenty percent mark. Take into consideration your current life situation and your life goals, and refer to your personal Three-Tier Money Map to make this most effective. You may consider bringing on a financial planner or money coach to help you plot things out. Remember: this is only a starting point, and you are welcome to create your own equation based on your values, phase of life, and what feels best to you.

Big Life Transitions

Our lives are filled with ups and downs, rhythms and cycles, initiations, crossroads, and those in-between spaces: *transitions*. All of these

---

22 Elizabeth Warren and Amelia Warren Tyagi, *All Your Worth: The Ultimate Lifetime Money Plan* (New York: Free Press, 2005), 27.

impact (and are impacted by) our financial reality, both practical and emotional. That's why it's so valuable to consciously and intentionally dance with your Money Map as you enter, undergo, or exit a big life transition.

Transitions can be positive, negative, or somewhere in between. They can be sudden or long-time-coming, subtle or un-miss-able. But almost all of them are at least a little disorienting: at the beginning of a transition, old strategies and familiar ways of being simply don't work anymore. If you are facing a transition like a death in the family, a divorce, a big health challenge, or a career change, this can be a pivotal moment to lean into your strengthening and deepening money relationship for support.

Many of the stories already told in this book are, in fact, about transitions: the middle-aged mother who got divorced and suddenly needed a crash course in money management; the woman who moved cross-country to Portland and felt anxious about bringing in enough money through her fledgling coaching business. The story about my own postpartum health recovery and ensuing business shift at the beginning of this chapter is one of the biggest transitions I've ever experienced—and it certainly had immense impacts on my money relationship.

Big life transitions can affect all five "money areas": a health crisis, for example, might lower your earning potential, raise your expenses, and put a hold on your debt repayment (or even increase your debt). In moments like this, it is helpful to remember that nothing is permanent, in life or in money. Transitions may be joyful or incredibly stressful— but they do eventually pass.

Be especially gentle with yourself during transitions, as you might not feel like yourself. Be patient as you identify the new rules of the game, realizing it may take some experimentation before you get a new system and groove in place. Add in Body Check-Ins often. Have compassionate Money Dates with yourself to keep current with your finances. Consider whether it would feel good to create an expense category just for this transition, and what category name might feel honoring and good. Forgive yourself if you neglect your Money Practice for a time, and simply begin again when you are ready. Zoom out, review where you have been, where you are, and where you hope to go in your life. Check that North Star of your heart, and trust that the clarity will come, all in the perfection of time.

Shifting Visions

Each person's definition of the Three Tiers shifts and morphs, over time. Rose, a high-powered corporate attorney for many years, had an Ultimate lifestyle dream that included partnership in her own practice, a luxury convertible, and several beach vacations each year. Now that she's retired and in her seventies, she has a radically new vision for her Ultimate lifestyle, which doesn't include a convertible or a beach vacation but does include starting an orphanage in India.

When Belinda, a yoga instructor from Atlanta, first created her Three-Tier Money Map several years ago, her Ultimate lifestyle level was decidedly cosmopolitan. She dreamed of being a "digital nomad," globetrotting from the lavender fields of southern France to the tango floors of Buenos Aires and the moonlit beaches of Bali, weighed down by little more than her laptop. Now, her Ultimate vision is far simpler. She dreams of living a simple, rural life, raising a garden and small family, and having plenty of time for her meditation practice. While this may be a far cry from her earlier cosmopolitan dreams, it feels no less true and aligned, for Belinda. By regularly checking in with herself and her hopes for the future, she is able to track her evolving priorities and values.

> "Regularly reassess where you are and where you want to be in relation to your evolving values and priorities. Get comfortable with the truth of your money situation, no matter what it is. From here you can take action. This is where your true power lies."
> —Gayle Yamauchi-Gleason, Art of Money student

It is a big project to look at and assess your Three-Tier Money Map, evaluate what lifestyle tier you're at, where you'd like to go, and how you want to dance with money. Once you paint these broad brushstrokes, every specific money decision is an opportunity to bring your unique vision to life, in small and not-so-small ways. This is where strategy moves into tactics, and the big themes come to life through concrete actions. In the next chapter, I will share several ways to help you move from these generalities into specifics, so that you can make great money decisions that feel elegant, true, and right on time.

how to make a good money decision

I'M TEMPTED TO say it was one of those days that could only happen in a place like Boulder. My not-so-little-anymore Noah, a big boy of five and a half, pulled at my arm in excitement. "Look, Mama! This one likes me!" He stuffed another handful of hay through the fence and bleated back at the goats. I took a long sip of my mocha and admired the orange-pink rays of sunshine reflecting off the mountains. My husband tapped his foot to the twangy beat of the acoustic duo playing outside our favorite cafe, The Laughing Goat.

Despite its name, The Laughing Goat doesn't normally have real, live goats in the parking lot. This was a special party, celebrating the coffee shop's tenth anniversary. My husband and I have been friends with the cafe's owner for years, and we visit his cafe almost daily for work dates and quickie mocha runs. So, of course we were there to celebrate his big day. But what I thought would be a relaxing "play day" downtown ended up including one of the biggest money decisions my husband and I had made in many years.

As we learn to dance with our Money Maps—through life's inevitable twists, turns, and rhythms—making specific money decisions on a day-to-day basis can still be tricky territory. How do we know when to invest, risk, and say, "Yes," or when to tighten our belts and say, "Nope" or "Not now"? When we have a *process* for making a money decision (even a simple one), we can feel clear and empowered with every money decision.

I was contemplating a second mocha and watching Noah hop from foot to foot with the music when I noticed *that look* on my husband's face. I could see the mental gears churning in his mind and the tiniest hint of a smile at the corners of his mouth. He was staring at something just beyond the goat and music-filled parking lot. I followed his gaze to a "green" used car lot right next to the cafe. There they were: not one but two Nissan Leafs, the exact model and blue color I knew he had his heart set on.

The Big Money Question, "To Nissan Leaf or not to Nissan Leaf?" had been the subject of a heated debate in our household ever since we first test-drove one, four years prior. We loved the idea of owning one of these 100 percent electric cars. Not only would driving a Leaf help reduce our carbon footprint, we would also be funneling our money into an industry we believe can accomplish a lot of good in the world. Yet buying a second car wasn't a simple spending decision: we needed to consider a host of important lifestyle pros and cons, and how it would impact our buying, saving, and debt repayment priorities. Even the simplest money decisions occur within a grand ecosystem of our values, our Money Story, our hopes and dreams, and the entire landscape of our income, savings, debt, and cash flow. And this was a big one. If we bought the Leaf, we would be reversing a decision we had made and stuck with since before Noah was born.

Back when I was pregnant, we consciously chose to become a one-car family. Relying solely on our little Toyota hybrid allowed us to save money and work less—and because our mountain town is so tiny, it's fairly easy to get by with just one car. Plus, it got great mileage (fabulous for family road trips) and, being a hybrid, it helped reduce our carbon footprint. Yet there were significant downsides to our One Car Feat, too: while I was out safe and comfy in the car, my husband had to travel by bike to do errands or work out of a cafe, often freezing his tush to buy groceries in the winter or arriving at the cafe in the summer drenched in sweat.

So a few years after our Noah was born, we began seriously pondering buying a second car. My husband channeled his Geeky Researcher gifts into the project, studying the best pricing, interest rates, and tax breaks. He studied smart negotiation tactics and began conversing with eight different dealerships. As opinionated entrepreneurs ourselves, we both hate high-pressure sales and quick financial decisions, so we wanted to be fully prepared should the day come to walk into a big scary dealership.

Of course, the Leaf debate wasn't just about the numbers—this was emotional territory, too. My husband had been dreaming of owning an electric car ever since he was ten years old, and he couldn't hold back this glee as he poured over efficiency and sustainability specs. I cycled through my own array of personality aspects, as well: I do quick math in my head, so sometimes I would focus solely on the monthly payments we would be facing; other times, my own Gleeful Dreamer mode would come to the forefront, and I'd remind my husband that buying this second car would delay our big dream of someday owning our own home.

Over that year leading up to the goat party, we devoted many Money Dates, spreadsheets, Body Check-Ins, and more than a few bars of dark chocolate to the Leaf conversation. We shared as openly and compassionately as we could about the numbers, our emotions, and all of the pros and cons involved in this purchase. So when my husband started casually strolling toward those two used Nissan Leafs on that warm summer day, he did so confidently, knowing he was carrying with him a vast inner vault of knowledge, emotional awareness, and clarity of vision. He was also smart enough to assure me that this was merely a fact-finding mission, and he had no intention of buying a car that day.

After chatting with the dealership owner for a while, he returned to the cafe and the goats, equipped with some surprisingly good news. Because those Nissan Leafs came originally from California, they were considered "new" in Colorado (even though they were used). That meant a significant tax rebate: a hardly shrug-off-able four thousand dollars. Forest pulled out his phone and studied this tax rebate, along with the pros and cons of leasing versus buying a car. Noah and I continued to enjoy the goats, the music, and the delicious drinks until my husband eventually emerged from his Geeky Researcher mode, gave me a playful nudge in the side, and asked, "Wanna go test drive one, Bari? Just for fun?" *Uh-huh*, I thought. *Just for fun, my foot!*

We left Noah with some dear friends at the cafe and sauntered over to the lot. I drove the Leaf around the neighborhood, and I couldn't help myself: I *loved* this car. My husband astutely pointed out the huge grin that simply wouldn't leave my face. Each time I checked in with my body, I noticed how good, relaxed, and exciting everything felt: the car, the dealership, the whole day.

When we returned from the test drive, my husband introduced me to the owner of the dealership: a bright-eyed, wonderfully laid-back man named Luke. As I looked around the lot and listened to my husband talk numbers with Luke, I appreciated how very un-dealership-like the place felt: there wasn't a high-pressured, schmaltzy sales tactic in sight. Of course, a big reason I was so relaxed was knowing that we weren't serious about buying a car *today*.

Yet as Forest and Luke dove into the pricing and financing discussion and I watched Forest calmly take in all the information, a little switch flipped inside me. Suddenly, I was almost hyperventilating. Our casual little fact-finding mission was rapidly turning into a real-deal, it-could-happen-today money decision.

We all have our "triggers" when it comes to money. Some people become overwhelmed when naming their fee or asking for a salary increase; others panic when they don't have enough information to make a sound money decision, as my husband did back on that beach in Santa Cruz when I pushed him to extend our vacation for a few days. For most of my life, my two biggest money triggers have been big purchases and quick money decisions. I like to be very deliberate and intentional about any money decision. I need to *feel* things in my body before knowing whether I can give a full "yes" to something, and sometimes this takes time. That's why I always try to give myself plenty of time when making money decisions, both in my personal and professional life. I'm also very intentional about not selling my products and programs with high pressure, gotta-buy-it-now tactics. The weight of a decision pushes on me all the harder when the ticket price is high, as it certainly was with that Nissan Leaf that summer day.

Forest and Luke did everything they possibly could to put me at ease. Luke reassured us that he loved these electric cars, and would certainly be getting more in, so if now wasn't the right time for us, we could simply return when we were ready. My husband suggested we talk about it outside the dealership. But by that point, I needed a little time and space alone so I could think, breathe, and settle back into my body.

"I'm going to the bathroom!" I announced.

Pro tip: the bathroom is a fabulous place to do a Body Check-In. I used to feel a little embarrassed about taking the time and space I needed in moments of anxiety or overwhelm to recenter and ground myself. Yet I've found that a trip to the bathroom is always socially acceptable. Over the years, I have released layer after layer of shame around taking time for myself in this way. There are so many situations in which a mindful, self-caring pause like this is helpful, and facing a big Money Decision is near the top of the list.

Some of my students take this pause even farther and use the H.A.L.T. questions, commonly cited in Alcoholics Anonymous-type programs, before entering any big money conversations. This stands for:

H Are you hungry?
A Are you angry?
L Are you lonely?
T Are you tired?

If you answer "yes" to one of the above, it's probably not the best time to make a money decision; if it's at all possible to give yourself a little more time, that might be very wise. These four factors are some of our most basic, fundamental human needs. When we're depleted in one or more of them, we're more prone to making bad decisions:

relapsing into an addiction, getting overwhelmed by anxiety, or making an unwise money decision. The "H.A.L.T." method has become a huge help for many people I know in avoiding money mistakes.

During those few moments in the dealership bathroom, I patiently gave myself the solitude and time I needed to come back home to myself and feel into the full range of everything I was experiencing, thinking, fearing, and hoping. I took a few deep breaths. I felt my feet firmly supported by the tile floor. I shimmied my shoulders and tuned into my pelvis, my heart, and finally my mind. After a few moments, I emerged from the bathroom with a plan.

A Thirty-Minute Conversation Four Years in the Making

Right then and there, in the middle of that car dealership that didn't quite feel like a car dealership, my husband and I had a full-on, spontaneous Money Date.

As you know by now, many of our Money Dates are planned in advance. We put them on the calendar, bring treats and spreadsheets, light a candle, and make a lovely, intimate mini-ritual out of it. But spur-of-the-moment, life-is-happening-right-now-so-let's-talk Money Dates are necessary too (if a bit more challenging). In this case, it turned out to be exactly what we needed.

By the end of our thirty minute Money Date, not only did Forest and I have a clear, confident decision, we also had a rock-solid and versatile framework for making all sorts of money decisions: spontaneous or planned, small or huge. Here's what we discussed:

SHORT-TERM MONEY GOALS

Things change. Time passes. Money and life unfold over time. This sounds simple enough, yet when it comes to making a money decision, it can be a real challenge to factor in the timing. That's why I decided we needed to think about the impact of this money decision over the short-term, mid-term, and long-term. Frankly, a clear "yes" on one of these levels might not mean a clear "yes" on the others. While many of the more complex money decisions we face won't check every box on the list, it's incredibly valuable to at least name and understand how they will affect us over each of these spans of time.

....

HOW TO MAKE A MONEY DECISION: BARI'S GO-TO FRAMEWORK

Consider five main factors:

1   The Numbers
Do you have enough money right now to make this purchase?
If not, is there some creative way you can cut other expenses or
bring in extra money to make up for it?

2   The Timing
Is now the right time for you to make this investment? Have you
been longing for this for some time now, or is it a spontaneous
desire? How does this decision intersect with this unique moment
of your life and Money Story?

3   The Value
Is this valuable to you? Consider both tangible and intangible
benefits. How would your life be different or better with these
benefits?

4   The Cost
What will happen if you *don't* make this purchase?

5   The Intention
Is this a self-loving decision? Are you ready to receive the full
value of this investment?

....

Right there in the dealership, we asked ourselves:

Do we have the cash flow for this, right now?

When we looked at the down payment needed for the car (once we
factored in the tax rebate), the answer was a clear "yes."

Will this stretch us in an uncomfortable way, right now?

We felt comfortable with the expense. Sometimes, in the past, we have said "yes" to expenses that we knew would push us into "Maximum Lockdown Mode," our version of tightening our belts to the extreme. While sometimes this is a necessity, it's always preferable to make an informed, lucid decision around this.

MID-TERM MONEY GOALS

There's certainly no hard-and-fast definition for "mid-term": it might mean the next six months or five years, depending on a multitude of financial and lifestyle considerations. For the Leaf decision, Forest and I defined "mid-term" as the next two years. This was a manageable timeframe for us to consider, given what we knew about our income and expenses at the time.

We asked ourselves:

> How does this fit in with our cash flow and life plan for the next two years?

Thanks to our regular Money Dates, we already had a good sense of our life and money goals for this timeframe. We had recently chosen to re-sign a two-year lease on our lovely rental house to lock in a tiny rent increase. Plus, we were just about to pay off our business debt, and knew this would free up more cash flow in the next few months.

LONG-TERM MONEY AND LIFE GOALS

We considered the questions:

> Where are we, right now, in the grand scheme of our lives?

> Where are we heading?

> Does this purchase contribute to our dream, or detract from it?

We have long loved the idea of living in an Earthship: a home that produces all the water, heat, cooling, and food we need—including electricity from the sun for our electric car. So, in one sense, purchasing the Leaf was fully aligned with this big dream; the Leaf would literally be parked *inside* the bigger dream, in the garage. The larger dream of buying that house was going to require so much time and money, this purchase wouldn't impact or postpone our big dream significantly. Also, we could see that our immediate and mid-term needs, desires, and values, were just as important as our big goals: it's important to us to live comfortably and joyfully, here and now, even as we work toward bigger dreams.

VALUES

Remember all of that values inventorying, spending plan categorizing, and re-naming we did in the Values-Based Bookkeeping practice? Every money decision you encounter is an opportunity to translate that work from the abstract into the literal, to consider how well a particular purchase aligns with what truly matters to you, and to put your values into action.

In the case of the electric car, the answer to this question was a hearty, *yes*! This purchase was completely aligned with our commitment to reduce our ecological footprint in big, small, and creative ways. And, it also contributed to another core value of ours: family fun. The idea of plugging in our car at solar-powered charging stations around town, using this as a teaching opportunity for our son, sounded like a fabulous time to us.

NEEDS, WANTS, AND DESIRES

Finally, we considered which of the three "lifestyle tiers" this purchase might fall under. Was it Basic Needs, Comfortable, or Ultimate, for us, in that particular moment of our lives? Would we call it a need, a want, or a desire? The answer wasn't exactly clear-cut.

While we had enjoyed being a one-car family for seven years, I had noticed the increasing toll biking was taking on my husband. Our desires for safety, warmth, and convenience nudged this purchase out of the Ultimate, "wouldn't it be nice someday" tier into the stronger need/ want zone of our Comfortable tier.

This lifestyle consideration felt like the final piece of the puzzle for our Leaf decision. Like so many money decisions, this one was truly a case where we couldn't just talk about the numbers and cash flow: it was about so very, very much more than that. It was about our dreams and goals, our values, our comfort, and our day-to-day well-being.

The Three Pots: Balancing Money, Time, and Energy

One of my wise students created her own method for considering all of these factors in a money decision, which she calls "The Three Pots." It's a wonderful alternative framework for making sound money decisions that takes into account numbers *and* important lifestyle factors—especially when combined with a Three-Tier Money Map.

Annie had been mostly bedridden for close to two months due to severe respiratory challenges and knee surgery. One day, she looked up from her recovery bed to see her husband, Jack, tackling the mountain of dishes in the sink, his face betraying deep exhaustion. He turned off the water, leaned on the edge of the sink, and took a moment to catch his breath, his eyes welling with tears. Annie could tell that Jack was having one of his "low days," when his autoimmune condition hit him a little harder. Jack suffered from chronic fatigue; on a good day, he could make it to his office job and still have energy for family dinner—yet on a bad day (and there were many of them), he could barely get out of bed.

Because of Annie's knee surgery recovery, Jack had done the lion's share of the housework for the past several months, and it was taking a big toll on him. Even before this latest round of illnesses, housework had been a constant struggle in their relationship. Annie *hated* cleaning: not only did her respiratory problems make it physically challenging, it also triggered old, painful memories of being punished as a child. While it was draining for Jack, as well, it was important for him to live in a clean home: mess and dirt only made him feel more stressed and depleted. The Great Cleaning Struggle felt like a classic, damned-if-you-do, damned-if-you-don't conundrum.

Watching Jack struggle to finish the dishes, Annie knew that something had to change, quickly. So that evening, at their weekly Money Date, she shared a possible solution she'd been mulling over for the past few weeks—along with a new way to think about their money/time/energy balancing act.

Annie and Jack were living at the low end of their "Comfortable" lifestyle tier. But as two people with chronic health issues, energy was perhaps an even more precious resource than money. Additionally, like many people, time was a big factor in many of their spending decisions. Jack worked a full-time job and even when he had the energy to run errands or clean, sometimes he simply didn't have the time.

As Annie considered the resources they had and how they could best leverage them, she had an image of three pots, filled to various levels. One pot represented the *money* she and Jack had at hand, the second, their *energy*, and the third, their *time*. The level of each of the pots fluctuated, somewhat independently of the other two. On any given day (or week or month), they might have very little money, but a little extra time and energy; sometimes, their "money pot" was fuller, but they were both exhausted; other times, all three pots might be dangerously low.

Annie realized that they had already been making decisions based on these three pots. Some evenings, when they were both too exhausted to cook, they dipped into the "money pot" and treated themselves to dinner from their favorite Thai restaurant, delivered straight to their door. Other times, when they had a little extra energy, they kept their "money pot" from dipping any lower by putting forth the effort to go to the discounted grocery store and farmer's market, both a long drive from their home. Annie had a sense that by becoming even more conscious and intentional about their "three pots," they could make some truly sound money decisions that would respect the demands on their time and energy, as well.

She decided to apply the "three pots" analysis to their house-cleaning conundrum. At that particular moment in their marriage, Annie and Jack's "energy pot" was dangerously low, too low to do the house cleaning they needed. Yet their "money pot" was at a more comfortable level and just might afford them a house cleaner. Annie spent some time researching house cleaning companies and found one she knew Jack would love. They were locally owned, used eco-friendly products, and seemed very friendly—just the sort of people who could bring some emotional brightness into their home, as well. She did some quick math and realized they could afford to hire the "house sparklers" once a week without stretching themselves too thin, if they cut back on dinners out. Plus, if they weren't expending so much energy cleaning, they would have more energy available for cooking nutritious, cost-effective meals at home.

Jack loved the idea, and when he saw that they truly could afford it, he eagerly agreed. After the very first visit from the "house sparklers," Jack and Annie noticed a significant up-tick in their energy and decrease in their stress levels. They bickered less about the state of their home, and both had a little more energy *and* time for things that truly brought them joy and restored their energy, like a Saturday picnic in the park or a luxurious afternoon at a coffee shop.

After about three months of having the cleaners visit their home every week, Annie and Jack found their money pot getting a little low—but their energy levels had perked back up. They went down to having the cleaners visit twice a month, and both of them contributed to the chores a bit more in between. By monitoring the levels of their "three pots," Jack and Annie had found a beautiful way to dance with their Money Map—and make smart spending decisions on the fly.

Each of the three pots fill and empty with the shifting, evolving dimensions of their lives. This framework un-shamed Jack and Annie around many of the choices they were making—expenses that they wouldn't need to make if their health were better, for example. Noting how each of the three pots drained and became replenished over time also helped them tune into and honor the ever-shifting, rhythmic nature of their lives. Finally, this approach to money decisions provided them with opportunities for celebration; each time they found themselves low in one "pot," they always found themselves more resourced in another, and took a moment to be thankful for the resource they did have.

· · · · ·

After our spontaneous Money Date at the car dealership, Forest and I emerged crystal-clear about our money decision: the pros, the cons, and what ultimately felt best to both of us. We signed the papers and left with our new electric car, feeling ecstatic not only with the car

....

HOW TO MAKE A MONEY DECISION:
THE THREE POTS METHOD

1   Check in with yourself and your three pots. How full are your
    resources, right now, in terms of Money, Energy, and Time?
    What pot is full? What pot is running low?

2   Will this money decision help replenish a pot that is running
    low? Will it further deplete a pot that is already low?

3   Check in with your heart, your gut, and finally your mind.
    What truly feels right to you, here?

4   Trust the answers you get. Release any shame that arises
    (physically shake it off, it that works for you). Celebrate your-
    self for taking the time to make such a wise, well-informed
    decision. Enjoy the result of your decision.

There is no One Right Way to make a money decision: we
all must create our *own* criteria, reflecting and honoring what
matters most to us, at each point in our lives. Annie came up with
the Three Pots method because it made sense to her, but another
couple might consider three different pots when making a money
decision, such as career, spirit, and children. Should Jack and
Annie suddenly find themselves at their Basic Needs or Ultimate
lifestyle tier instead of Comfortable, they might need to come up
with a whole new set of factors to consider as well.

....

but with the entire process of deciding to buy it. As we drove the car
home, our son waved triumphant fists in the air, shouting, "Wahoo!
Wahoo!" While he hadn't seen the complex decision process behind
our purchase, he could tell that something big and wonderful had just
happened in our little family.

CHAPTER 15

solving money koans

"Be patient toward all that is unsolved in your heart and try to love the *questions themselves* like locked rooms and like books that are written in a very foreign tongue. Do not now seek the answers, which cannot be given you because you would not be able to live them. And the point is, to live everything. *Live* the questions now. Perhaps you will gradually, without noticing it, live along some distant day into the answer." —*Rainer Maria Rilke*[23]

SOME MONEY DECISIONS have no quick and easy solutions, no matter how many spreadsheets and maps and lists we make. How can I earn the money I need to have the life I want *and* work little enough to have the life I want? How can I release this primal anxiety around enoughness? How can I get from here to there when I'm stuck?

"Money Koan" is the term I use to describe those big, complex questions and challenges: those nuts that take some time to crack. Whether you're longing to release a deeply ingrained money belief or struggling to break through a money ceiling, sometimes it can be helpful to reframe the questions, themselves, as koans.

The concept of a *koan* comes from the Zen Buddhist tradition, where it's used to describe a question or paradox to be meditated upon (sometimes for years) to lead the practitioner into a vaster place within

---

23 Rainer Maria Rilke. *Letters to a Young Poet*, trans. M. D. Herter Norton (New York: W. W. Norton & Company, 1934), 35.

themselves, beyond their ordinary, rational mind. A koan is a bit like a riddle—except it transforms *you* into the answer. So long, that is, as you sit with it patiently, as Rilke suggests.

I think we all have money koans to work on and solve at different points in our life. These are questions and conundrums that cannot be ignored nor rushed, and that often we can not solve alone. When we sit with a money koan long enough, we can discover (or create) new solutions, new possibilities, and new ways to do things around money, even when stress is high or things seem impossible.

Home: A Personal Money Koan Story

Some money koans take years to solve: my husband and I "sat" with the koan of "home" for three years before solving it this year. It's no surprise that housing was such a big, complex money issue; a place to live is both a basic physical need *and* a fundamental emotional need. It's also an extremely significant financial matter: most people in the United States spend more money on housing than on any other single expense. And many people struggle to afford even basic shelter, let alone a home that nourishes them on an emotional level.

In my own life, I have always been fortunate enough to have a warm, dry, safe place to live, and I feel incredibly grateful for this. In my younger days, I was happy to live in an apartment with roommates, on a kibbutz in Israel, or in that ridiculously small, 400-square-foot cottage with Forest in Northern California. Yet as my husband and I have grown a little older, created our own businesses (run mostly from home), and become parents to our little Noah, finding a place to live that we can afford *and* that feels like home has become one of our biggest money koans.

While many of my friends and colleagues bought their first homes in their twenties and early thirties, my husband and I put off buying a house until our forties. We simply had other financial priorities, including Montessori schooling for our son and weathering the inevitable financial ups and downs of being a dual-entrepreneur family. Plus, we were quite happy renting our hundred-year-old Victorian home, right at the foot of my favorite mountain in Boulder (this made my daily hike, one of my most important self-care practices, very doable). I sometimes felt a twinge of money shame when I compared myself to all the homeowners in our circle of peers, but for the most part, I knew Forest and I were making the right choice for our little family, at that point in our life-and-money journey together.

Still, when I reflected on my ultimate lifestyle dream, it always included our little family owning a bit of land near Boulder to build an Earthship—a super sustainable, off-the-grid home. We'd fallen in love with these creative, ultra-eco-friendly homes over several vacations spent in one in New Mexico. They were the tangible marriage of my husband's passion for all things eco-friendly and my love of the beautiful and unique. What started as a soft whisper of a dream grew, over the course of three years and countless conversations and research, into a full-blown goal. Or, more accurately, a money koan.

We knew we wanted to make the Earthship happen, but it felt like a riddle we couldn't solve. How would we come up with the money to build the house, let alone to buy the land to build it on? Eventually, after talking about the Earthship dream from every possible angle, doing research on building codes, and getting quotes for land, we realized that we would need to take an intermediate step: buying a house or townhome in Boulder. This would be a more affordable way to get into the pricey Boulder real estate market; plus, our house would surely appreciate enough over a few years to help us achieve our Earthship dream. This steppingstone goal felt good, but only led us to the heart of our big money koan: How were we going to buy a home in the crazy-fast, competitive, expansive Boulder market?

As we continued to sit with this riddle, I watched my mind try to solve it. Some old, worn, unhelpful tapes played themselves in my head: *there's nothing close to our price range that we will actually like; only folks with family money or big successes in the tech world can afford homes in Boulder; we'll be outbid as soon as we make an offer.* But thankfully, I had enough experience with money shame and seemingly unsolvable riddles that I stuck with the money koan. I noticed those thoughts, felt those feelings, took pauses when I needed to . . . and kept moving forward. In our weekly Money Dates, Forest and I discussed everything related to this money koan, from our emotions and values to a host of practical considerations and compromises.

Forest and I considered moving somewhere other than Boulder that would be more affordable, and tried and tried to find somewhere else that could offer us a similar constellation of community, lifestyle, landscape, culture, and environmental factors. But our hearts kept leading us back to Boulder. It's our home, and we wouldn't have wanted to build our dream anywhere else. We also discussed how important building or buying a home was, where it fit in our values and priorities at the moment, and how it aligned with this phase of our lives. We searched for houses and land online for a solid year. Forest tracked homes in our price range and watched how fast they sold, what they sold for, and studied the Boulder real estate scene so we'd be prepared if we ever figured out how to get all the pieces in place to buy a home here. Meanwhile, we kept growing our business revenue—but the longer we waited, the more expensive home prices became. We began to worry that we might not break into the market before home prices climbed too far out of our reach.

Then our business consultant, Sara, whom we had hired a few months earlier to do some branding and marketing, sent us an email out of the blue: "I'm not sure if you're ready for this right now, but I think you should go look at this house."

During our very first meeting with Sara, she had asked us what our big dream was in life. We shared with her our Earthship dream, along with the steppingstone dream of buying a house in Boulder. Then it was as if she took that vision of ours, placed it in her magician's cauldron, and began stirring the pot. Three months later, she sent us that email about a house she thought would be perfect for us. And as soon as I walked in the front door, I had a feeling I'd never had before. It was as if the house itself was talking to me: *This is it. You are home.*

We met with Sara's trusted realtor, and hit it off immediately (she was familiar with my first money mentor, Tamara Slayton—a big, beautiful coincidence for me). Next, we went to a great credit union and met with a lender who understood the special challenges that self-employed entrepreneurs face when trying to get approved for a loan.

As the lender asked us incredibly direct and sensitive questions about our money, Forest and I found ourselves answering simultaneously, over and over again. All our regular Money Dates (solo, as a couple, and for our business) had prepared us for this. We had all of our information readily available and without surprises, from our net income, our bank statements, several years of tax returns, and credit scores, to our savings accounts and how much we could afford for a down payment. The lender actually told us, "I can't believe how honest and comfortable you two are about all this money stuff. That's really helpful to me—but it's also rare."

Within a few hours of meeting with the lender, we got the call: we were preapproved for a loan. That same day, we made an offer to the seller, complete with a family selfie taken in front of the house and a personal note explaining how much we loved the house. Our offer was accepted the very next morning. The entire experience, from first seeing the home to having our offer accepted, happened within a whirlwind, 36-hour period. The final pages of this book were written in my very first and very wonderful home.

As I unpack boxes in our new home, the balcony door open and the view of my beloved Mount Sanitas in the distance, I realize that this money work has not only changed my relationship with money—it has changed *me*. This is true in practical ways, such as having clear credit scores and tax returns. But it is also true in deeper, quieter, more internal ways, such as the calm and confidence I felt making this huge money decision, and the presence and gratitude I feel in this very moment, settling into my new home with my family.

. . . . .

There are so many types and flavors and sizes of money koans we can sit with and solve along our life-and-money journeys. We can face big, important money koans in every "money area" (earning, spending, saving, debt repayment, and giving). Some of these take months or years to solve, like my little family's decision to buy our first home. Some feel clear to us, in an instant, yet take a little time for others to understand—like the decision Forest and I made to stay on that beach in Santa Cruz a few more healing days. How to break through a money ceiling is a common koan, as is striking the right balance between work and leisure.

Sometimes, solving a money koan takes grieving, forgiving, and letting go of dreams. Sometimes, it asks us to recognize new dreams, just waiting to be born through us. Compromises that leave us feeling icky, anxious, and unsettled are often signs that we have not fully cracked the nut of our money koans. Many money koans are "tough luck miracles," which confound us for years before we recognize, in a flash of inspiration, the solution. Sometimes, we don't even realize we *have* a money koan until we start doing the work, get brave, and take a hard look at our numbers. Often, we can *feel* the solution to a money koan before our minds understand what it really looks like; other times, we *know* what we must do, but don't fully understand *why* for a long while. While money koans don't always feel welcome, they are always an opportunity for growth—if we seize them.

. . . . .

While I wish you every success in your money and your life, engaging with this money work will support you even when you don't get the answer or result you wish for. As you sit with your money koans, you may hit a brick wall and get stuck: you might receive a "no" on that loan application, lose your job, or receive any number of other troubling financial news. In challenging moments like those, please return to the Money Healing work, and return to this concept of "money koans." In the thick of my more difficult financial riddles and tough times, simply relating to my circumstances in this way, as koans, has helped me find some calm, some hope, and some trust that, even if I don't have the answers right now, they will come. Money koans require patience, persistence, and focus. Here, all of our hard work, intention, and a little magic swirl together, until they finally combust in a flash of insight and fresh possibility.

....

FOUR WAYS TO WORK WITH A MONEY KOAN

"Some of life's questions, conflicts, and problems are so big, so deep, so complex, that we cannot simply solve them. These are invitations into transformation. These are moments when life is calling us to expand. Here, our task is to soften, open, and allow these 'problems' to solve us." — *Rob McNamara*

1   MAKE YOUR KOANS LIVING QUESTIONS.

Write them down.
Ask them over and over.
Live them, breathe them, take them on walks.
Set the clear intention to solve them.
Stay with the questions.
The answers will come.

2   ACCESS YOUR WILD, CREATIVE MIND.

Allow your rational mind to relax a bit.
Brainstorm as many different ways as possible to solve your
money koan.
Let yourself dream, vision, and get wildly creative.

3   HOW DOES YOUR MONEY KOAN FIT INTO YOUR THREE-TIER MONEY MAP?

What phase of life are you in, right now? Basic Needs,
Comfortable, or Ultimate lifestyle?
How does your current money koan-riddle-challenge fit within
your values and priorities right now?
How will each of the solutions you come up with affect your lifestyle level right now, or how soon you'll reach the next level
you want to reach?

continued

4   TALK ABOUT YOUR KOAN WITH FRIENDS.

In traditional Zen koan practice, you don't talk about your current koan with your friends. You only talk about it with your teacher, but they don't exactly help you solve it, either: you must solve it on your own, because that's the only way the deeper spiritual insights will stick with you. With money koans, though, talking them through with good listeners (friends, family, your partner, or a financial professional) is a great way to get insight. If it feels good to you, discuss your money koan with others: the answer may come from an unexpected source.

5   STAY WITH IT.

Be as patient as you can, without losing focus and determination.
    Many money koans take a long time to solve.
Don't give up.
Keep returning to a practice of trust, patience, and gratitude.
Keep working on your koan, internally and externally. Keep with
    it. Keep working these practices, over and over, patiently and
    gently, determined and trusting.
Allow the question to transform *you*. Stay present until a new
    solution emerges.

your money legacy

THE HOSPITAL ROOM was quiet, the hush broken only by the hypnotic *beep beep* of my father's heart monitor. The lights were soothingly dim, though I could glimpse the brilliant white snow out of the window, blanketing Madison in silence. Nurses and doctors moved slowly, meditatively, through the ICU, and I squeezed my father's hand again, ever so gently, careful not to disturb the IV in his vein. My father, who had always been such a strong, stoic figure, was now utterly vulnerable.

Earlier that day, I'd received the phone call. My mother, her voice cracking, told me that my father had suffered a severe stroke, and they weren't sure whether he would live. By what felt like miraculous timing, I was only a five-hour drive away from my parents, celebrating Christmas with my husband's family in St. Louis. I packed my overnight bag and, with quick and emotional goodbyes to my family, drove straight to Wisconsin.

When I arrived, my father was conscious. He knew I was there. I held his hand, and he held mine back. I stayed by his side that whole night in the ICU. And throughout that long night, listening to that *beep beep* as doctors and nurses shuffled in and out of my father's room, sitting there, I had a lot of time to think, to remember, to pray, and to feel.

We plan our lives like crazy, and then . . . life happens. The unexpected, the tragic, and the wonderful, too. It is often in those unexpected moments that we transform. That night in the ICU with my father and the days that followed felt like a rite of passage: one of those sacred moments that brings us face-to-face with what truly matters. For me, this is: love, family, and health, connecting with one another, and the simple sacrament of holding a loved one's hand. My years of professional training as a therapist and hospice worker had prepared me to offer tender, clear-headed support to my mother during that difficult time. Yet within myself, I could also feel deep, emotional stirrings. My whole relationship with my father was being transformed.

Before his stroke, my father was an intense, Chicago-tough entrepreneur. My whole life, he had focused intently on business, work, and money. He was proud of my own entrepreneurial path, but we didn't always agree with each other's business values. I fought to carve my own path, in life and in money, knowing I needed it to include a creativity, intuition, grace, and gentleness that hadn't been prioritized in my father's life-and-money relationship.

All of this hard stuff came up for me during that week in the ICU. I held my father's hand for days, as wave after wave of grief, fear, and love passed through me. And each time one of those tough memories, harsh judgments, or past fights bubbled up, it dissolved in forgiveness and love. None of that mattered any more. I simply loved my father, held his hand, and loved him some more. In those few days, I made peace with what had defined my father and challenged me my entire life. I felt deeply that his legacy was living in me, and wondered what legacy I would eventually leave.

The Paradox of Legacy

Legacy is paradoxical. It is what we receive and what we leave behind. Like Janus, the Roman god of beginnings and endings, legacy simultaneously looks to the past and to the future. On the one hand, it is our connection to our roots and all the ways our parents and ancestors continue living, through us. We have all received gifts from those who came before us: some tangible (money, inheritance, or property), and some intangible (beliefs, attitudes, wisdom, and strength). We have also all received suffering: forced migration, exile, unpaid debts, unhelpful beliefs, wounds, and traumas. Our legacy includes all the gifts *and* challenges bestowed upon us by our family, our ancestors, and our culture.

Yet legacy also refers to the future and what we will leave behind after we are gone. All of the tangible and intangible assets, values, and gifts we will pass on to our children (if we have them) and our community and society at large. Sometimes, this includes unhealed suffering, unconscious patterns, and pain. To consider our legacy, then, is to honor and aspire, to be aware of our lineage and consciously nurture its growing branches. This is incredibly poignant territory, full of reverence, brave honesty, and certainly hope.

As I held my father's hand in that ICU room the days following his stroke, I considered what he would leave behind: the businesses he created and grew, the money he may pass on, the passion and drive he had for his work, and the smarts he'd passed down to my siblings and myself. I thought of all the countless lives he had touched—for better and for worse, in big ways and small. I also thought about his money legacy.

A "Money Legacy" is everything you pass on that's related to money, including how you lived your life. It's the wealth you accumulate during your life, your attitudes about money, and everything that money meant to you. A Money Legacy is how your personal Money Story lives on after you die. Just like a Money Story, your legacy has at least three levels:

The Practical Level. Any cash, properties, trusts, or other assets (or sometimes liabilities) left behind.

The Mental-Emotional Level. Any attitudes or practices modeled or taught to others about money, as well as beliefs about work, value, and the vast spectrum of other concepts intertwined with money.

The Spiritual Level. The profound beliefs about the "big picture" of our place in the universe and how money ties into this. This includes our relationship to trust (or mistrust), thriving, and generosity (or scarcity).

Reflecting on the Money Legacy we have received from our ancestors entails both honoring the positive aspects of these three levels and
unraveling the complicated challenges that may accompany them. We
can receive huge gifts. And we can also inherit deep wounds that need
to be acknowledged, un-shamed, and healed.

On the practical level, my father would leave behind some money,
properties, and investments from his business, which would go to my
mother. On the emotional level, for me, my father had taught me the
value of hard work. From a young age, I had watched him create and
grow his business. He had modeled the chutzpah it takes to work for
yourself as an entrepreneur: to take risk after risk and create something out of nothing. And though my father rarely talked to me directly
about money, I could tell that he enjoyed making money, managing it,
spending it, and sharing it. He taught me how to work *and* enjoy the
fruits of my labor.

Of course, the Money Legacy I have inherited comes from many
more people and sources than my father. My mother was thrifty in
many ways (and still uses coupons), which provided a nice balance to my
father, who enjoyed spending more. Yet my mother never hesitated to
spend money supporting my interests, such as paying for dance classes.
I didn't realize until my early thirties that the women in my lineage had
been the money trackers for generations before me. My mother was
the behind-the-scenes money person in the business my father started,
and by the time I learned QuickBooks in my thirties, she had already
used it for years. My grandmother before her had carefully tracked the
cash flowing in and out of her family's lives, too. Despite my utter lack
of financial education or training from my family, I unknowingly lived
out this aspect of my Money Legacy when I began working as a bookkeeper in my early thirties, and have continued to deepen and expand
it through my own money-related teachings and business.

Sometimes legacies are consciously, even intentionally, carried on
and lived out. Yet other times, they flow in deeper waters, in our col-
lective and individual unconsciousness, and spring forth in unknown
or surprising ways. Just as I never knew part of my matrilineal Money
Legacy was bookkeeping, it also took me a long time to realize that

I had inherited my father's entrepreneurial spirit. As a young adult, I didn't know what I wanted to do with my life, and didn't realize entrepreneurship was even an option for me until I hit thirty-two. This spirit of professional and financial freedom, creativity, and choice is certainly something I'd like to pass on to others, but it's only one part of the Money Legacy I hope to leave.

Creating Your Money Legacy

I squeezed my father's hand once more before venturing into the dimly lit hallway, passing the nurse's station and the blurry cascade of white coats and blue paper footies doing their silent dance through the ICU. I found a secluded corner and, as I called my husband, I became aware of just how dry my mouth was. I reported the facts of my father's situation: the severity of the stroke, his current condition, and the prognosis. Forest listened and loved and listened some more. Then I talked to my son; he was enjoying his Christmas visit with his grandparents, and told me how excited he was to track Santa by radar that night. He also strummed his guitar and sang me the "Get Well Soon" song he had written for his Grandpa Jeff.

"Mama, when will you be back?" he wanted to know. I explained to him that his Grandpa was very sick, and I was there to take care of him, and I would be back just as soon as I could. I spoke to him as honestly as I could, telling him what I felt was appropriate for his age. Forest and I have always tried to be as honest with Noah as possible, about emotions, life, and, yes, money: this is part of the legacy we want to leave him.

While my father taught me a lot about money, most of it was in indirect and circumstantial ways. We never sat down for direct, clear money teachings. Forest and I both want to speak directly and honestly with Noah about money, and are still feeling out, day by day, what attitudes, beliefs, and practices we want to share with him about money.

From the time he was three, we started giving Noah age-appropriate money lessons. At the toy store, we would acknowledge and honor his desire to Buy All the Toys, without needing to indulge it: we taught him to make a big wish list, instead. When he wanted *two* pairs of new sneakers, we helped him imagine which pair he would really love, for a long time—this was our way of helping him make a good spending decision. We have also given him small paid "jobs," so he can start feeling empowered about earning and spending. Throughout it all, I have taught him to check in with his body, slow down, take a fuller breath, and express his feelings. This child-sized version of a Body Check-In is a life-and-money tool we have used with Noah since he was very little, and I hope it serves him for the rest of his life.

When he was six and a half, we felt he was ready for a little teaching on savings, focused on the small weekly allowance we give him. We pointed out that he was welcome to spend that money any way he likes (which was usually immediately, on small toys), but that if he could save it until his seventh birthday, we would match it, so it would double and he could buy one of those big Lego sets he had been drooling over for so long. He loved the idea, and soon, both sets of grandparents jumped on this bandwagon, pledging to match his savings, as well. Motivated by the awesome power of Legos, he successfully saved his weekly allowance for six months (an eternity for a child that age) and, thanks to the grandparent-matching programs, quadrupled it. Our next step, now that he is seven, is taking him to the credit union, where he will open his very own bank account before buying those exalted Lego sets. It took me *years* to learn to save money, so I am thrilled to pass on this aspect of a Money Legacy to Noah so directly and early on.

Whether we're conscious of it or not—and whether we are thinking about our own children, future generations of the whole human family, or the entire Earth, we all leave a Money Legacy behind. As we know, this entails literal money, property, or even debt. For the friends and family around us, it also includes our attitudes and philosophies about money, work, value, and trust.

When considering the Money Legacy we'd like to leave, we zoom out to the very largest view of our Money Story and the broadest scope of our Money Map. We look into the past at the legacy we've inherited; we look at how we've evolved and changed the money attitudes we've received; and we take the time to name what's truly, wildly important to us: what's so vital, we want to pass it on to that which continues.

SQUIRRELS AND FOOD PANTRIES

When Angela, a freelance writer in her thirties, reflected on the Money Legacy she wanted to create, she thought immediately of her Grandpa Dale. Dale grew up in rural Missouri during the Depression. Putting food on the family table was a daily struggle, and by the age of nine, Dale went hunting with his rifle almost every day, bringing home squirrels and rabbits for dinner. His family scrimped and saved for everything they had and truly lived by the World War II slogan, "Use it up, wear it out, make it do, or do without."

After becoming the first in his family to attend college (and eventually becoming the well-respected pastor of a large congregation), Dale broke free from the financial hardship of his youth and achieved a comfortable lifestyle later in life. Yet he never changed his frugal ways. If holes appeared in his socks, he asked his wife to patch them; he bought groceries at the cheapest discount store he could find; and he never threw away anything that could be repaired. He felt incredibly fortunate for every dollar, possession, and meal he had, and sought to be the best steward of his earnings he could possibly be. For Dale, this meant sharing as much as he possibly could with others—especially those in need.

Dale created a thriving food pantry at his church, and while other pastors warned him to watch out for "scammers," he was resolute. "I will not risk a single child going hungry," he proclaimed. No one was ever turned away from Dale's food pantry, and he often invited people in need to his house for a warm meal (or ten). Later, he cofounded a city-wide food bank. Today, many years after his death, Operation Food Search has grown into the largest provider of food in the region, feeding more than 190,000 people each month, one third of whom are children. Dale's grandchildren and great-grandchildren volunteer there in honor of his name. Angela's own attitudes about money and her hopes for her own Money Legacy are directly influenced by her Grandpa. "He loved to say, 'We're all here to prop each other up on the leaning side,'" she said. "I might not leave behind vast sums of wealth, but I hope that my legacy can carry on some of his generous spirit."

INHERITING WEALTH, CONSCIOUSLY

By the time he reached his early fifties, Elliott, a single father to three young children, had amassed several million dollars thanks to his successful online businesses and some smart investing. As his sixties began looming on the horizon, Elliott began thinking seriously about how his wealth could support his children after his death.

Leaving behind emotional, spiritual, and financial resources for those who survive us can help empower future generations to create the lives they most want. Yet the sad truth is, distributing wealth after a death is often poorly planned, if at all. I've heard countless, heart-wrenching stories about the stickiness that can arise when a wealthy parent, family member, or friend dies. Far too often, a *financial* trust contains no *real* trust. What could be a beautiful Money Legacy gets soured by unconsciousness, poor planning, and general emotional wonkiness.

Mindful of all of this, and wanting to truly empower his children financially and emotionally, Elliot reached out to an estate planner who specializes in helping families pass on their Money Legacies in a more positive, conscious way. She helped him create a comprehensive plan to pass on both his wealth and the wisdom to direct it well. He created a step-by-step plan to entrust more and more fiscal responsibility to his children as they grew, so they would have excellent money management skills by the time they were adults. He made sure they were involved in his charitable ventures, instilling generosity and a commitment to philanthropy in them. And he established structures that required his children to work as a team as they directed funds, because he knew inheriting great wealth can leave us prone to isolation. Finally, the estate planner helped Elliott record a "family legacy interview" to be viewed after his death: a joyful retelling of his life story, memories of his children, and the life lessons he most wanted to pass on to them. By the time he completed his estate planning process, Elliott felt confident that his children would receive the wealth he most wanted to pass on to them—financial *and* emotional—in ways that would honor the gravity of this legacy and support them in bringing their own, unique visions to life. As his wonderful estate planner, Martha Hartney, shared with me,

When people plan their estate—and plan consciously—they have a better shot at leaving their children in a place where their resources can be leveraged for something good. Conscious estate planning is about resourcing the next generation's vision for the future, harnessing the power of human and financial capital, and nurturing each individual's vision and values.

Putting money in stocks and bonds may compound and preserve assets. But great wealth comes from investing in humanity, in each person's particular vision and unique gift. The families I know who really leverage their wealth recognize their children as visionaries. We should see each family member as our treasure—this is what we're investing in.

A LIVING LEGACY

Vicky wanted something different—not just to leave behind, but to live, now. For a few years, she had felt a little stuck: her private life-coaching business no longer felt fulfilling, but she kept working at it to keep current on her monthly debt payments and to afford her expensive life-style, living on a houseboat in Vancouver, British Columbia. Vicky was an independent-minded woman in her sixties, but felt trapped on a financial treadmill and she was ready to find a way off.

Some people make big life changes gradually—but for Vicky, all signs were pointing to a drastic overhaul. She sold her houseboat (which allowed her to pay off her debts and create some savings), temporarily cut back on her coaching business, and moved to her native New Zealand. She bought a bus to travel and live out of, and embraced a radically new and simple lifestyle. She had done the hard work of inventorying her values, and gotten brave enough to change *everything* to live (and spend) according to them. She valued freedom, so she adored exploring the countryside in her bus, coming and going as she pleased. She valued community, so she connected with a cohousing group full of like-minded folks and made sure to regularly visit her family. She valued sustainability, so she connected with a local eco-village, and is considering joining them someday soon, building straw-bale homes and tiny houses, growing fruits and veggies and wine, and continuing to live as simply as she can.

During this transition, Vicky started tracking her spending for the first time in her life and created her Three-Tier Money Map. Much to her surprise, she found herself living just barely shy of her "Ultimate" lifestyle tier. Even though she was no longer earning much money (she was mostly living on her savings), she felt more wealthy than ever before. As she recently shared with me,

> I used to feel envious of people who had a lot of money, but I don't anymore. Something major has shifted within me: I have finally connected to my values of freedom, simplicity, curiosity, and saving the planet's resources. Now that I'm living so simply and don't have that financial pressure anymore, I have the ultimate freedom to listen to what's really true for me. Even though I'm living so simply, I never feel deprived: I'm living my values, by choice. I'm happier than I have ever been.

Vicky's unique "retirement" is such an inspiring money-and-life legacy. As her story illustrates, so often, leaving behind a legacy means being willing to do something different, *now*. It means writing a new story, making brave choices, and consciously impacting the world and future generations, through our actions here and now. Sometimes, this means inventorying inherited beliefs and patterns around money and doing the deep inner work to release those that no longer serve us, so they don't carry on to future generations. Sometimes, it means paying off debt or creating wealth, to secure our children's financial security. But most importantly of all, it means being conscious and intentional about the life and money choices we live and create, ourselves, each and every day. Perhaps the most powerful way we can serve those who come after us is to create our own happiness, here and now.

My Own Money Legacy: Looking Forward

After several intense, touch-and-go weeks in the hospital, my father recovered enough from his stroke to be discharged. Though he was told he might never walk or talk again, after a tremendous amount of work, he's now doing both. Thanks to my father's retirement planning (and my mother's strict spending plans), they have enough savings to pay for this phase of their lives. My father and mother have moved into a retirement community, which they both love; she gets to play mahjong and ping pong everyday, and they're both much closer to their grandchildren. After his brush with death, my father is still strong, yet also far gentler and more loving than ever before. He and my mother have entered a sweet new phase of their lives together that is more beautiful than I could have imagined. And holding his hand for those days in the ICU has forever shifted my relationship with my father. I now appreciate him, his work ethic, his strength, and everything he brought to my life in a new, far deeper way.

One of the surprising twists of this new chapter in my parents' lives is how it has shifted my mother's relationship with money. Before my father's stroke, he took care of all the big money decisions in the marriage and in his business. While she was the tracker, he was the negotiator, the decider, and the buyer. But now, at sixty-eight, my mother has taken on all of this "money stuff" for the first time. She refinanced and then sold their house, sold one of their rental properties, and bought a car, in addition to working out all of the financial ins and outs with the hospital and insurance companies. Late in life, she has rapidly become an absolute financial superstar. She's a living, breathing example of how we all have the power to shift our relationship to money—and consciously create or even recreate our Money Legacy—at any age, at any moment.

Coming Full Circle

A short while after those intense nights in the ICU with my father, I took my questions about my own Money Legacy on my daily hike up the mountain. I consider my hikes a moving meditation, a self-care practice where I reconnect with myself and everything greater than me as I listen to the crunching leaves, behold the soaring pines, and feel the steady, strong, vulnerable beating of my heart.

....

CREATE YOUR OWN MONEY LEGACY

First, take a look back at the legacy you have received.

- Who has impacted your money relationship? Family, friends, ancestors, teachers? What have you learned from each of them?
- What beliefs, practices, or attitudes have served you? Are there some you're ready to release?
- What are you grateful for in your past? What do you want to honor? How can you bring this to life more, as you look forward?

As always, take your time with these questions. Breathe. Check in with your body. Be gentle with yourself. This is tender, beautiful, challenging stuff. Go at your own pace. Take dance and chocolate and journalling breaks as needed.

Now, take a look forward.

- What's an important nugget of money wisdom you'd like to pass on? To your own children—or the next generation?
- What financial practices, insights, and attitudes have truly "worked" for you, which you'd love to leave behind?
- Are there any money shames you need to heal, and make sure you don't pass on? (I believe we all have these!) Any money "messes" or loose ends you want to tie up?
- What have you learned about earning, spending, saving, giving, and receiving that you think could benefit others to know?
- When it comes to money, what do you want to be remembered for?
- If it helps you, consider these questions on the three levels of money work: the practical, the emotional-psychological, and the spiritual.

Finally, take action.

- Is there anything you feel called to do, to bring your Money Legacy to life in a tangible way? Do you want to hire an estate planner and set up a will or trust? Do you want to have a conversation with your children, partner, or friends about money?

- What tiny day-to-day things can you do to breathe your Money Legacy to life, now? If generosity is part of the Money Legacy you'd like to leave, for example, be on the lookout for ways to show it.

As you reflect on your past and look forward to the legacy you'd like to leave, remember to bring great doses of gentleness and self-love to the process. This question—like everything with money—touches upon so many aspects of you: health and body, emotions, beliefs, relationships, right livelihood, gender dynamics, personality types, nuts 'n bolts practices, big visioning, and so much more.

....

On this particular hike, I remembered another time when I had brought weighty questions to the woods, back when I lived in that tiny cottage in Sebastopol, and was preparing to lead my very first money workshop. That day, my question was: *What can I offer those around me who have so much suffering around money?* The answers I received were the seeds that became the Art of Money methodology. As I surveyed the horizon at the top of my mountain on my recent Boulder hike, my mind drifted to all the other areas of my money relationship that I am still working on, or rather, are still working *me*.

One of my biggest money koans, at the moment, is learning to think of the future. Until my early thirties, I couldn't even conceive of my finances more than a few weeks in the future. Like so many Americans, I was living month-to-month, paycheck-to-paycheck, and even imagining the future felt like a luxury I couldn't afford. The way someone thinks about their financial future reveals a great deal about their personality, financial planner Christopher Peck recently explained to me during an interview. You might be a dreamer with rose-colored glasses—or you might be a doom-and-gloom type. Or, you might experience the future more like I once did: as an inscrutable blank canvas, beyond your imagining.

My challenge now is to stretch my ability to think about the future, to prioritize and plan for it, and to start taking action steps now to provide for it. Future planning brings us face-to-face with our relationship with trust, optimism, and darkness. It also reveals the tricky balance between present-moment well-being and future planning.

We all must find our own solutions to the now vs. future equation, but simply asking the questions openly is, in my mind, a big victory. The question of a Money Legacy brings us to the future's doorstep. You may choose to sock away money in stocks and investments for your own future (or your children's and grandchildren's). You might focus on philanthropy as the gift you will pass down through the generations, as Angela's grandfather did. And certainly, you will create a Money Legacy through the attitudes and choices you embody during your life, as so brilliantly illustrated by Vicky's unique "retirement" on a bus in New Zealand. I hope my legacy strikes a balance between present-moment self-care and lovingly caretaking the future. I haven't yet found my own right balance, here, and I keep bringing my questions to my heart, to my bookkeeping, to the mountain. No matter how far we travel along our money journey, we will uncover new questions and koans and growing edges. Thankfully, the farther we explore our money relationship, the deeper our reserves of self-trust become.

As I mused on this past-present-future money stuff, I remembered long-forgotten hikes on this same Colorado mountain back in my early twenties, during graduate school. Back then, over twenty years ago, I hiked the exact same trail, over and over. Nowadays as back then, each day is different. Some days, it's sunny, hot, and calm, and I wear a sundress and shades. Some days, the mountain is cloaked in grey, wet rain clouds. Some days it's snowy and I watch my breath before me.

My life is so much different now than it was when I first hiked this mountain in my twenties. Back then, I was still finishing up my graduate program, struggling to make ends meet, head firmly planted in the sand around money, without a clue about my true value or how I would create a livelihood from it. I hadn't yet received that first student loan bill that became my money wakeup call. Now, I am a mama, a wife, and a creative entrepreneur. I am more sovereign, soft, and strong, in my financial world and beyond. My sense of value has ripened, and even though I still have my normal, human moments of freakout and doubt, I feel more empowered and clear-hearted than ever before. It's no exaggeration to say that many of these changes are directly due to my shifting, deepening, evolving relationship with money.

I believe we can and must re-think how to "do" money, work, and life. We can look this "elephant in the room" directly in the eye, call it over, and welcome it back into the full, rich expanse of our lives. We can offer our money relationship love, consciousness, deep meaning, and playfulness. We can gift ourselves a financial education: learning tools and practices that support this precious area of life. We can make our money relationship a cherished training ground for growth, mindfulness, and ever-deepening connection with ourselves. By engaging with our money relationships in this way, we can shift every area of our lives for the better.

From the summit of my mountain trail, I paused, drinking in the view from all directions. I felt myself at the crossroads of past, present, and future. Each breath connected me with the woman I had been and the woman I hoped to become, both within the woman I am, now. Amidst all the doubt and changes and evolving, what arises in this crossroads, for me, is gratitude: celebrating what is now, what has been, and what will be. I know that this glimpse of radical gratitude is part of the answer to my money koan about the future.

As you live your own money koans and questions, blazing a trail into a new, more mindful and joyful relationship with money, please know that I am grateful for you and for all of your brave work and heartfelt considerations. It is my greatest hope that, in this way, we will create a lasting Money Legacy of gentleness, compassion, smarts, and peace, for generations to come. Together, we truly will move mountains.

resources

Tracking Systems

Excel Spreadsheets: Some people love creating their own DIY spreadsheets to track income and/or expenses or for complex forecasting and projections once they collect data from other systems.

iBank: Simple personal finance tracking system. Similar to Quicken, but geared toward Mac users. www.ibank.com

Kashoo: Cloud-based business bookkeeping system. Simpler and easier to use than QuickBooks. www.kashoo.com

Mint: Great cloud-based system for beginners. Syncs with your bank to give you a quick glance of your income and expenses. Helpful for tracking cash flow (on its own or in conjunction with another accounting system). www.mint.com

MoneyMinder: Personal and business finance tracking systems created by two of my pioneering money coach colleagues. Offers income and expense tracking but also helps you create values-based spending plans using personalized categories. www.moneyminderonline.com

QuickBooks: The gold standard for business bookkeeping. Includes all the basics (tracking income and expenses, categorizing, etc.), plus: invoicing, payroll and cash flow projections. Great for businesses of all sizes. www.quickbooks.intuit.com

Quicken: Desktop system for personal finances (or very simple business finances). Offers simple income and expense tracking. Choose to automatically sync with your bank (for speed and ease) or manually enter transactions (for greater awareness). www.quicken.com

YNAB: Includes expense tracking but also has a built-in philosophy of money management (budgeting and saving), including the idea, "give every dollar a job." Can be very helpful for working with your values and goals. www.youneedabudget.com

Xero: Hip, beautiful, cloud-based international business bookkeeping system. www.xero.com

Additional Financial Support

Credit Karma: Offers a free copy of your credit score, access to your full credit report, and tools to help you track and raise your score and work with discrepancies. www.creditkarma.com

DailyWorth: A daily e-newsletter for women to help them see money not as a source of stress and anxiety, but as one of freedom and empowerment. www.dailyworth.com

Debtors Anonymous: Twelve-step program based on the principles of Alcoholics Anonymous (and other recovery groups) treating debt as a form of addiction. Offers support meetings, literature, sponsors, and more. www. debtorsanonymous.org

Gerri Detweiler: Consumer debt advocate offering a free blog and radio show to help people understand and work with their debt. www.gerridetweiler.com

Go Girl Finance: Tips and stories to support women's financial literacy and confidence. www.gogirlfinance.com

Heather Jarvis: Student loan advocate offering many resources to help students (and those who love them) understand and work with student loans. www.askheatherjarvis.com

LearnVest: A company that pairs you with a financial planner and helps you create a plan to tackle difficult financial decisions. www.learnvest.com

Building Your Financial Support Team

See chapter 11, "Your Financial Toolbox," for full descriptions of financial support team members.

Financial Recovery Institute: Find (or become) a Certified Financial Recovery Counselor. www.financialrecovery.com

Financial Therapy Association: Find (or become) a Certified Financial Therapist. www.financialtherapyassociation.org

Hartney Law: Conscious estate planning attorneys in Boulder, Colorado. www.hartneylaw.com

Heart Based Bookkeeping: My personal bookkeeper, who specializes in working with small business owners. www.heartbasedbookkeeping.com

Money Coaching Institute: Find (or become) a Certified Money Coach. www.moneycoachinginstitute.com

Natural Investments: Offers socially responsible financial planning, portfolio management, and consulting for individuals and nonprofits. www.naturalinvestments.com

Somatic Experiencing Directory: Learn more about Somatic Experiencing Therapy and find a practitioner near you to work with. www.traumahealing.org

My Eighteen Favorite Money Books

Baylor, Byrd. *The Table Where Rich People Sit*. New York: Aladdin, 1998. A wonderful, illustrated children's book that reflects on the true meaning of wealth.

Benson, April. *To Buy or Not to Buy: Why We Overshop and How to Stop*. Boston: Trumpeter Books, 2008. If you are a compulsive or chronic shopper, you will want to read this book, which integrates emotional, spiritual, and practical wisdom to overcome shopping addiction.

Butterworth, Eric. *Spiritual Economics: The Principles and Process of True Prosperity*. Lees Summit, MO: Unity School of Christianity, 2001. Spiritual principles and practical advice for rethinking your relationship to prosperity and abundance. If you love the idea that changing your thoughts can change your reality, this book is for you.

Hughes, James E., Jr. *Family Wealth: Keeping it in the Family*. New York: Wiley, 2004. If you come from a wealthy family where resources (financial and otherwise) are passed down to the next generation, this book will be very helpful for you. It expands our definitions of wealth and provides thoughtful and practical guidelines for providing for future generations.

Kinder, George. *The Seven Stages of Money Maturity: Understanding the Spirit and Value of Money in Your Life*. New York: Dell, 1999. This foundational book for financial planning and wealth building is written by a renowned Buddhist teacher—who's also a leading voice in the financial planning world.

Lieber, Ron. *The Opposite of Spoiled: Raising Kids Who Are Grounded, Generous, and Smart About Money*. New York: HarperCollins. The best book I know of on parenting and money. Advocates open conversations and includes clear suggestions about everything from the tooth fairy to allowances, chores, and tuition.

McCall, Karen. *Financial Recovery: Developing a Healthy Relationship with Money*. Novato, CA: New World Library, 2011. This pioneering money coach offers her holistic system for money health, inspired by the twelve-step recovery movement.

Needleman, Jacob. *Money and the Meaning of Life*. New York: Doubleday, 1991. The first money book I ever read. Written by a philosopher and combining psychology, poetry, myth, and personal exploration, it presents money as a path into greater self-knowledge.

Nemeth, Maria. *The Energy of Money: A Spiritual Guide to Financial and Personal Fulfillment*. New York: Ballantine, 1999. One of the original books on money psychology. It incorporates spiritual and psychological practices to help us understand our emotions, history, and money stories.

Northrup, Kate. *Money, a Love Story: Untangle Your Financial Woes and Create the Life You Really Want*. Carlsbad, CA: Hay House, 2013. A fun and modern money book for millennials and creative entrepreneurs.

Peck, Christopher, Michael Kramer, and Hall Brill. *Resilient Investor: A Plan for Your Life, Not Just Your Money*. Oakland, CA: Berrett-Koehler Publishers, 2015. From my favorite Socially Responsible Financial Planners, this book teaches you to think about investing in a new, holistic way, including your time, energy, and more.

Price, Deborah L. *The Heart of Money: A Couple's Guide to Financial Intimacy*. Novato, CA: New World Library, 2012. A framework to transform money from a source of tension and stress in a relationship into a realm of intimacy and understanding. Includes conversation prompts, support for understanding your own and each other's psychological patterns around money, and a set of money "archetypes" to work with.

Robin, Vicki, Joseph R. Dominguez, and Monique Tilford. *Your Money or Your Life: 9 Steps to Transforming Your Relationship with Money and Achieving Financial Independence*. New York: Penguin Books, 2008. Known as one of the original money books. It blazed a trail for many people to start thinking about integrating their values and their money, and "helping folks create a life, rather than just make a living."

Roth, Geneen. *Lost and Found: One Woman's Story of Losing Her Money and Finding Her Life*. New York: Viking, 2011. Geneen Roth and her husband lost their life savings in the Bernie Madoff scandal. This important book reveals what happens when we lose a lot of money, our home, or our job . . . and offers provocative strategies for finding true security.

Stanny, Barbara. *Overcoming Underearning: Overcome Your Money Fears and Earn What You Deserve.* New York: HarperCollins, 2005. A ground-breaking book offering stories and strategies for working through fear and self-sabotage to claim greater empowerment, freedom, and self-worth.

Twist, Lynne. *The Soul of Money: Reclaiming the Wealth of our Inner Resources.* New York: W. W. Norton & Co, 2003. One of the best books on helping us understand the mindset of scarcity and transform it into sufficiency and prosperity, while making an impact in the world.

Thakor, Manisha, and Sharon Kedar. *On My Own Two Feet: A Modern Girl's Guide to Personal Finance.* Avon, MA: Adams Media, 2014. Grasp the basic principles of money management: how to get out of debt, save for retirement, and take financial control of your life.

Warren, Elizabeth, and Amelia Warren Tyagi. *All Your Worth: The Ultimate Lifetime Money Plan.* New York: Free Press, 2005. Simple, step-by-step money management plan created by a mother-daughter team and based on 20+ years of research on women and bankruptcy.

Resources for Exploring the "Macro" Side of Money

Eisenstein, Charles. *Sacred Economics: Money, Gift, and Society in the Age of Transition.* Berkeley, CA: North Atlantic Books, 2011. A scholarly and provocative re-examination of the history of currencies, the attitudes they foster, and a bold invitation into radically new modes of exchange.

Frontline. *The Secret History of the Credit Card.* PBS Video. DVD. This PBS documentary reveals the tactics credit card companies have used to become powerful and lucrative—much to the detriment of many cardholders.

Lietaer, Bernard, and Jacqui Dunne. *Rethinking Money: How New Currencies Turn Scarcity into Prosperity.* San Francisco, CA: Berrett-Koehler Publishers, 2013. The economist I always turn to for inspiration. This book traces the surprising origins of our current monetary system and its built-in drawbacks, but also paints a hopeful picture of new, alternative currencies.

Teague, Katie. *Money & Life.* DVD. I've watched this documentary over and over again: it asks *big* questions and weaves together the current economic crisis, planetary interconnection and wellness, the origins and evolution of money, personal practices, and so much more. Plus, it features interviews with Bernard Lietaer, Lynne Twist, Jacob Needleman, and other financial thinkers.

Money Management Resources

Please note: there are hundreds of books already written about traditional financial management (paying down debt, saving for retirement, investing in the stock market, etc.), and while I don't agree with 100 percent of their life-and-money philosophies, learning these tools and strategies can be incredibly positive and empowering. Here are a handful of authors I think offer this ultra-practical piece well. Please take what works and leave the rest, and rely upon the gentle, healing approach in this book as you explore these methods.

Ramit Sethi
Dave Ramsey
Suze Orman
Tony Robbins
Farnoosh Torabi
Jean Chatzsky

Non-Money Books to Support Your Journey

Beck, Renee, and Sydney Barbara Metrick. *The Art of Ritual*. Berkeley, CA: Apocryphile Press, 2009.

Brach, Tara. *Radical Acceptance: Embracing Your Life with the Heart of a Buddha*. New York: Bantam Dell, 2003.

Brown, Brené. *Daring Greatly: How the Courage to Be Vulnerable Transforms the Way We Live, Love, Parent, and Lead*. London: Penguin UK, 2013.

Caldwell, Christine. *Getting Our Bodies Back: Recovery, Healing, and Transformation through Body-Centered Psychotherapy*. Boston: Shambhala, 2013.

Campbell, Joseph. *The Hero's Journey*. Novato, CA: New World Library, 2003.

Chödrön, Pema. *When Things Fall Apart: Heart Advice for Difficult Times*. Boston: Shambhala: 2002.

Estés, Clarissa Pinkola. *Women Who Run With the Wolves*. New York: Ballantine Books, 1997.

Frankl, Victor E. *Man's Search for Meaning*. Boston: Beacon Press, 1997.

Gendlin, Eugene T. *Focusing*. New York: Bantam Dell, 1981.

Hendricks, Gay, and Katie Hendricks. *Conscious Loving: The Journey to Co-Commitment*. New York: Bantam Books, 1990.

Hillman, James. *Suicide and the Soul*. Berkeley, CA: University of California Press, 1973.

Kübler-Ross, Elisabeth. *On Death and Dying: What the Dying Have to Teach Doctors, Nurses, Clergy and Their Own Families.* New York: Scribner, 2014.

LaPorte, Danielle. *The Desire Map: A Guide to Creating Goals with Soul.* Boulder, CO: SoundsTrue, 2014.

Lesser, Elizabeth. *Broken Open: How Difficult Times Can Help Us Grow.* New York: Villard Books, 2008.

Levine, Peter. *Waking The Tiger: Healing Trauma.* Berkeley, CA: North Atlantic Books, 1997.

Palmer, Amanda. *The Art of Asking: How I Learned to Stop Worrying and Let People Help.* New York: Grand Central Publishing, 2014.

Pressfield, Steven. *The War of Art: Break through the Blocks and Win Your Inner Creative Battles.* New York: Black Irish Entertainment, 2002.

Riso, Don, and Russ Hudson. *The Wisdom of the Enneagram.* New York: Bantam Books, 1999.

Steinem, Gloria. *Revolution from Within: A Book of Self Esteem.* New York: Little, Brown, 1993.

Tharp, Twyla. *The Creative Habit: Learn It and Use It for Life.* New York: Simon & Schuster, 2009.

acknowledgements

With Deep Gratitude for My Lineage and Village

From the very first talk I gave on my money methodology (almost fifteen years ago) right up until today, folks have asked me: *When is the book coming out?* They could feel what I felt: there was a book here, growing. But these teachings needed time to mature and evolve. And, frankly, so did I. I needed to live this work myself. And I needed a community to join me on this adventure.

For years, then, I gave the same answer to that question: *Not yet, but soon. The book is coming.* Well, the day has finally arrived. I am thrilled . . . and grateful beyond belief. It's no exaggeration to say that this book and the teachings it contains took a village to create. My gratitude begins with this, my wonderful village.

I am eternally grateful to all of the participants, students, and clients who have shown up over the years and done this money work with me, from those early days when I called this Conscious Bookkeeping, up until today. Thank you for saying YES to this work. Thank you for trusting me. Thank you for diving in so bravely. Thank you for confirming what worked, revealing what didn't, and opening my eyes to ever-greater, ever-deeper pieces to share. It has been an honor to co-create this content with you.

My life and this work have also been graced by a whole lineage of treasured mentors. To my teachers and fellow students at my wonderful Somatic Psychology Master's program at Naropa University: thank you. This training was the foundation for *everything* in my life—parenting, business, and money work—and taught me how to be a therapist and a guide. From you, I learned the self-examination, openness, mindfulness, and practices to fully live all of the beauty and pain, ebbs and flows of life.

During my graduate program, I was guided by four seasoned somatic therapists: Christine Caldwell, Cassie Bull, Susan Aposhyn, and Nicole McGough. I also felt the loving spirit of Mary Whitehouse, the late founder of Authentic Movement, present with me during those transformative years. To my favorite dance teachers, Rujeko Sarah Dumbutshena, Rosangela Silvestre, and Donna Mejia: I carry you with me, in gratitude. And I wish I could dance with you every single week.

I am grateful-beyond-words to Tamara Slayton, my first spiritual money mentor. We met in 2001, at key junctures in both of our lives. She was the first to see my path clearly, and helped me bridge my two worlds: psychotherapy and bookkeeping. She also asked me to step up and become a teacher of this work. Tamara left this world in 2003, but her spirit and wisdom carry on in this work and everyone who is touched by it. Tamara, you will always be remembered.

When I first created my money methodology, I didn't know this field even existed. In the years since, I have discovered the pioneers who blazed this trail before me, and I am lucky to call some of them dear colleagues and friends. Joe Dominguez, Vicki Robin, Jacob Needleman, Olivia Mellan, Maria Nemeth, Lynne Twist, Karen McCall, Deborah Price, Barbara Stanny, George Kinder, and Dick Wagner: I honor you, my wonderful money lineage.

From 2005 through 2008, my Conscious Bookkeeping business blossomed into a whole team of wonderful bookkeeping trainers and financial coaches. These three years were foundational to my business, to this methodology, and to my dear community. My thanks to everyone involved in this phase, especially Joetta Johnson (financial coach) for being my business partner, and to Eva Konigsberg (financial coach and tax expert) for being a key part of our team.

Because money is such a vast and multifaceted topic, I constantly collaborate with and interview other money experts and colleagues from different, related fields. Many of the stories in this book come from the hundreds of interviews I have done over the years, and I want to thank my wonderful colleagues for being willing to talk with me and share their stories: Fabeku Fatunmise, Hiro Boga, Barbara Stanny, Ben Saltzman, Rachel Cole, Christopher Peck, Mark Silver, Jess Salzman, Karin Robbins, Amy Bradbury, Galia Gichon, Deborah Price, Sara Avant Stover, Julie Daley, Kate Swoboda, Andrea Scher, Rebecca Lewis McLoughlin, Jacquette Timmons, Mikelann Valterra, Heather Jarvis, Kristen Wheeler, Nona Jordan, Maketa and Jesse Rey, Catharine and Julie Clarenbach, and Terry Jordan.

While writing this book, I consulted with many trusted financial colleagues who quickly and lovingly responded to my S.O.S. messages, especially in the final hours of editing. For this, I am forever grateful to: Jess Salzman, Christopher Peck, Michael Kramer, Galia Gichon, Martha Hartney, Rick Kahler, Gerri Detweiler, and Deborah Price.

My original team of Teaching Assistants (or, as we prefer to call them, Transformational Assistants) for my year-long Art of Money program, Karin Robbins (Somatic Experiencing therapist) and Jess Salzman (bookkeeper extraordinaire): you have given so much to our community, and I am forever grateful.

While writing this book, I laid on Elena Guilini's acupuncture table every two weeks. Elena was my teacher at Naropa, twenty years ago, and today, she's not only my acupuncturist, she also gave me endless council on editing and book-writing. Tanya Geisler, my awesome coach, has given me endless mama-love, support, and piercing clarity over the last few years. Lisa Grace Byrne: thank you for your love, support, and sister-mind during our monthly meetings.

When I wrote my Master's thesis in 1997, it brought me to my knees. My teaching tradition is an oral one: I love to speak, guide, coach, and create content, but simply don't know how writers do their thing. I knew I needed to find a way to bring my teachings to the page. When I discovered collaborative writing, I knew I had found that way. The fact that I could go back and forth with a writer, ensuring every story, concept, and sentence felt accurate and authentic has been a revolutionary gift for me. No co-writer comes close to the one and only Miss Angela Raines. She is able to bring my voice into written form, enhancing the teachings along the way, beyond anything I could do or imagine. She honors my commitment to depth *and* playfulness, and truly values this body of work. She has also been immersed in the Art of Money, doing her own money work; it means so much to me that she understands this journey so personally. We have co-written all of my articles for years, now (and she also writes the copy for my website). A year into our collaboration, I could sense I had found "the one" to help me birth this book.

I'm not sure I have the words to describe how grateful I am for my collaboration with Angela. We were given a challenging timeframe for this book, and we did it: we birthed it together. I am forever grateful for her keen mind, creative spirit, brilliance with words, deep sense of practice, and wisdom beyond her years.

I had no idea that Angela would additionally come with a super smart, well-read, and wise mother. Sue Jackson was our first reader for many chapters of this book, providing thoughtful feedback. Thank you!

My masterful tarot reader, Theresa Reed, knew I would get a book deal in the fall of 2014. Laurie Wagner co-created this kismet; she invited me to write a guest article for her website, which got the attention of the team from Parallax Press. My thanks to her for all of her counsel throughout the book-writing year, and to Janet Goldstein for helping me to review the contract.

In my wildest book dreams, a publisher would simply call me up one day. This is exactly what happened! As Angela and I were finalizing the book proposal, I got the call from Parallax Press. I did a huge, thorough examination of all the things I hoped for in a publisher, and realized Parallax was a perfect match. It was, literally, a dream come true.

Rachel Neumann is my publishing angel. She not only believed in this book enough to publish it, but she stepped in after a challenging, growth-filled first round of edits and took on the developmental editing herself. She provided editing the way my team had always hoped for, which means the world to me. I can now say that I share the same publisher *and* editor as Thich Nhat Hanh—what an honor. Rachel, thank you for being such a champion for me, and my work, and for taking me under your wing.

I am grateful for my dear parents for giving me this physical life and having always been so supportive of my dreams and business endeavors. They have always believed there was a book (or a few books!) inside of me, and I feel so lucky to be able to finish this project while they are still alive. I also want to honor my family lineage of Tesslers, Rosens, Brahills, and Zippersteins, all of whom traveled far from their homelands to arrive here in America, and all of whom live on in me.

Mount Sanitas, my blessed mountain that I have hiked almost daily for many years now: I go to you for my sanity, strength, clarity, vitality, and peace of mind. I bring you my questions and always receive my answers. Your natural glory served me so well during this book-writing year.

Forest, my husband, my love, the father of my child, my partner in all creative business endeavors: I might be the lead singer of the band, but you are the producer, always behind the scenes, putting your heart, brilliance, and creativity in everything I do and that the Art of Money creates. Forest was there at the very beginning when this money work was conceived, and has been here every step of the way since. He was part of every book-visioning meeting, discussing every chapter and providing invaluable creative direction. I am forever grateful for his partnership in every area of my life.

Noah, my one and only child: I am so lucky to be your mama. Thank you for choosing me. And may everything in this book inspire you—and all of us—to create a beautiful, lasting life legacy for our little family and beyond.

With my deepest gratitude to my lineage, my village, and all I have been given. Thank you for the gift of a lifetime.

RELATED TITLES

Awakening Joy James Baraz and Shoshana Alexander

Be Free Where You Are Thich Nhat Hanh

Beginning Anew Sister Chan Khong

Buddha Mind, Buddha Body Thich Nhat Hanh

Deep Relaxation Sister Chan Khong

Fidelity Thich Nhat Hanh

Happiness Thich Nhat Hanh

Love's Garden Larry Ward and Peggy Rowe-Ward

Making Space Thich Nhat Hanh

Mindfulness Survival Kit Thich Nhat Hanh

No Mud, No Lotus Thich Nhat Hanh

Solid Ground Sylvia Boorstein, Norman Fischer, Tsoknyi Rinpoche

Ten Breaths to Happiness Glen Schneider

Work Thich Nhat Hanh

PARALLAX
PRESS

Parallax Press is a nonprofit publisher, founded and inspired by Zen
Master Thich Nhat Hanh. We publish books on mindfulness in daily
life and are committed to making these teachings accessible to everyone
and preserving them for future generations. We do this work to alleviate
suffering and contribute to a more just and joyful world.

For a copy of the catalog, please contact:
Parallax Press
P.O. Box 7355
Berkeley, CA 94707
Tel: (510) 540-6411
parallax.org